Enlightened Pleasures

**THE LEWIS WALPOLE SERIES
IN EIGHTEENTH-CENTURY CULTURE AND HISTORY**

The Lewis Walpole Series, published by Yale University Press with the aid of the Annie Burr Lewis Fund, is dedicated to the culture and history of the long eighteenth century (from the Glorious Revolution to the accession of Queen Victoria). It welcomes work in a variety of fields, including literature and history, the visual arts, political philosophy, music, legal history, and the history of science. In addition to original scholarly work, the series publishes new editions and translations of writing from the period, as well as reprints of major books that are currently unavailable. Though the majority of books in the series will probably concentrate on Great Britain and the Continent, the range of our geographical interests is as wide as Horace Walpole's.

Enlightened Pleasures

*Eighteenth-Century France and
the New Epicureanism*

Thomas M. Kavanagh

YALE UNIVERSITY PRESS   NEW HAVEN AND LONDON

Published with assistance from the Annie Burr Lewis Fund, from the Kingsley Trust Association Publication Fund established by the Scroll and Key Society of Yale College, and from the Frederick W. Hilles Publication Fund of Yale University.

Copyright © 2010 by Yale University.
All rights reserved.
This book may not be reproduced, in whole or in part, including illustrations, in any form (beyond that copying permitted by Sections 107 and 108 of the U.S. Copyright Law and except by reviewers for the public press), without written permission from the publishers.
Set in Fournier type by
Westchester Book Group, Danbury, Connecticut.
Printed in the United States of America by Sheridan Books, Ann Arbor, Michigan.

Library of Congress Cataloging-in-Publication Data

Kavanagh, Thomas M.
Enlightened pleasures : eighteenth-century France and the new epicureanism / Thomas M. Kavanagh.
p. cm — (The Lewis Walpole series in eighteenth-century culture and history)
Includes bibliographical references and index.
ISBN 978-0-300-14094-1 (cloth : alk. paper) 1. France—Intellectual life—18th century.
2. Philosophy, French—18th century. 3. France—Civilization—Greek influences.
4. Epicureans (Greek philosophy) 5. Pleasure. 6. French literature—18th century—
History and criticism. I. Title.
DC133.8.K38 2010
944'.034—dc22
2009027231

A catalogue record for this book is available from the British Library.

This paper meets the requirements of ANSI/NISO Z39.48-1992 (Permanence of Paper).

10 9 8 7 6 5 4 3 2 1

To Monique, Charlotte, and Matthew

Trahit sua quemque voluptas.
—Virgil, *Eclogues*

Cet atome est, selon moi, un joli petit corps.
—Mérard de Saint-Just, *L'Esprit des mœurs*

Contents

Introduction: A New Epicureanism ... 1

1. The Pleasures of Failure:
   Jourdan's *Le Guerrier philosophe* ... 10

2. Mirroring Pleasure:
   La Morlière's *Angola* ... 31

3. Life-Writing as Epicurean Allegory:
   Thérèse philosophe ... 52

4. The Esthetics of Pleasure:
   Du Bos and Boucher ... 71

5. Rousseau's Eudemony of Liberty ... 103

6. Laclos' Anthropology of Pleasure ... 128

7. Recasting the Epicurean Novel:
   Mirabeau's *La Morale des sens* ... 149

8. Theaters of Pleasure ... 171

Conclusion: From Pleasure to Happiness ... 207

Notes ... 219

Illustration Credits ... 243

Index ... 245

Introduction
A New Epicureanism

Pleasure lies always to the dark side. Most often reduced to a dubious luxuriance within sensation, it is condemned by the Christian as an appetite of fallen nature, by the Marxist as a perquisite of expropriated value, and by the Freudian as a surrender to raw id. Whatever one's ideological position, pleasure smacks of egotism or shameful privilege. When Roland Barthes chose to use the word in the title of *The Pleasure of the Text*, he felt obliged to make explicit his understanding that, at the very mention of that word, two censors always stand ready to pounce: "the political policeman and the psychoanalytic policeman: futility and/or guilt, pleasure is either idle or vain, a class notion or an illusion."[1]

Yet it was not always so. Eighteenth-century France—the France born in John Law's multiplication of wealth and swept away in the Terror's bloodbath of civic virtue—was a century of Pleasure. Setting aside absolutism's *régime du bon plaisir*, the period's major figures, novelists and artists, *philosophes* as well as *libertins*, set out to describe, analyze, and systematize the multiplicity of pleasure. Pleasure was the elixir to be found not only in a glass but in an intimate encounter, a novel, an opera, or a painting. It was consecrated as a force driving individual action and constituting the essence of existence. *Sentir son existence*, to be alive through the senses and their pleasures, was the goal motivating works as different as Julien Offray de La Mettrie's programmatic *Art de jouir* of 1751 and Jean-Jacques Rousseau's plaintive *Reveries of the Solitary Walker* of 1776–78. Be it the eroticism so dear to the *libertins* or Rousseau's final consolation of solipsistic ecstasy, pleasure was a defining hallmark of eighteenth-century France. The ability to take and multiply pleasure as a gift shared with one's companion, reader, or public became a signature of the century's conviviality. Pleasure was the shared endeavor of individuals savoring what their senses perceived as well as of a larger community knitted together by the expression and communication of its pleasures.

This tension between pleasure as idiolect and pleasure as lingua franca—between sensation as specific to the sentient self and as an energy seeking to communicate itself to others—generated a conundrum that would become the century's defining question. Pleasure is utterly personal; yet representing that pleasure, making it real for the other, must occur not as an objectification but as a pan-subjectification—an enticing seduction of one's audience. The Enlightenment's *pleasure principle*—so unlike the later Freudian variant of a dangerously immediate gratification that refuses the salutary deferrals of the *reality principle*—sought to parlay the pleasure of the one into the exuberance of the many. The optimism of the French Enlightenment flowed from its faith in pleasure as a universal currency whose exchange could both define the self and bind together society. What the Epicurean called hedonism, no longer a mark of shame, became a fundamental human right promising the social concord of pleasures shared and multiplied. Many, of course, would claim that civic virtue or happiness was the great invention of the Enlightenment. While those values are part of the story, the specific texture of the French eighteenth century can be felt most tangibly in the changing fortunes not of socialized happiness but of idiosyncratic pleasure.

Both as an experience of the senses and as the foundation of a new social contract, pleasure emerged during the eighteenth century from the minatory shadow of Christian asceticism. The trauma of France's wars of religion, resurrected by Louis XIV's revocation of the Edict of Nantes in 1685 and in the religious cleansing that would continue until the Revolution, led an ever growing number to see the conflict between Catholic and Protestant as proof of a shared absurdity. The scandal of Christianity at war with itself established agnosticism and atheism as intellectually responsible options for those who rejected religious intolerance. At the same time, the body's senses, relegated by both religious camps to the realm of the dangerous and sinful, became the touchstone of a new empiricism that looked to the data of the senses as the bedrock of all knowledge. By midcentury, the *philosophes*, reversing the Cartesian primacy of mind, insisted not only that sensation preceded thought but that only the data of the senses was truly clear and distinct.

This privileging of the senses and their pleasures took many forms: an eroticism freed from religious prohibition, a mastery of the physical world grounded in empirical investigation, and an *art de vivre* augmented by the new commodities of international trade. What I am calling enlightened pleasures rarely proclaimed themselves openly. If this new valorizing of pleasure was enlightened, it was because it set itself against a lingering darkness of benighted superstitions and metaphysical chimeras that spoke of sin and the baseness of the body. The eighteenth century's practitioners of pleasure appealed less to some fulgent sun meant to banish all shadows than to a more circumscribed light illuminating in private a freedom of experience eked out from within the limits imposed by prevailing religious norms. By the end of the century this ethos of pleasure would fall under a different shadow that had nothing to do with the Church. Pleasure, always grounded in the personal and the individual, succumbed instead to the new strictures of civic duties and communal responsibilities imposed in the name of the Revolution's universalizing orthodoxies of happiness.

My analysis of eighteenth-century France as an interlude of pleasure's primacy will borrow concepts from two schools of classical philosophy: Epicureanism and Stoicism. Looking at their confluence, at what might paradoxically be called an Epicurean Stoicism, has the advantage of underlining a complexity that is too often overlooked when we speak of the more familiar *libertinage*—a term which has come to mean little more than sexual license set within the ancien régime.[2] On the face of it, Epicureanism and Stoicism represent opposing traditions. As a system of thought based on the premise that pleasure is life's goal, Epicureanism retained throughout the eighteenth century its sense of an adherence to that philosophy as described by Lucretius. Stoicism, on the other hand, was a concept that underwent an important evolution. The Stoicism of the early eighteenth century designated a regimen of individual discipline, a self-mastery achieved through a commitment to reason's power to preserve balance by distancing oneself from and controlling the destructive force of passion. During the 1740s and 1750s—a focal period for this study—the distance and control associated with Stoicism were, especially in relation to the novel and the arts, imagined not as an abstention from pleasure and its dangers but as protocols for its extension and refinement. What one read in a novel or saw in a painting offered vividly vicarious experiences of pleasure, with none of its dangers. As esthetic objects, the novel and the image promised a merging of the Epicurean's pleasure with the Stoic's distance and control. Finally, during the three decades leading up to the Revolution, Stoicism would once again be refashioned as the shibboleth of the voices raised against a pleasure they denounced as aristocratic hedonism. The evolving political and cultural agenda of the late Enlightenment produced a Stoicism which hypothesized a duty, not to reason's tempering of individual appetites in even greater pleasure, but to the civic ideal of an imaginary community whose collective happiness became an individual responsibility.

In the context of the Enlightenment, the classic opposition between Epicureanism and Stoicism became less important than their similarities as differently accented versions of a shared subversion. In the entry on Epicureanism which he wrote for the *Encyclopédie*, Diderot denounces the way this philosophical perspective had been vilified and misrepresented as vulgar hedonism. He begins by imbuing its founder with a distinctly Stoic coloration: "Never has a philosophy been less understood and more calumniated than that of Epicurus. . . . Portrayed as an apologist for debauchery, he devoted his life to a constant practice of all the virtues, especially that of temperance."[3] Diderot's Epicurus may speak of pleasure, but it is a pleasure to be found in the calm and measure of life in the garden where he taught his philosophy. Likewise, in his entry on Stoicism, Diderot takes the position that the doctrine Zeno of Citium taught at Athen's Painted Portico (the Stoa, from which his philosophy took its name) conveyed the same message as Epicurus, only differently—to seek a minimizing of pain and suffering was, after all, the obverse corollary to the Epicurean goal of maximizing pleasure.

Epicureanism and Stoicism became, in this sense, two sides of a single coin. In the context of the century's growing rejection of Christian metaphysics, these enemy twins from antiquity became allies in a shared struggle. As Diderot notes in his *Encyclopédie* entries, both Epicureanism and Stoicism owe their rebirth in the modern world to the work of the seventeenth-century cleric, Pierre Gassendi, whose commentary on Diogenes Laërtius initiated a challenge to orthodoxy that, according to Diderot, was the common inspiration of the most important modern philosophers.[4] Beneath their surface differences, Epicureanism and Stoicism share a materialist philosophy that presupposes continuity between the physical world of things and human world of consciousness. For the Stoic, matter and mind stand as manifestations of a single "divine fire" that manifests itself as order within things and as reason within the mind. For the Epicurean, both mind and matter are composed of atoms falling through space in trajectories deflected by their random swerves and collisions. Mind differs from matter only because its smaller and more fragile atoms are motile, igneous, and ethereal. As Diderot makes clear, these two philosophies of classical antiquity are equally antithetical to the Christian belief in an immaterial soul fundamentally different from the material body. This opposition is what establishes them as the dual source of all that might qualify as true philosophy. As Diderot puts it, "The human soul is corporeal. . . . Were it incorporeal, it could neither act nor be acted upon by the body, its heterogeneity would render impossible any connection with the body" (1:1196).

If the terms *Epicurean* and *Stoic* were rarely combined during the eighteenth century, then, it was not because they were incompatible but because Cartesian physics had driven a wedge between them. René Descartes, while embracing the Stoic emphasis on the control exercised by reason, rejected Epicureanism because of its belief in an atomistic universe. For Descartes, the world of matter was a plenum, a fullness irreconcilable with any void or vacuum through which Lucretian atoms might be seen as falling. Diderot, a partisan of the Epicurean rather than the Cartesian understanding of matter, challenged Descartes' plenum of vortices and whirlpools by drawing even his description of the Stoic conception of matter toward the Epicurean model: "Matter is never stable," he writes in his entry on Stoicism, "it varies ceaselessly, everything is carried away in a torrent, all passes, nothing of what we perceive stays the same" (3:618). For Diderot, Epicureanism and Stoicism, rather than being opposites, are different points on a shared continuum of age, experience, and wisdom: "We become Stoics, but we are born Epicureans" (1:1196).

Diderot's reconciliation of the Epicurean and the Stoic is an illustration of how the French eighteenth century, from the death of Louis XIV to the upheavals of the Revolution, can be seen as a continually evolving attempt to reconcile these twinned philosophical alternatives to Platonism within a new understanding of the individual and society. An unstable synthesis of attitudes toward experience and consciousness usually assumed to be antithetical, what I am calling Epicurean Stoicism is resolutely hybrid. The changed valence it would give to the notion of pleasure provided the nuance of the eighteenth century's interwoven rethinking of literature and art, philosophy and political theory, theater and social practice.

My decision to focus on how specific novelists, artists, and philosophers refashioned the tenets of Epicureanism and Stoicism as wellsprings of their own iconoclastic syntheses is also meant to help us step outside a calcified orthodoxy of Enlightenment studies that obfuscates the period's real tensions and continuing importance. The canonical story of the French Enlightenment is a familiar one. Freed by the death of the Sun King from the ever more disastrous consequences of military and absolutist ambitions, the Regency ushered in a period of license presided over by the dissolute Philippe d'Orléans. The hyperinflation and massive increase in buying power triggered by John Law's System set the stage for increasingly refined practices of an elegant joie de vivre symbolized by the passing dalliances of *libertinage* and the alluring emblems of the rococo. During the 1760s, however, as the rising bourgeoisie challenged aristocratic privilege and excess within an ever expanding public sphere, a countervailing force began to emerge. When the monarchy and its institutions turned a deaf ear to the spokespersons of this new order, in which the values of virtue and sentiment replaced those of birth and wealth, the explosions of the Revolution and the march toward democratic republicanism became inevitable.

This narrative, born in the second half of the nineteenth century, has endured not so much for what it captures of the past it purports to describe but because it provides a myth of origins. First articulated in the wake of 1848 and the end of monarchy in France, the parable of Enlightenment universalism became, after the interlude of the Second Empire, a reigning orthodoxy during France's Third Republic. Between 1871 and the outbreak of World War II, the new discipline of literary history played an important role in elaborating an eighteenth century that legitimized the moral values invoked by the Third Republic in its struggle to reconcile *bourgeoisie* and *peuple* within something other than socialism. As early as the 1930s, however, a different and more cosmopolitan Enlightenment began to displace France's domestic version of its eighteenth-century past. Conceived as a response to the rise of fascist and soviet totalitarianism, the Enlightenment as it is most widely understood today came to be articulated as two quite different but equally Germanic retellings of what was originally a French story. For the most influential spokesperson of that story's first version, Ernst Cassirer, the dismantling of religion's hegemony; the recourse to empirical fact; the divided powers of government, free debate, and a tolerance of republicanism-in-the-making became the shared virtues of Enlightenment science, philosophy, epistemology, history, and esthetics. Cassirer's Enlightenment stood as an anticipatory indictment of everything Hitler and Stalin were proposing as their different visions of Europe's New Order. Cassirer's version of the Enlightenment recast what had happened in France as but one part of a larger, pan-European story. France's *philosophes* may have broadened the scope and implications of what began with British empiricism, but their work would achieve its full flower only in the crowning achievements of German idealism. Cassirer's Enlightenment became the condemnation of Nazism as the betrayal of all that had been best about the German nation.[5]

A far darker yet equally premonitory version of the Enlightenment emerges from what stands as the foundational text of the Frankfurt school: Max Horkheimer and Theodor W. Adorno's *Dialectic of Enlightenment* (1947). Insisting that, behind the calm resolve of Kant's "daring to know" (*sapere aude*) as a summary of enlightenment, there lurks the drive toward totalitarian domination, Horkheimer and Adorno abruptly redefined Kant's optimistic empowerment: "Enlightenment, understood in the widest sense as the advance of thought, has always aimed at liberating human beings from fear and installing them as masters. Yet the wholly enlightened earth is radiant with triumphant calamity."[6] More than anything else, Enlightenment must be seen as a "disenchantment of the world" that stands as the poisoned fruit of its "corrosive rationality." Embracing utility above all other values, the defining ambition of Enlightenment man and his demythologizing of nature was the domination of all and everyone: "What human beings seek to learn from nature is how to use it to dominate wholly both it and human beings. Nothing else counts.... Enlightenment stands in the same relationship to things as the dictator to human beings. He knows them to the extent that he can manipulate them" (2–6). For Horkheimer and Adorno, the call to maturity which Kant equated with Enlightenment becomes the universal will to power of a Nietzschean *Übermensch* who would go on to orchestrate the horrors of totalitarianism in all its forms.[7]

As even so rapid a summary makes clear, these very different narratives of eighteenth-century France and its legacy are considerably taxed by the heavy lifting this Enlightenment must do in the service of ideologies born long after it. As opposed as Cassirer's optimism and the Frankfurt school's pessimism may be, their versions of the Enlightenment share the postulate that the eighteenth century reveals its full meaning only in the Revolution that was its defining endpoint. For both interpretations the Revolution becomes an event so portentous that its very existence necessitates a teleological rereading of its history as extending beyond its actual dates into both the past that prepared it and the future that would fulfill it. For Cassirer, the Revolution as telos is mankind's throwing off the shackles of error and superstition. For Horkheimer and Adorno, the Revolution as telos is the proto-totalitarian fanaticism of the Terror.[8]

My examination of the Enlightenment's new Epicureanism and its privileging of pleasure is a way of stepping outside the orthodoxies that postulate eighteenth-century France as the preparation of a future it had never anticipated. The play of pleasure and virtue within Epicurean Stoicism reconfigured tensions long at work in early modern France. The Epicureanism of Democritus and Lucretius speaks of pleasure, but of a pleasure always threatened by the fictive creations of passion. The Stoicism harking back to Zeno of Citium and Epictetus speaks of virtue, but of a virtue aimed at the pleasure of living in accord with a natural order alien to religious and metaphysical precepts. Epicureanism and Stoicism, each with its distinct inflection, came together over the course of the eighteenth century in a shifting synthesis that challenged all variants of idealism—Platonic, Christian, and Cartesian. Monist rather than dualist, Epicurean Stoicism was first and foremost a naturalism, a leveling within the oneness of matter of all hierarchies that subtended the institutions of Church and Monarchy. Reworking a Democratian atomism inherited from Ovid and rearticulated by Gassendi, this new Epicureanism refused any cleavage between body and soul, sensation and thought, perception and knowledge. A radical materialism that rejected any transcendence separating the virtuous exercise of the mind from the sentient pleasure of the body, it grounded its secular morality in nature as it was experienced by the senses.

Eighteenth-century France's fascination with pleasure went beyond the classical heritage by reason of the vitality and philosophical ambition its materialism drew from the empiricism of Bacon, Newton, and Locke. The senses and their pleasure moved to the center not only of how the individual might know the world but of how society might achieve concord within it.

Consciousness and subjectivity fused perception and reflection in a dialectic that remained resolutely within the realm of the material. This primacy of pleasure provided the eighteenth century with a new epistemology, a new ethics, and a new esthetics. Knowing the world, experiencing pleasure, and creating beauty became the complementary components of a materialist cosmology, a secular morality, and a sensationist esthetics.

The chapters that follow examine the challenges involved in the enterprise of depicting pleasure. The very notion of representing pleasure opens a dilemma. By its nature, pleasure is both exhilarating and frustrating. It exhilarates as the experience of a present so complete that it seeks no foundation beyond itself. It frustrates because that exaltation within a unique moment implicitly forecloses its integration within any more enduring supplement. Each of the chapters that follow will focus on an instance of this dialectic by looking at how key works from the French eighteenth century—novels, paintings, philosophical treatises, and plays—reveal what were the shapes and stakes of its enlightened pleasures.

1. The Pleasures of Failure
Jourdan's *Le Guerrier philosophe*

Pleasure may well, as Hegel said of history, exist only in writing, only in the stories that portray it. As an experience, pleasure is one with, and limited to, the senses. As a reality endowed with meaning, however, pleasure becomes perceptible for others only through representation. Only written or pictured pleasure extends beyond its present and offers itself to others who might experience it vicariously. To represent pleasure is to strain toward a form that must be as tangible and immediate as possible. Yet, try as it might, the enterprise of writing pleasure always comes up short, always turns pleasure into something else.

This dilemma of pleasure's relation to writing lies at the core of the Enlightenment novel. No literary genre was more closely associated with—or more vociferously denounced for—its proximity to pleasure. On the one hand, in a novel the description of pleasure, especially pleasure of the senses, was seen as exercising a dangerous power not only to reenact itself in the mind of the reader but to encourage that reader, even in her conduct, toward acts of unbridled license. On the other hand, as the century's novelists never tired of repeating, the novel, more than any other literary form, could fashion its portrayals of pleasure to illustrate a moral lesson. To give pleasure and to instruct—*plaire et instruire*—summarized the defining ambitions of the genre. As responses to the ambiguities of pleasure's representation, the eighteenth-century French novel—a grab bag of vastly different narrative forms—has no more curious trait than its ability to renew itself through its failures. Prodding the form in ever new directions, the gap between experience and representation as well as between pleasure and instruction established the novel both as a story of failure and as a failure of story.

Toward the middle of Jean-Baptiste Jourdan's *Le Guerrier philosophe* of 1744, Sophie, the young yet already widowed sister of the narrator's closest friend, wishes above all to overcome an unrequited love for the narrator. This narrator, the warrior-philosopher of the title, happens to notice, while accompanying Sophie on a visit to one of her relatives, that she is carrying a book. When he asks her what it is, Sophie replies that she has just finished reading, for the second time, Mme de Lafayette's *La Princesse de Clèves* of 1678. Complimenting her on her excellent taste, the narrator remarks that it is certainly the best of what people call novels, but that its title is poorly chosen, that its real value would be better reflected by a title such as *L'École des femmes* (School for Wives). Sophie agrees with him—but only up to a point. "You are right, and I know of no reading better suited to fortify wavering virtue. . . . But there are unfortunate situations in which even good examples are of no help to us. We may, in the sway of a violent passion, admire virtue, but that does not give us the fortitude to follow its promptings, and our best intentions remain without effect."[1]

Sophie's point is an important one: though a masterpiece of exemplary fiction, *La Princesse de Clèves* has miserably failed Sophie as a reader who asks only to learn its lesson. This *mise en abyme* of what one asks from a novel takes place while Sophie and her brother Saint-Julien, accompanied by the narrator, are visiting the richly appointed home of Mme de Chat*** on family business. Sophie, it happens, particularly enjoys these visits because her aunt has transformed an entire room of her house into a picture gallery in which she displays her collection of paintings depicting characters from classical literature. Shortly before her exchange with the narrator on the failure of exemplary fiction, Sophie insisted on giving him a guided tour of the picture gallery. During that tour, she draws his attention to three works depicting scenes from Homer and Virgil. The first is of the tearful Ariadne as she watches Theseus leaving the island of Naxos. The second shows Ulysses as he sails away from Ogygia, where he has been the lover of Calypso for ten years. The third depicts Dido as she prepares to die on her funeral pyre while the ship carrying Aeneas away from her can be seen in the distance.

For the young narrator, an easy identification with the heroes portrayed in these paintings makes their lesson an obvious one. As he puts it to

Sophie: "No sooner is the torpor into which their passion has plunged them interrupted by the voice of a duty to greater things than reason draws force from it and overcomes the promptings of their hearts" (116). For Sophie, to the contrary, these same images, filtered through her identification with the abandoned heroines, are illustrations of a very different lesson. "I admit that each time I come here, I cannot stop myself from sympathizing with the fate of these three unfortunate women. Their lovers' ingratitude touches me and I can think only of men's treachery" (115).

These painted scenes from antiquity, evoking the classical epic as the most distant origin of the novel's dialectic of pleasure and instruction, also foreground the act of reading as inevitably ambiguous. The young narrator sees in these images the confirmation of an ideal to be imitated, a model of what he might become. Sophie, to the contrary, sees in them a consolation, a distancing of herself from her own suffering as she sees it shared by another. This scene juxtaposing the quest for a model and the balm of consolation brings into focus the broad and contradictory spectrum of the pleasures a reader might ask of the novel. Jourdan, as we shall see, inscribes both these postures within the very form of his work. This story of a young hero obsessed by the question of how pleasure relates to virtue will begin with him trying to learn from the intercalated stories told by others. Later, when his own story becomes one of seemingly irretrievable loss, he will discover the novel's other more muted pleasure of consolation as it is enunciated by the enigmatic character of Mlle Du ***. That encounter, as the work's penultimate episode, allegorizes the way the novel's pleasure, as a representation rich with a presence that recedes into the inaccessible, draws its force from an always asymptotic relation to the real. When, to the contrary, the muted pleasure of consolation is replaced by what is accessible within the real, the novel as novel can only implode.

Born in Marseille in 1711, Jean-Baptiste Jourdan was the son of a ship captain. As a young man, he distinguished himself—not unlike the narrator of his novel—in a number of naval battles while under his father's command. Rather than pursuing a military career, however, Jourdan spent most of his adult life in Paris. His various attempts to establish himself as a playwright (his *L'École des prudes* was performed at the Théâtre italien in 1753, but no script has survived), as a translator, as a music critic (his two *Lettres du correcteur des bouffons* defend the cause of French as opposed to Italian opera within the context of the 1750s *Querelle des bouffons*), and as a novelist had only limited success. The entry on Jourdan in Michaud's 1854 *Biographie universelle* describes his career with a merciless irony: "He was not born to poverty, but earned it."[2] *Le Guerrier philosophe, ou mémoires de M. le duc de **** was the only one of his works to have any real success. Reprinted in 1752 and 1764, it has not been edited since and has received little critical attention.[3]

Presenting itself as a memoir, *Le Guerrier philosophe* tells the life story in the first person of an unnamed Chevalier, the younger son in a family of the minor nobility that had emigrated from Italy to Provence in the second half of the fourteenth century, during the time of Urban V's Avignon papacy. The narrator, inducted as a child into the celibate Knights of Malta so as to protect his older bother's inheritance, begins his military career when he goes to sea at the age of fourteen. The novel covers the period during which he transfers to the elite corps of the *mousquetaires gris*, purchases a regiment, and goes on to participate in the Italian campaign of the War of Polish Succession between 1733 and 1738.

As a young man in Marseille, immediately after his first exploits at sea, the Chevalier becomes fast friends with the older Saint-Julien, the son of an influential noble family in that port city. Committed to the goal of incarnating the *guerrier philosophe* of the novel's title, the narrator's dreams of military glory make him impervious to the obsessive love which Sophie, Saint-Julien's sister, feels for him from the moment they meet. Divided into four parts, the novel's first half is structured as the loose and digressive narrative of that unrequited love. Parts 3 and 4, which could well be subtitled "Sophie's Revenge," tell the story of the narrator's own discovery and loss of love in the person of Geltrude, a member of the Italian nobility, whom the Chevalier first meets at an officers' ball in Milan. Unconstrained by this central plot, the novel also tells, through a series of intercalated narratives, the tumultuous story of Saint-Julien's life-long love for an elusive Spanish noblewoman named Doña Clara.

Le Guerrier philosophe opens with a preface in which an unnamed *rédacteur* explains why he has chosen so striking a title for the life story that will follow: "This title seems particularly apt to me because of both the character's ardor for combat and his love for learning. He hopes to find the source of the true good in philosophy. He lives his life, he wishes to be happy—and that idea guides all his desires" (xv). The main character's goal of becoming a philosopher has less to do with allegiance to a school or intellectual doctrine than it does with parrying a danger—a danger, however, that is at the same time so attractive that the Chevalier might well be seen as a masculine twin to the self-mastering Princesse de Clèves: "As love seems to him the greatest enemy of that perfect peace of soul he seeks, he fears both its turmoil and its seductive charms. He avoids it, but he wants to experience it" (xv).

As the *rédacteur* sees it, it is the dilemma of fearing the pleasure of love yet longing to know it which makes the life story of this young knight (he will become the duke referred to in the title only in the novel's closing paragraph) a subject worthy of a memoir, a genre usually reserved for the lives of kings and generals. If the Chevalier's story deserves to be published, it is because of its exemplarity: its ability, like what we call history, to provide for its readers a story from the past that will serve as a lesson for the future. "What in fact is the point of this story? It is to offer us a panorama of what has happened before us, so that, when we compare that panorama with the events of our own time, both the general and specific reflections it provokes can provide us with a lesson for our own conduct" (ix). To publish the thoughts and actions of someone who is neither a prince nor a statesman, but someone very much like the majority of the work's readers—"characters to whose rank and station we can relate" (ix)—is not to debase the memoir as a genre, but to enhance it as a didactic and heuristic enterprise. This first-person narrative revealing the hidden workings and disavowed motivations behind the pleasures and passions that prompt the Chevalier's actions—the "thousand small details" which "reveal the hidden wellsprings of our actions and our passions" (x)—is offered to its readers as a point of comparison that will help them to better understand themselves as well as to learn from mistakes and errors while remaining safely removed from the consequences of such failures. As "a faithful mirror of our errors," the Chevalier's memoir will move its readers to "censure themselves in secret." It is through a subtle dialectic of identification and disassociation that this novel will achieve its aim of providing "the seed of a virtue which must necessarily produce a positive effect" (xi).

The choice to narrate failures in a diction devoid of moral condemnation may, the *rédacteur* admits, appear to some as an indulgence in frivolity and licentiousness. To the contrary, he insists, the nonjudgmental story of the narrator's failures establishes *Le Guerrier philosophe* as an instrument of reform far more effective than the minatory disquisitions of such classical moralists as Pascal and La Rochefoucauld. As eloquent as those castigators of human folly may be, their "too starkly drawn portraits" give the impression that they are "raging against human nature," producing a discourse that alienates more than instructs: "I am repulsed by such moralizing. There is no point in my being crudely told I am ambitious, miserly, libertine, conceited, etc." (xiii). Those dark visions of human nature not only ill dispose the reader to any positive message but compromise a fundamental dimension of sociability by exacerbating their readers' mistrust of their fellows: "Alas, we are born with enough dislike of our fellows that there is no need to make everyone seem odious" (xii). This memoir's choice to represent experience in all its moral ambiguity will, to the contrary, have the positive effect of serving to "foment a mutual compassion which becomes a bond of friendship between all men" (xiii).

The moralist, measuring humankind against a standard of inflexible virtue, can only denigrate and condemn. His single and ever-repeated lesson is the universality of human frailty and duplicity. *Le Guerrier philosophe*, to the contrary, will speak in the uncertain first-person voice of a consciousness caught up in the difficult process of discovering itself, the world, and its challenges. The course of the narrator's life—its interplay of hypothesis, experience, and chastened apprenticeship in the pursuit of true pleasure—will be useful for the reader because it captures experience as the performance of an always unscripted role forged at the intersection of an opaque self and an ever-changing world.

The Chevalier, passing quickly over his birth, his youth in Avignon, and his early military career of heroic rescues at sea, points out that it was only when he found himself based at Marseille shortly after the plague years of 1720 to 1722 that he made it his "principal occupation to observe and reflect on the actions of men" (10). This initiation to the reflective life leads not to the moralist's certainty, but to the philosopher's perplexity. "All that study which had been the principal occupation of my moments of leisure served only to increase my confusion as to crucial points of metaphysics and morality. I felt I glimpsed truth, but could not yet see it clearly" (11). Embarking on a program of reading that includes history, novels, and poetry, he deduces from his study and experience not the moralist's vision of virtue but the Epicurean's conviction that it is the force of passion and the promise of pleasure that drive humankind: "One of the things that most struck me was to see that in all ages it is love that rules our world and agitates the whole of humankind—and that, in spite of its devastating disorders, no one had been able to hold himself safe from it" (11). Be they gods or kings, magistrates or philosophers, wise men or fools, all are equally subject to pleasure's fickle illusions. Looking both to what history teaches and to what the conduct of his fellows confirms, the Chevalier comes to see clearly not the steadfastness of virtue but the evanescence of pleasure: "How can it be that so many sighs and tears serve only to obtain a good which a moment later no longer touches you? Love must therefore be madness and all the more so because its goal is an illusion whose possession abolishes all feeling. Furthermore, it clearly makes us run the risk of losing all reason and virtue. Does the wise man need any further justification for holding himself safe from it?" (12).

At the beginning of his story, the Chevalier approaches life armed only with abstract convictions—abstract both because they are book-bound beliefs and because their unifying principle is the Stoic imperative of refraining from passion and its pleasures. The situations and characters he later encounters will, through their interlocking stories, provide multifaceted illustrations that reveal the inadequacy of the regimen adopted by the would-be *philosophe*. Starting from the Stoic premise that the world and the self can be dominated by reason, he will discover a consciousness never able to move outside the warring dictates of passion and the pleasures they elect. On the level of the novel's form, the frequent use of intercalated stories underlines the equivalence between narrator and reader. As he listens attentively to the stories told by other characters, the Chevalier himself becomes a version of the reader. The most extensive example of this mirroring comes with Saint-Julien's narration of his past. Taking up the greater part of book 1, this novel-within-the-novel confronts the narrator with the lesson that people and things are rarely as they first appear.

Drawn to Saint-Julien by a calm self-mastery that he seeks only to emulate, the Chevalier will learn from his friend's story a quite different lesson. Returning to events situated five years in the past, Saint-Julien begins his story with the arrival in Marseille of a young Portuguese gentleman named Don Elzear. Moving in the same social circles, Saint-Julien and the foreign visitor quickly become good friends. In the same way that the narrator is drawn to Saint-Julien by his aloof seriousness, so also it is Don Elzear's disdain for petty pleasures—what he describes as "the frivolous delights of a passing affair" (34)—that lead Saint-Julien to choose him as his companion and model.

This male bonding based on a shared devotion to Stoic calm abruptly becomes something else. Having received an unsigned letter in a place where only Don Elzear knew he would be that day, Saint-Julien follows its instructions and lets himself be taken by the mysterious messenger to a small boat on which both embark. Several hours later, when Saint-Julien awakens from a sleep induced by a glass of drugged wine, he finds himself in a remote *bastide* on the coast. Decorated as a temple of Eros, this dwelling is presided over by a bewitching young woman whose unsettling beauty so excites Saint-Julien that his two attempts to respond to her obvious passion result only in premature ejaculation. Later, when Saint-Julien awakens in his own bed after what must have been a second glass of drugged wine that accompanied the exotic supper his *inconnue* provided, the fractured memory of that evening becomes a dream of pleasure that makes all else seem pointless and insipid. The mystery of what happened to him finds its resolution only days later. Following the instructions of a second letter, this one thrown down to him from the parapet of a convent wall and written in the same hand as the first, Saint-Julien develops and executes a plan that will allow him to help the letter writer escape from the convent where she is being held prisoner. Once freed, that letter writer turns out to be not only the mystery woman of his dream but also Don Elzear: "'Good God!,' I cried as I embraced her tightly. 'What happiness is mine! I have found in the same person my mistress and my friend! How sweet it is to pass in that way from friendship to passion!'" (56). Revealing herself to be a Spanish noblewoman named Doña Clara, the woman he had thought was a man explains how she had taken the papers and assumed the identity of her own Portuguese admirer, Don Elzear, when he was killed while helping her to escape a plot by her half-brother to kidnap her and steal her inheritance.

The second chapter of Saint-Julien's story becomes even more baroque. No sooner are the two lovers united in pleasures only intensified by previous gender assumptions than the plague breaks out in Marseille. As panic overcomes public order and all flee the city, Saint-Julien refuses to accompany his family, remaining instead with Elzear-Clara and their two faithful servants. First the servants die of the plague; then Clara falls ill. She is saved when Saint-Julien rescues her from a mass grave where her seemingly lifeless body had been thrown by the guard that inspects every house for corpses.

But, just as the worst seems over, Saint-Julien again discovers that Clara has disappeared, this time leaving no trace as to where she might have gone.

To the Chevalier's great surprise, Saint-Julien is hardly the calm devotee of reason he had imagined. He is instead the product of a story whose roller-coaster itinerary, from erotic paradise to streets flowing with corpses, places him at the antipodes of the narrator's ideal of Stoic self-containment. Summing up his life, Saint-Julien illustrates the powerlessness of reason in the face of pleasure and its fantasies: "It is in vain that we try to exempt ourselves from the tribute the two sexes reciprocally owe one another. . . . Wisdom dissolves into folly when confronted by two beautiful eyes" (106). The challenge that Saint-Julien's story levels against the narrator's naïve Stoicism expresses itself both in the rhetoric of Epicurean materialism—"Our hearts hold within them a seed of tenderness, a seed whose fruits a beautiful woman will sooner or later claim. We live so that we might love, and to our dying breath our actions have no cause or goal other than love" (108)—and as a celebration of passion as the driving force of all civilized life: "Love holds society together. It inspires eloquence, poetry, music, and literature. . . . It sweetens our conduct, making us polite, mild, honest, and sometimes virtuous" (108). Even as it brings book 1 to a close, Saint-Julien's lesson of acceptance fails to allay the Chevalier's misgivings: "He did not succeed in changing my ideas. All that had happened to him seemed disastrous and the very story I had just heard was proof of that" (109).

Structuring his novel as an inventory of attitudes toward the pleasures and dangers of passion, Jourdan next leads his narrator to an encounter with a very different kind of character. As the antithesis of Saint-Julien's devotion to a love that exists only in memory, the Comtesse de *** is a frank and avid champion of Epicureanism. Amused by the Chevalier's prim dismissal of sensual pleasure as meaninglessly evanescent, she delights in contradicting everything his study of philosophy has taught him. " 'How sadly mistaken you are!' replied the Comtesse. 'Even if, as you claim, our passions are fleeting and frivolous, we have only to repeat them over and over to know true delight' " (139). Passion, she concedes, may be fickle, but the variety and multiplicity of its pleasures provide the perfect remedy for that shortcoming: "What if your beloved no longer pleases you? Simply leave. What if she no longer loves you? Console yourself for her faithlessness with someone else. What if several appeal to you at the same time, and find themselves beguiled by your charms? Discourage none of them, and enjoy all your conquests"

(140). Even as the narrator defends his allegiance to self-contained calm, his words become a comic denegation of his actions as the Comtesse proceeds to provide him with his first real experience of what all the fuss is about: "The Comtesse's caresses only intensified my ardor. Covering me with kisses, she took advantage of the impetuousness with which I embraced her to lead me to her bed, where love took care of the rest" (147).

While book 1 was centered on the Chevalier's inability to understand the force of the remembered pleasures still alive in Saint-Julien's narrative of a passion made sacred by loss, book 2 is structured around the narrator's discovery of passion's antipleasure, jealousy, as the first flickering of a conflagration to come. The pleasure he discovers with the Comtesse may have left him with his "imagination still dazzled by the delights of the previous night" (148), but his philosophical pretensions soon whip up his virtuous indignation at the thought that any continued liaison with such a woman can mean that he will find himself forced "to see [himself] tossed aside for whomever might come along, tormented by jealousy, stifling [his] regrets, and gnawed by [his] pain" (148). Repulsed by the thought of such degradation, our philosopher resolves to eschew the dangers he associates with any woman "who lives entirely through her senses" (148).

There is, however, no easy exit for the Chevalier from the dilemma of jealousy that shapes book 2. Sophie, Saint-Julien's recently widowed sister, is more obsessively committed than ever to having the Chevalier as her husband. There is something almost comical in the narrator's half-hearted attempts to show some enthusiasm for that possibility and for making the case to his own family that a marriage to Sophie would in no way jeopardize his older brother's inheritance. The coldness of the letter he writes to his uncle in defense of this position leaves the anxious widow with no illusions: "Could anything be more tepid!" (174), is her reaction when she reads what he has written. When his family's refusal of the marriage allows the Chevalier to breathe an all too audible sigh of relief, Sophie abruptly decides to cure herself "of a passion that can only destroy" her (187), receiving as her guest a young magistrate from Aix whom her father sees as a perfect match. To the Chevalier's enormous surprise, the simple presence of this new suitor as the apparent object of Sophie's attentions triggers a reaction he would never have expected: "I admit that I was unable to watch with calm even the slight signs of favor with which Mme de Viler [Sophie's married name] greeted him. I found myself upset by them without understanding why, as it was clear to me that I felt no love for her. Could it be that I felt jealousy even without feeling love?" (188).

Jealousy—experienced as a vague risk in relation to the Comtesse and as a curious surprise with Sophie—becomes the driving force of books 3 and 4. Everything the narrator has failed to learn from the stories told by others now becomes the very stuff of his own story. Leading a regiment sent to northern Italy during the War of Polish Succession, the narrator abruptly finds himself stepping into another world—not only of war, but of love. While attending a ball given by the French commander in honor of the ladies of Milan, the narrator is unexpectedly approached by a striking young woman. "My surprise was accompanied by feelings entirely new to me. My eyes remained fixed on her without my intending it, and looking at her gave me a feeling of pleasure and affection I had never before experienced" (205). Anticipating the leitmotiv of all that will happen between them, he focuses, not on her taking the initiative of speaking to him, but on the question she asks him—the name of a man dancing with one of her friends—and the jealousy it triggers. When that same dancer, the Duc de la Trimouille, then requests the next dance of the unknown woman who spoke to him, the Chevalier finds that "her every glance penetrated to my very heart" (205). Hardly able to speak when she rejoins him after the dance, the narrator is even more intensely affected by her departure: "At that moment a part of my soul left me. I felt a profound regret when I could no longer see her and a secret longing fell over my senses" (206).

Book 3 begins with a sentence that captures the new opacity of self born of the Chevalier's unexpected encounter: "From that day on I felt I had become a different person" (209). Struggling to understand what is happening to him, the narrator discovers that what had always been his surest source of guidance has run dry. The calm wisdom provided by his revered philosophers has been replaced by a need for different pleasures that consolidate a single omnipotent image: "The image of my *belle inconnue* had so totally taken possession of my mind that all serious reading became impossible. Only poetry and novels now held any charm for me" (210). Struggling with an obsession for which his studies have in no way prepared him, the Chevalier's devotion to philosophy is replaced by the anticipation of pleasures he can only imagine. "What a crowning blow to my vanity! What good, I asked myself, have all my study and meditations done me? Yet I am delighted with my sorry state! I adore it, and everything related in any way to my love thrills and enchants me. What a ridiculous state for a philosopher who wanted only to attain true happiness through wisdom" (235).

Books 3 and 4, a chronicle of the Chevalier's courtship of Geltrude, *la belle inconnue*, are structured as a dialectic between the pleasures of love reciprocated and the tortures of jealousy as love's enemy twin. For the Chevalier, the Duc de la Trimouille, who triggered his insecurity, will be replaced first by the Marquis de Roz, a fellow officer bent on courting Geltrude, and far more seriously by Comte Novati, a cousin of Geltrude whom her mother is determined for her to marry. When the narrative's focus is not on the Chevalier's jealousy, it shifts instead to how Geltrude's discovery of Sophie's portrait and letters convinces her that the Chevalier is a liar unworthy of her love. These permutations of pleasure and suffering, punctuated by the narrator's military campaigns, lead the Chevalier to recast his devotion to philosophy as an egotism whose indulgence erases any boundary between passion and masochism. "I reproached myself for my pride, for my having spurned a penchant so essential to all humanity. It is only fitting, I said to myself, that I should suffer more than another. If I had followed the natural inclination toward love which all men share, I would have experienced moments of discomfort in the midst of numberless pleasures. But I chose to rebel against the law that subjects all to beauty's power. Now I am punished, and fully deserve to be" (308).

At one level, the Chevalier's dilemma is a reenactment of his earlier debate with the Epicurean Comtesse. What has changed, as we saw when his tastes as a reader abruptly shifted from philosophy to novels and poetry, is his perception of the relation between reading and life. The question now raised is not whether pleasure is positive or negative, but how reading relates to experience as an apprenticeship of pleasure. The sharpest formulation of that question comes from the Marquise de Marignan, Geltrude's mother, as her reaction to the intercalated story told by her companion Brigide—who turns out to be none other than Clara, Saint-Julien's long-lost beloved.

Beginning her story at the moment we last saw her—when she disappeared from Marseille because she was kidnapped by bandits who intended to sell her as a slave in North Africa—Clara recounts how she was rescued at sea by a Dutch vessel on which one of the passengers happened to be the Marquise's brother. Resolved to help this destitute but clearly honorable young woman, that brother arranged for Clara to be escorted to his sister's villa near Milan. There, renamed Brigide by the Marquise in honor of a lost friend, she has since lived as a sister to her hostess and as a cherished aunt for Geltrude. "When Clara had finished her story, the Marquise posed a peculiar question: Would life be happier lived in unchanging tranquility, or agitated by the misfortunes that are the products of our passions? We might never, she continued, be plagued by passing troubles; but neither would we know those sweet outpourings, that vital and pure joy, the elation that comes with the end of longing when we rejoice in the possession of the beloved we have chosen" (262–63). This summary of Clara's story in the form of the question it poses accomplishes two things. It acknowledges the ideal of Stoic tranquility to which the Chevalier has so long been attached. At the same time, however, it refocuses the implications of that ideal on a different kind of choice: as we live our lives, should we do so as readers of philosophy or as readers of novels? Should life be approached with the expectations the reader brings to a philosophical treatise, or with the expectations one brings to a novel?

The lesson the Marquise draws from Clara's narrative is that the novel's value lies not so much in its content, in how much or how little its story might coincide with our own, but in its very form, in the ways the genre's surprising and unanticipated concatenation of events speaks to the shape and limits of the expectations one should bring to life. As a reaction to Clara's tale of coincidences, reversals, and last-minute rescues, the Marquise's question invites the reader to see even in a novel's most baroque elements, not the gratuitous devices of an overheated imagination, but the very underpinning of the genre's relation to pleasure. Conversely, she suggests that to live life as a quest for the calm mastery of the philosopher is to confuse abstraction with reality and thought with experience. What the Chevalier must finally understand is that the novel's form is consubstantial with its lesson: that the philosopher's insistence on a logical continuity between past, present, and future will produce only delusion and suffering. To refuse pleasure's hallmarks of the unanticipated, the precarious, and the uncontrollable is to ask from the chaos of experience an equanimity that consolidates ignorance with pride.

What is most original in *Le Guerrier philosophe* is Jourdan's choice to allegorize within his novel the complex interplay between reading, pleasure, and fiction. As we saw, the event holding the two halves of the novel together is the narrator's encounter, in the closing pages of book 2, with the woman who will transform him from philosopher into lover. During that first meeting at the Commander's ball the Chevalier has no idea who that *belle inconnue* might be. Book 3 opens as the French army prepares to take up its winter quarters in Milan. As chance would have it, the Chevalier meets there the Marquise de Marignan—the woman whose life he saved some fifteen years earlier when he was a young cadet in the Galères du roi. Remembering well the young man whose sword cut down the pirate about to kill her and the infant daughter she held in her arms, the Marquise insists that he stay at her villa as her guest. It is, of course, her own daughter, now finishing her studies at a local convent, who turns out to be the beautiful young woman he met at the ball. As events unfold, the Chevalier learns from the Marquise both the good news that Geltrude has no fonder wish than to thank the brave knight of Malta who saved her life and the bad news that the Marquise intends to have her daughter marry her nephew Count Novati, an officer fighting on the side of the Austrians.

Obliged to leave Milan on a family errand, the Marquise suggests that the Chevalier not wait until her return to meet her daughter, but that he visit her at the convent. It is during his first such visit that, as though enacting a scene from Marivaux, the narrator chooses to mask his identity as a way out of the dilemma of being in love with a woman he knows is promised to another. When he visits Geltrude, he introduces himself as the Chevalier de la Garde, claiming to be a friend of Geltrude's long-absent father, who has been living in Paris as a political exile. After shedding filial tears for the father she so misses, Geltrude ravishes the narrator when she then asks if he might also have any news of a fellow knight of Malta: her gallant rescuer, who, she explains, is the only other man from France she would wish to meet.

This mininovel of the narrator's masquerade begins to weave its own plot when, under his assumed identity as the Chevalier de la Garde, he launches into the sad story, told to the very woman he loves, of how that rescuer of long ago has since been transformed by an ill-fated love. "Ah, Mademoiselle, the Chevalier is now a different man. He defied love, and love has punished him. Two bewitching eyes have subjugated him to a passion which inspires a thousand others. He sighs night and day, all the more unhappy because his suffering is without remedy" (221). This conversation, continued over many visits, allows the Chevalier, under cover of the third person of his absent friend, to luxuriate in a prolonged description of the intensity of his feelings and of the suffering he endures at the thought that the woman he loves is promised to another.

Everything changes, however, when the Marquise, back from her trip, insists that her daughter join them for a celebration of their reunion with their rescuer. No longer able to pose as the Chevalier de la Garde, the narrator finds it unthinkable that he disavow the passion he has so eloquently described to Geltrude under cover of talking about someone else. He resolves his dilemma by adding an additional character to the novel he has created. Yes, he is their rescuer. And yes, he is deeply and tragically in love—but with a different woman. This new character of the other beloved not only allows his novel to continue, but sets up a scene that will confirm the power of fiction to shift the contours of even the most intractable reality.

Torn between a desire to declare his love to Geltrude and the fear that doing so will end any relation he might have with her, he loses control over the boundary between fiction and life, between the third person of the absent beloved and the first and second persons of his conversation with Geltrude. One afternoon, trying to draw for Geltrude and Brigide-Clara a verbal portrait of the woman he loves, he offers a metaphor that coincides with reality: "As for her person, I can imagine no one comparable to her. She has your bearing, your grace, your complexion, your mouth, your eyes—these beautiful eyes [*ces beaux yeux*] which I cannot behold without dying of love" (236). Hearing "*these* beautiful eyes" (*ces beaux yeux*), as opposed to the homonymic "*her* beautiful eyes" (*ses beaux yeux*), just as the Chevalier intended it, Geltrude, less surprised than the Chevalier might think, interrupts him to confirm aloud what the wise Brigide-Clara has long been whispering to her: "Ah, Brigide, your suspicions are all too well founded!" Having discovered the reality behind his story, Geltrude asks just what it is he proposes to do. Stepping outside his fiction, the narrator replies, "To love you tenderly and, as I can expect no return of that sentiment, to merit at least your sympathy" (237). The Chevalier's mininovel, now recognized as fiction, has created its own reality. Regardless of its conditional tense, Geltrude's response—"If only I were not engaged and could listen to you without guilt" (237)—opens the way to the protracted minuet of pleasure and suffering that will punctuate their love and jealousy to come.

Within this topsy-turvy love story, the summit of passion and pleasure reciprocated even as they are declared occurs in a scene that directly allegorizes writing's power to go beyond what, as unmediated experience, would have been shot through with fear, suspicion, and insecurity. Over the three months the narrator must spend with his regiment in the field and separated from his beloved, his only contact with Geltrude is through the letters he writes during pauses in the battles between the French and the imperial coalition. In December, when impassable roads make continued military maneuvers impossible, the Chevalier is at last able to return to Milan. Once again at the Marquise's villa, where the wounded Saint-Julien has been reunited with his long-lost Clara, the narrator's only wish is to see Geltrude. Told she is "busy reading and has asked not to be disturbed" (341), the narrator nonetheless hurries to her room. As he arrives there, he finds her so absorbed in her reading that he begins to experience his arrival less as the long-anticipated surprise he will offer her than as his intrusion on a private moment: "Geltrude was seated at a porphyry desk on which she had placed both her arms. Although she was facing a large mirror, her eyes were lowered toward a paper which she read with such obvious satisfaction that she did not notice my arrival. I expected that, as soon as she happened to glance at the mirror, she would see me. I stood perfectly still waiting to surprise her, but she did not look up" (341–42). What he calls his "slight impatience" with Geltrude's absorption in her reading becomes something else when, as he examines her reflection in the mirror, the narrator realizes that what she is reading is a letter written in his own hand. Announcing his presence now yields to the attraction of a different yet unexpectedly intense pleasure. "My love for her was so flattered at seeing in her hands that proof of my tenderness that it did not even occur to me to interrupt her. I stood perfectly still so as to savor for as long as possible so delicious a sight" (342).[4]

As she reads the Chevalier's letter, Geltrude is present, absent, and finally more completely present for him because of that absence. The lovers may share the same physical space, but, for the duration of her reading, Geltrude inhabits and reacts to the written world of the letter. Her reading body—"she sigh[s] over certain passages" (342)—becomes the direct expression of the pleasure she finds within that other world of the letter. Thanks to his letter, the Chevalier is able to perceive both Geltrude's reading aloud of the words he has written and her own reaction to those words—a reaction that confirms a reciprocity so complete that their two subjectivities become one. "She was visibly moved, as though the words that expressed *my* love had sprung from *her own* thought" (342; italics mine). Watching unseen as Geltrude reads his letter, the narrator discovers a "delirium of love," which, had Geltrude been aware of his presence, would have been disguised as something else. Geltrude's response to the letter's closing plea—"Remember that my entire happiness depends on your loving me"— unleashes a power of what is read so complete that, when she raises her eyes from the letter to the mirror, the image of the Chevalier she discovers there exists for her not as reality but as a fantasy inspired by the letter's more perfect world: " 'Yes, I do, dear Chevalier,' she repeated as she lifted her eyes to the mirror and looked at me with a passion that proved she took me for an illusion sprung from her own feelings rather than as someone actually present and able to hear the declaration she had just made" (343). Geltrude's other world of the letter she is reading will yield to reality only when the Chevalier, overwhelmed by what he has been privileged to see, inadvertently brings about this change: "I was so moved that, taking a step forward as though I were about to throw myself before her, the spell was broken. 'Good God!,' she cried as she turned toward me, 'It is actually him' " (343). Returning to a reality reshaped by the world of the letter, they share a kiss that brings with it "everything most touching and most delicate in love's pleasure" (344).

This staging of the narrator as unseen but ravished spectator repeats and recasts a very different scene of voyeurism. Shortly before leaving for maneuvers, and determined to overhear the secrets he is sure Geltrude shares with Clara, the Chevalier had followed the two women to the secluded *grotte des bains* on the villa's grounds. Hiding in a small changing room, the Chevalier was able, as he watched Geltrude undress and enter the pool of black marble, "to admire for almost an entire hour a beauty and grace so delightful that I felt I would die of rapture and love" (314). In this earlier scene, however, the voyeur's pleasure was promptly punished when Geltrude decided to nap in the very changing room where the Chevalier had hidden. "Gripped by the worst fear I had ever known" (314), he was forced, contorted and suffering, to hide almost without breathing under the very bench where Geltrude lay. Because she locked the room's door from outside when she left, the Chevalier was also obliged to remain there until nightfall when, as his last punishment, he nearly broke his arm as he fell from the high window that provided the only exit. A masochistic variation on the episodes of voyeurism so frequent in libertine fiction, this ordeal from before his departure prepares and anticipates the later moment of voyeurism and shared ecstasy that will be made possible by writing and reading.

Book 4, after its opening scene of shared pleasures, depicts the declining fortunes of the Chevalier. Geltrude's mother may finally consent to her daughter's marrying the man she loves, but that option disappears when the narrator is forced to kill Geltrude's putative fiancé, Comte Novati, when he and his henchmen attack him in the courtyard of the Marignan villa. As blameless as he may be, it is now unthinkable for the Marquise that she might ever "welcome into my family the murderer of my sister's son, and place him in my daughter's bed" (376). Because the Comte's death also risks touching off an uprising against the French troops, the Chevalier is ordered by his commander to leave Italy immediately. Once back in Paris, he is greeted with the sad news that both his father and his beloved uncle have recently died. Later, when Saint-Julien returns from Italy, the final blow comes with his report that both Geltrude and Clara have disappeared without a trace.

During his first stay in Paris, it was the vivacious Comtesse who had provided the young Chevalier with his first inkling of an Epicurean alternative to his naïve Stoicism. Now, as an echo of that earlier encounter, it is another alluring female character, Mlle Du ***, who will provide the bereft narrator with a different lesson, which in turn prepares the novel's final implosion. What the narrator learns from Mlle Du *** also relates to the novel's function of consolation as it first emerged in the narrator's exchanges with Sophie on her aunt's paintings and *La Princesse de Clèves*. Paralyzed by what he sees as the "hideous revolution" that has transformed his life into an "abyss of sadness" (398), the Chevalier will begin to imagine the possibility of something better only when he happens to visit the Parisian salon of Mme D***, where he discovers the "company of distinguished people who eagerly cultivated her friendship, and made her circle one of Paris's most charming" (399).[5] The effect these gatherings have on him is slow but certain: "Still too preoccupied and melancholy to pay much attention to anything . . . I nonetheless felt less depressed than had become my custom when I left that delightful gathering" (401). Discovering the pleasures of Mme D***'s salon much as distracted readers might find themselves intrigued by the opening pages of a novel, the narrator is particularly fascinated by one woman he meets there. The embodiment of charm, wisdom, and beauty, Mlle Du *** emerges as a focus not only for the Chevalier but for all who are present: "The eldest daughter of M. Du *** was the center of everyone's attention. Even I, much to my surprise, found myself intrigued by her. My sadness seemed to disappear while I was with her" (401). As when the Chevalier listened so attentively to Saint-Julien's story of Clara, what happens between the narrator and Mlle Du *** becomes a novel within the novel. As the person on whom all desires seem to converge, Mlle Du *** is portrayed as a synthesis of qualities compelling the interest and admiration of all around her. "Never were so many graces united in a single person. In addition to the most noble bearing and a stature that was both delicate and attractive, Mlle Du *** added the flair of a worldliness which augmented even more the charm of her every action" (401).

What establishes Mlle Du *** as an allegory of a novel that might be read by the narrator is the fact that her consummate grace and charm never come together as a seduction, as the possibility of some accessible pleasure: "What makes her all the more desirable is that, for all her charming qualities, she makes no effort to please" (402). The antithesis of the *petite maîtresse*, Mlle Du *** exists only within the inaccessible realm of her own alluring performance. She is the central and animating figure within this salon in the same way that, in the different register of a mythological painting, the alluring body of a naked goddess might draw the spectator's attention to a display of charms that are by definition inaccessible. The magic of Mlle Du ***, like the magic of a painting's pigment or a novel's words, lies in her power to provide the texture of experience without evoking any of its dangers.

Personifying the novel's ability to console, Mlle Du *** revives the narrator's interest in a world that extends beyond the paralysis of his suffering. "Mlle Du *** often shared with me her reactions to the events that took place around us. As we considered their implications, I discovered to my surprise a deeply reflective side in this spirited young woman. I delighted in drawing out her feelings because I wanted to understand them as fully as possible" (405). In keeping with the novel's rule of combining pleasure with instruction, the Chevalier describes her effect on him: "Well aware of my own character, I decided I needed to cultivate pleasures that would make my life enjoyable" (406). That personal regimen, which she calls "philanthropy," is defined as her choice to "love nothing seriously yet profit from everything" (406). Turning her philanthropic power toward the specific situation of the Chevalier, Mlle Du *** whispers to him that, as concerns his ill-fated love, it is the novel's law of chance that will have the last word: "'Fortune has separated you,' she said to me, 'and fortune will reunite you'" (405). Fascinating yet never fascinated, she offers consolation that may be *for him* but is never *of herself*: "Each time I saw her she consoled me in the same way, devoting her attention to me more out of sympathy with my suffering than out of any preference for my person" (405). Like the events of a novel for its readers, Mlle Du *** remains asymptotic to the Chevalier's reality: no matter how much she brings his world back to life, she is never accessible within that world. Her charm and wisdom produce the spark of pleasure reborn— but that spark illuminates a reality of which she herself is never fully a part.

Mlle Du *** is more than simply another character within the novel. Like a mirror held up to the genre, she reveals the dilemma at the core of the novel's ambition to offer both pleasure and instruction. Once her own and the genre's asymptotic exemplarity come together in the lesson that one must accept the bitter and the sweet of what life chooses to give, the Chevalier is ready for the final turn of chance's wheel that will leave the novel with nothing more to tell.

At a ball to celebrate the impending marriage of Sophie and Clara's first protector, the now resurrected Don Elzear, two masked women suddenly appear. Not only do they turn out to be Geltrude and Clara, but the narrator and Saint-Julien now learn what took them away without a trace. If they disappeared from Milan so abruptly, it was to accompany the Marquise to the sickbed of her long-absent husband, Geltrude's father. Before dying, he insisted that his daughter marry the man who saved him from drowning— none other, as chance would have it, than the Chevalier, who, during his trip back to France, had pulled him from a raging river. Finally coinciding with its subtitle, *les mémoires de M. le duc de ***,* the novel comes to a close in two brief sentences. "We returned to Italy where we established ourselves in the duchy of ***, which Mlle Marignan's aunt had left to her on the condition that I assume its title as my name. I lead there a quiet life and fear death only because it will separate me from my beloved Geltrude" (421).

The Chevalier had begun his story as a relic from a bygone age. Having imagined what he called philosophy to be a Platonic refusal of the senses as threats to the calm sovereignty of reason, his hubris was brought low by everything he discovered through Geltrude. Jourdan's allegory of the novel demonstrates how it is the conjoined failure of pleasure lost and of instruction misunderstood that propels the narrative along its always chance-driven itinerary. Imploding upon itself in its closing marriage scene, the novel ends its story by lifting its characters outside the genre's defining pursuits of pleasure and understanding as quests that can continue only so long as they fail.

2. Mirroring Pleasure

La Morlière's *Angola*

In spite of its publication date of 1744, Jourdan's *Le Guerrier philosophe* remains close in spirit to the culture and preoccupations of the much earlier novel it invokes as its explicit model: Lafayette's *La Princesse de Clèves*, of 1678. Rooted in an esthetic of exemplarity, *Le Guerrier philosophe* assumes that pleasure's depiction will, no matter how complicated its course, ultimately serve the goal of moral instruction. Jourdan's novel includes, seriatim and often as intercalated tales, stories of characters who intersect with and determine one another's fates. The stories they actually tell, however, concern each of them separately as individuals trying to find their way in a world of apparent and real pleasures that provide only ambiguous instruction. *Le Guerrier philosophe* may present itself as a memoir, but it is far more a juxtaposition of the exemplary stories of Sophie, Saint-Julien, Clara, and Geltrude, each of whom moves on and off center stage to narrate his or her past. What anchors Jourdan's novel in the seventeenth century is the artifice of a first-person narrative that effortlessly accommodates itself to the disguises, sex changes, and baroque plot devices of the stories told by other characters.

Jacques Rochette de La Morlière's *Angola, histoire indienne*, published only two years after *Le Guerrier philosophe*, places its reader in a world in which the novel's relation to pleasure and instruction is profoundly different. La Morlière speaks, not of how love and life temper a bookish commitment to the self-mastery of Stoic reason, but of what the novel became for a readership whose primary concern was to be in step with the stylized yet giddy, ritualized yet free-wheeling, and above all Epicurean life-style of Parisian high society. At the same time, the reader is continually invited to laugh mockingly at the frivolity of a world where only fashion reigns. La Morlière's characters exist as functions of their pleasures: the theater, the opera, receptions, reading, hunting, gambling, and—above and before all else—the dynamics and delights of the bedroom. While the narration of these pleasures can never be the equivalent of experiencing them, what La Morlière does offer is a diction of flippancy and cynicism that invites his readers to share an assumed superiority to characters whom in most cases they would be delighted to replace.

Born in Grenoble in 1719 to a distinguished family within *la noblesse de robe*, La Morlière, the son of a city official, completed his legal studies at eighteen; when his father obtained for him a clerkship to a crown magistrate, he seemed destined for high government office.[1] But, at least from his family's perspective, things quickly went wrong. A propensity for brawls and a series of indelicate seductions forced his father to dispatch him to Paris, where he had arranged an appointment to the King's Musketeers with the hope that a position in that elite police force would straighten him out. In fact, the result was the opposite: La Morlière was soon discharged for dishonorable conduct. Living off an allowance from his mother, La Morlière spent the rest of his life trying to make ends meet as a novelist and playwright, but *Angola* would be his only successful and often republished work. Frequently banished from Paris and even imprisoned for various seductions and swindles of young married women, he became a figure of intimidation and braggadocio in the venal world of writers-for-hire and never hesitated to serve as a police informant. He was perhaps best known as the person who, from 1747 to 1758, headed up the most powerful theatrical claque in Paris. With, according to Favart, as many as five hundred hirelings at his disposal and ready to supply applause or boos on command, he could make or break reputations at the Comédie-Française as well as at the Théâtre italien.[2] The effectiveness of his machine (even Voltaire was careful to secure his services for the opening of his *Sémiramis* in August 1748) put La Morlière in a position where he was able to impose, for his own benefit, what amounted to a tax on Parisian theatrical productions.

Be it at the theater or in his private life, La Morlière was an unsavory character who knew the rules of the game, manipulated them to his advantage, and never hesitated to laugh out loud at his dupes. While hardly an admirable human being, his style of mastery, manipulation, and mockery produced *Angola*, a novel whose provocation and wit were perfectly in step with the spirit of his time. Setting aside the mystery of how it happens that bad people write good books, let us look at what *Angola* tells us about French society at midcentury and about the novel of pleasure that came into fashion between Marivaux and Rousseau.[3]

The plethora of prose forms we now group under the rubric of the eighteenth-century French novel—*histoires, nouvelles, mémoires, correspondances, récits de voyage, vies, aventures, contes*, and so on—is a corollary to the fact that, throughout the century, writers systematically avoided the term *roman*, or novel.[4] As early as 1700 *roman* already carried heavy baggage, associated as it was with two different yet equally rejected traditions. On the one hand, it evoked imaginary romances of heroic sentimentality in the tradition of Honoré d'Urfé's *L'Astrée* (1607–19). On the other, it brought to mind burlesque parodies of lower-class life in the tradition of Paul Scarron's *Le Roman comique* (1651–57). Both associations marked the novel as a genre far removed from any serious portrayal of a world that authors actually shared with their readers. The genre's protracted denial of its status as *roman* comes through clearly in the way the English terms *romance* and *novel* are translated into French; the former becomes *le roman romanesque* while the latter becomes *le roman vraisemblable*.

Over and over, the eighteenth-century French writers we now refer to as novelists introduce their works with warnings that what will follow is distinctly different from what readers expect from a novel. In his preface to *La Vie de Marianne* of 1731, Pierre Carlet de Marivaux explains that what we are about to read is certainly not a novel because it eschews that genre's overwhelming emphasis on adventures, those plot-heavy concatenations of unexpected events that were so frequent in *Le Guerrier philosophe*. In a novel, Marivaux points out, "people want only adventures."[5] *La Vie de Marianne*, he insists, is something quite different. It is the story of a real person told in her own voice, "her reflections about life's strange events" (47). What the reader will discover in this work "is not an author, but a woman who thinks" (85). Marivaux's readers, rather than being swept along by surprises of plot, will become privy to the complexities and ambiguities of a real person, of an actual woman the reader might meet or be. As such, Marivaux promises to provide his reader with something far more valuable than the novel's "stories intended only to entertain" (85).

Beginning with his title page, La Morlière pokes fun at this concern with realism and seriousness. Not only is *Angola* an *histoire indienne*, but immediately below that title, a single phrase proclaims it to be "a work destitute of all probability" (*un ouvrage sans vraisemblance*). The irony here is that the apparent exoticism of an oriental fairy tale in fact goes no deeper than the names of places and characters. The story may be situated in some purely imaginary Orient, but each page describes the details, fashions, and even verbal tics of aristocratic society with a specificity that gives it the feel of a guidebook for those who would pass themselves off as insiders. We learn, for instance, how gauche one would appear in being overly attentive to one's ostensible partner during the ritual of the afternoon stroll in the Tuileries. "A lady and gentleman of fashion would never carry on a sustained conversation lest they be taken for some bourgeois husband and wife out for a stroll. Persons of quality speak only in monosyllables and are careful to go their separate ways and then rejoin each other *ten times*."[6] As in the false precision and exaggeration of this *"ten times,"* La Morlière uses italics throughout his dialogues and descriptions to highlight the more egregiously absurd clichés of the practices and parlance that defined high society's *petits maîtres* and *petites maîtresses*.[7]

La Morlière sets his satire in a register markedly different from the diction of Marivaux, whose concern is the complexity of a heroine's inner thoughts as she finds her way within society. La Morlière's focus is on the interplay of social expectation and action in a context larger than the single character or the single gender. The most striking aspect of this novel is the fact that it reads neither as a guidebook for masculine seduction (Claude Crébillon's abiding temptation) nor as an illustration of feminine resistance (Marivaux's abiding temptation). It is not that La Morlière excludes these options, but rather that he subsumes them within a larger and more fundamental dynamic proper to the couple as couple. The story that La Morlière tells is not about one couple or even of a series of couples. It is a story about coupling itself, coupling as a practice of pleasures sought and found within a conviviality that enfolds all who enact its rituals and run its risks. Concentrating on the dynamics of the couple, La Morlière opens up a third way within the traditional alternatives of eighteenth-century fiction. His chronicle of coupling highlights a protocol of social and sexual exchange that recasts the opposition between the libertine novel's celebration of masculine deception and the sentimental novel's travails of feminine passion.

La Morlière's choice of coupling over specific couples declares itself from the opening page. A preface—but a strangely prefatory preface, titled "We Will Soon Get to the Preface"—takes the form of a dialogue between the Comtesse de S*** and an unnamed Marquis as he arrives in her *appartement*.[8] Their banter of seduction and resistance is abruptly redirected by the Marquis' discovery on the Comtesse's night table of the very novel—here mockingly referred to as a *brochure*—we will soon be reading: " 'But what do I see here? A little brochure, *Angola, an Indian Tale. Well, well, this is something new! I have not had the honor of knowing it.*' 'Nor have I,' replied the Comtesse. 'It was given to me this morning, and I am not sure I should read it' " (677). When the Comtesse then suggests that the Marquis read *Angola* aloud, he responds that he will do so only if she can guarantee them the privacy appropriate to the kind of "dissertations" their reading as a couple is sure to initiate. "Close your door to everyone else, I beg you, as I am not at all accustomed to *speaking in public*. There are surely things in this book which we will want to *discuss*, and we don't want just anyone walking in on us as though it were a *public lecture*" (678).

This pre-preface of a couple in the making draws to a close as the Marquis opens the book they are about to read to the brief "Epistle to Coquettes" (*Aux petites-maîtresses*) which provides both a mirror of where they are and a guide to where they might go: "It is as though he were describing our situation. So let us see to it that none of his conjectures prove untrue. He even manages to combine passion with jest" (679). When the Comtesse declares herself less than enchanted to be cast as a coquette, the Marquis' final counsel is that they close the gap between themselves as readers and the characters they will read about by a particular kind of listening. "Listen carefully, and I hope that soon, so as to have your share of the honor paid them, you will be tempted to join their ranks" (679). This enfolding of specific individuals within coupling as a global trope is consolidated by the way the authorial voice within this second preface speaks directly to his female readers, encouraging them to read the novel that will follow in propitious company. "It should be read in company as you prepare your make-up, and it should be interrupted by the naughtiness of a flirtatious abbé, or by the loving attentions of some ardent warrior!" (680). Serving as both guide and witness, as knowing coach and passive watcher, *Angola* is intended to stand as an invitation to the pleasure of deliciously closing the gap between readers and what they read. The work's real ambition is to initiate a dynamic of pleasure between readers and text such that each, drawing from the other, moves toward the Epicurean ideal of coupling as the very essence of nature. "May you learn from its pages, after a few tender moments, still new lessons; and may you imbue it with that divine voluptuousness which is your essence and the very soul of earthly nature" (680).[9] Rather than any furtive liaison between only two individuals, this work, if its erotic charm is successful, will, as its epigraph from Horace makes clear, generate a boundary-abolishing laughter that will allow all readers to find their own story in this novel they are about to read. "Quid rides? Mutato nomine, de te fabula narratur" (Why do you laugh? Change the name, and this fable is your story) (675).

Angola speaks both of coupling's pleasure and of its pathology. That pathology, whose victim will be Angola, traces its genesis to an unfortunate incident involving a mirror. La Morlière's oriental tale opens as King Erzebcan and his wife Arsénide decide to mark the birth of their first child by inviting all the fairies of the earth to a huge celebration. Once they have arrived, the King presides over a *loterie galante*, in which a jeweled prize will be awarded to each of the fairies honoring his house. As luck would have it, Mutine, a fairy as ugly as she is mean-spirited, draws the number that marks as her prize "a hand mirror garnished with jewels" (686). When she holds it up and contemplates the mirror's portrait of her, she discovers "a kind of topsy-turvy face which expressed only dark and deathly malice. She had sunken bloodshot eyes, a flattened nose, and a toothless mouth which opened only to gush stupidity" (686). The mirror's portrait of Mutine as a sight immediately foreclosing any promise of coupling's pleasure is made only more insulting by a snidely ironic remark from the most beautiful of the fairies present, Queen Lumineuse. "Fate has not been blind, Madame, in awarding you so well suited a prize. It will faithfully portray for you those charms which touch every heart, and even dispose you to feel pity for all who fall under the full sway of their spell" (686).

Mutine, enraged and convinced that the King has rigged the drawing so that she would be insulted, avenges the mirror's proof of her exclusion from the realm of coupling by bestowing on the baby boy a poisoned gift meant to compromise all his chances for that pleasure. While the other fairies have given the child such gifts as courage, wit, and comeliness, Mutine confers on him, as the virtue she hopes he will most sorely need, the gift of patience. It is, however, a patience rooted in the Latin *patior,* to suffer. "'You have endowed the Prince with every virtue,' she said in a terrifying voice, 'but you have forgotten patience, which is the one he will need most. You will fall in love,' she continued, 'and the very thing that brings pleasure to others will be the source of your cruelest torments. The most consuming sorrows will devour you as you watch the object of your love pass into another's arms and you are forced to acquiesce. Terrible doubts will rip you apart, and even crueler certainty will crown my vengeance'" (687).

Queen Lumineuse, appalled that her witticism should redound to the detriment of the innocent baby, and realizing she cannot annul Mutine's curse, proposes the solution of having the child come to her court, the most illustrious of the universe, when he reaches puberty. As it is within the dynamics of the couple that Mutine's curse will have its effect, so also it is the tenor of the coupling at Lumineuse's court that will provide the most effective remedy to the fate that threatens him. "All his sufferings," Lumineuse explains to the anxious parents, "are premised on his falling seriously in love. But my court is the surest antidote for that poison. The variety of his pleasures there will keep his mind in balance—not only parrying the sad fate promised him, but, I dare say, assuring him the happiest possible future" (688).

Of course, what the robust adolescent will discover at Lumineuse's court is a thinly disguised Versailles at the acme of its devotion to pleasure in all its forms. Less than a year before *Angola*'s publication, the Maréchal de Saxe's victory at Fontenoy over the combined English and Dutch forces ushered in a new and fevered giddiness in the calendar of pleasures that defined life at court. As the Duc de Luynes notes in his memoirs, it was decided by royal proclamation that "there will be a musical performance on Mondays and Saturdays. A French comedy on Tuesdays and a tragedy on Thursdays. Italian comedies on Wednesdays and Fridays. Gambling on Sundays."[10] Replacing Louis XV with a ravishingly beautiful Queen Lumineuse also acknowledged the new effervescence brought to court when Mme de Pompadour became the King's official mistress in the spring of 1745. More than anything else, however, Lumineuse's realm is a utopia of Epicurean sexuality. At her court, as well as in the city nearby, to be part of a couple is to exist as pure surface and pure appearance. Celebrating life as a spectacle of pleasure in constant movement, this "glittering and boisterous court, where truth can hardly be distinguished from falsehood and where lies not only disguise themselves in the colors of truth, but add to them nuances which make their attraction all the more dangerous" (691), draws even the ponderous categories of true and false into the giddy dance of its mutating couples. Lumineuse, watching over her charge, will instruct Angola carefully in the ambiguities of "those seductive dangers and voluptuous illusions" (691). Mutine's curse of patience, passion, and suffering will be safely eluded so long as Angola is surrounded by women "who have no time for sentimental love, which they find more absurd than respectable" (692). Lumineuse makes clear to the young man that his goal is not to avoid passion and its pleasures but to retain his own Stoic mastery of their effects. More than any other, it is the potentially enslaving passion of love that must be carefully modulated. "Don't reject it completely, but carefully pluck its flower. Use it as a relish for other pleasures in order that it render them even more piquant. Let your heart, even in its deepest swoons, retain command over itself. Take pleasure, be happy; but remain free" (693).

What Lumineuse suggests to Angola as abstract theory will be completed by his budding friendship with Almaïr. A young man the same age as Angola, Almaïr's liaison with Aménis will provide the perfect example of "a peaceful passion which never blinds one to the merits of other women" (729). The ideal proposed here, the secret to endless pleasure and the remedy for Angola's anticipated woes, is an Epicureanism fortified by Stoic self-mastery. Its practice is a prophylaxis intended to prevent any confusion between process and state, between the dynamic of coupling and its transient pairings.[11] Angola must understand that to confuse verb with noun, coupling with any specific couple, is to set oneself futilely against the forces of change and movement. When the timid Angola finds himself infatuated with Zobéide, a close friend of Aménis and someone Almaïr also very much desires, their potential rivalry provides Almaïr with the perfect occasion to explain to Angola the libertine's version of patience—a patience that is safely insulated from suffering. Recognizing that the separation of individuals within the Epicurean clinamen is just as integral a stage of coupling as their coming together, Almaïr feels no jealousy toward Angola's feelings for Zobéide: "For me, all these beautiful women are like *goods in trade* to which all may aspire. I felt something for Zobéide before you did; but, guessing your aspirations, I stepped aside, fully resolved to try again once your fancy for her had passed" (734). The realization that tomorrow will be unlike today, that Angola and Aménis are just as probable a couple as Almaïr and Zobéide, endows all involved—Zobéide and Aménis as much as Angola and Almaïr—with a lucidity beyond all moralizing dichotomies. "After that conversation they went their separate ways, swearing eternal love to ladies they were already thinking about leaving" (735). Very much outside the clichés of predatory men and victimized women, La Morlière's couples embark on a process of feint and deception which is mutual and shared. Within the intimacy of the tight carriage known as a *vis-à-vis* that takes them from the theater to Zobéide's home, Angola and his partner discover that "everything favored passion, lessening timidity for the one and banishing all scruples for the other" (708). The fact that no one is a dupe in coupling's comedy, that each plays to and through the other, is confirmed each time one or the other recites what are defined as "all those courtly phrases with which people mutually agree to deceive one another" (767).

The merry-go-round of pleasures described in *Angola* is apportioned between two distinct yet mutually sustaining spaces. Within the *vis-à-vis*, the *alcôve*, and the *petite maison*, there is the private and personal space of intimacy, of victories and surrenders executed in such a way that those bellicose terms cease to have any real meaning. At the theater, the opera, and court ceremonies, there is the public space of spectacle and display. The locus of rituals performed by *les gens du bel air*, these are spaces in which pleasure is never associated with the purely passive role of watching what occurs on stage. To the contrary, the theater and the opera are points of assembly where, just as when strolling in the Tuileries, individuals indulge themselves in the double pleasure of establishing the self as spectacle and of scrutinizing their audience as a repository of clues as to who is coupled with whom. "The play could not have interested them less, and many asked in the middle of the fifth act what was being performed. It was their own seductive charms which were on display and all fixed their opera glasses on their prey" (739–40). This public space of mutual observation, rather than opposing the space of intimacy, serves indifferently as its preparation and unraveling. The couples move from public to private space not as a choice of the second over the first but as a movement to the second phase of an ever-repeating cycle. Existing within a world where everyone watches everyone and where no movement goes unnoticed, the couple is animated by a desire that is always triangular. To pass from public to private space with any given partner is to whet the appetite of all other potential partners in pleasure.

La Morlière's novel takes the trope of coupling well beyond an illustration of the dynamics presiding over the coming together and moving apart of *petits-maîtres* and *petites-maîtresses*. It deploys its couples in such a way that they tell us something otherwise unnoticed about Enlightenment reading practices, about how and why people consumed these scenarios of pleasure so central to the new Epicureanism. Chapters 10 and 11 of *Angola* take us to the crucial moment when the young prince, having comically missed his chance with the very willing Zobéide, finally loses his virginity—and this with none other than Queen Lumineuse herself. As with the Marquis and Comtesse we met in the preface, the ostensible reason for Angola's evening visit to Lumineuse's private quarters is so that they "might read together a little novel that has just come out" (717). Once they are ready to begin their reading, Lumineuse makes clear for her guest what might be the novel's exemplary value. "It portrays love so well and the lover is so skilled at choosing his moment that, without any tedious delays, he achieves his happiness while leaving his mistress neither the time nor the desire to reproach herself for her weakness" (719–20). Still paralyzed by innocence and timidity, Angola's response to Lumineuse is marked by the contradiction of his simultaneously longing to yet fearing to imagine a continuity between the third person used to describe the characters in the novel they read and the alluring proximity of the first and second persons that constitute his actual "conversation" with Lumineuse. "'How lucky he is!' cried the Prince. 'His enviable situation underlines how different he is from someone whose love is hopeless and whose lips are sealed by respect'" (720). Angola's problem is not in recognizing the pleasure he desires; what he cannot seem to manage is to bring together the third-person "he" and "she" of the novel they read with the first- and second-person readers, himself and Lumineuse.

When Lumineuse coyly proposes the intermediate solution of her serving as the messenger for the declaration of love that Angola finds he is unable to make in person, he timidly conjures up a question situated in a hypothetical middle ground between third and second person: "How could you accept to say things to someone else which I suspect would make you indignant if they were addressed to you?" (721). When their minuet of advance and hesitation threatens to degenerate into pure repetition, Lumineuse turns to their reading as a couple for a possible remedy. " 'But let's examine this book,' she added. 'Perhaps it will be useful for both of us, helping you to find a way out of such an embarrassing *situation*, and helping me to make you more sincere and less evasive' " (721). Now reading with Lumineuse, Angola finds himself more and more excited, not only because "the *situations* were intriguing" (721), but because the couple they read about—"who loved each other simply and charmingly without any of the interminable tediousness of an old romance" (721)—is delightfully unimpeded by the hesitations of Angola's timidity. Empowered by this reading as a couple, Angola is finally able to raise his eyes from the page and complete the transition from third person to first and second person. " 'Well then,' said the Prince, overcome by passion and kneeling beside her, 'let me admit to you the full extent of my rashness. It is to *you* that *I* address these timid vows which *I* never before dared to declare. It is *your* heart that *I* have dared desire' " (722; italics mine).

Their long-awaited movement toward pleasures available only in the first and second persons sets in motion a play of exchanged glances testing the commensurability between what is read and what is done, between the novel they read and the situation they live. "He read in a halting voice, every moment casting glances at Lumineuse that revealed his most ardent desires" (725). It is at this point in their story that La Morlière begins his own textual play with the conventions of the quotation mark as a sign tracing the boundary between what is read and what is done. Emphasizing the contagious pleasures flowing between the novel his characters read and the novel he himself writes, La Morlière's staccato alternation between those two registers erases the border between reading and acting in such a way that life becomes the perfect imitation of art. " 'Such delightful boldness!' continued Angola. 'He dares take from his lady's lips still less ambiguous pledges of her love.' As he read, the Prince, carried away by *the force of example*, dared to approach his mouth to that of the fairy and revel in sweet kisses whose hesitation only made them more precious. 'Still unsatisfied,' the Prince read on, 'his lady's bosom is no longer safe from his passion.' And at that instant, *still faithful to his model*, he threw himself upon the fairy, covering her alabaster breasts with kisses and eager caresses" (725).

In his study of the libertine novel, Jean-Marie Goulemot raises the question of how to define what he calls "pornographic books." A pornographic novel, he finally decides, is one which "has the physiological goal of inspiring in its reader a desire to climax, placing him in a state of tension and lack whose relief can only come from extraliterary means."[12] Goulemot's verbally convoluted definition is clarified by the phrase from Rousseau that he borrows for the title of his study: "Those books which one reads with only one hand." For any reader still too dense to catch his drift, the cover of Goulemot's study reproduces Emmanuel de Ghendt's engraving of Pierre-Antoine Baudouin's painting *Le Midi*. Goulemot lingers long over the details of this engraving of a fully-clothed young woman caught leaning backward against a gentle slope at the exact moment of a self-administered orgasm. Her left hand, slipped discreetly into her skirt, reaches furtively between her spread thighs. Staring fixedly ahead, her pupils are tightened to two black dots. Her slipper is balanced on the extended toes of her foot. Even more important for Goulemot's argument is the fact that the woman's right hand, extended downward and parallel to her pleasured body, seems almost to point to a book that lies open on the ground next to her—the book she had been reading until, its magic having taken effect, she let it fall from her hand.

While Goulemot's use of the Baudouin image is convincing, La Morlière's *Angola* makes clear the need for caution when one chooses Rousseau as a guide to how the eighteenth century conceived of reading and its pleasures. It is hardly surprising that Rousseau, always ready to sense in the presence of another a potential threat to his integrity and independence, should restrict the reading of what Goulemot calls pornographic novels to the solitary imagination. As *Angola* makes clear, however, that is hardly the whole story. What La Morlière began by staging his preface as a couple's coming together to read *Angola*, he repeats and completes in the bravura performance of chapters 10 and 11. With a constant movement between *reading as a couple* and *coupling while reading* as the structural and semantic center of his novel, La Morlière raises to the power of two what Goulemot, speaking of solitary masturbation, refers to as the *mise en abyme* of the standard scene in libertine novels, when a lone character is overcome by his or her reading of a "pornographic" novel.

In the same scene with Lumineuse, where the quotation mark's boundary between what is read and what is done so happily collapses, there also reappears that other instrument of replication that set Angola's story in motion. It was, we recall, the gift of a mirror that unleashed Mutine's fury against the innocent child. Here, as Lumineuse prepares for her late-night *explication de texte* with Angola, she begins to undress. Insisting that Angola need not leave the room, but only that he turn away from her, Lumineuse deftly exploits the presence of a wall mirror, a *trumeau*, in her bedchamber. Like the passages from the novel they will read, the mirror's surface generates its own exciting images. As she "reveal[s] the treasures of a lovely bosom whiter than snow and molded to perfection" (724), glancing at the mirror, she sees not only herself but also the effect which her body, glimpsed in the same mirror, has on Angola. "Lumineuse saw in her mirror how uneasy the Prince became at the sight of her charms. Sure she would increase his fervor by placing an obstacle on his path, and feigning upset at having been glimpsed even for a moment, she immediately raised her hand to adjust her tucker, knowing full well that it would immediately fall again" (724).

For Mutine, the mirror provided only a devastating scrutiny of the self. The repugnance she felt for what it forced her to behold provoked her decision to do the most harm she could to those she imagined responsible for the mirror's affront. For Lumineuse and the peeking Angola, to the contrary, the mirror's surface sets in motion not a scrutiny of self but an anticipation of the shared pleasures sure to come for the couple whose glances it reflects. The presence of mirrors and other instruments of replication and exchange emblematize this novel's commitment to reflecting and inspiring pleasure. In the same way that Mutine's mirror cast its shadow over Angola's birth, other mirrors and their equivalents will inflect the prince's destiny at crucial points in his story. While Zobéide prepares herself for what could have been Angola's long-awaited initiation, she uses her mirror to "casually tidy herself up" (709). More like Mutine than Lumineuse, Zobéide limits the use of her mirror to scrutinizing herself. For her, it provides none of the teasing and playful indirection of glances that will draw Angola and Lumineuse so happily together. In fact, Zobéide's entire strategy for seduction is based not on her beguiling presence but on a feigned absence. After carefully progressing through the usual stages of increasing proximity that follow their late-night supper in her private quarters, and at just the moment when Angola felt sure that "he was on the brink of happiness," Zobéide suddenly "seemed bereft of all feeling and plunged into a deep swoon" (714). Utterly confused by Zobéide's faint, Angola's reaction propels the scene from the erotic to the comic. The hapless young man, "too ignorant of the ways of the world to know the proper course when confronted with *a lady in a swoon*" (715), tries first to revive her with a whiff of the *eau des carmes* he finds on her nightstand. When it has no effect he calls her servants to his aid and tries a succession of other smelling salts until Zobéide finally opens her eyes. More than miffed at how egregiously Angola has misread her signs, she has no further interest in any remedies he might provide. "Your failure to use them when we were alone," she announces, "inclines me to doubt your powers" (715). It is only the next day that Angola's friend Almaïr explains to him that "nothing is more humiliating for a beautiful woman than to have *swooned in vain*" (716). Zobéide's seduction fails because, at the crucial moment, her ploy is to pretend that she is no longer there—that, as a body without consciousness, she is somehow abstracted from any frank exchange of pleasures. Lumineuse, to the contrary, will use both the novel she and Angola read and the mirror conveying their exchanged glances to accelerate and intensify the circulation of pleasure that brings them together.

Angola's real problems, and the fulfillment of Mutine's curse, begin when he encounters another variation of the mirror. During his first happy interlude in Lumineuse's chamber both *brochure* and *trumeau* provided images of couples coming together. Some days later, alone in Lumineuse's quarters and surreptitiously inspecting things that do not concern him, Angola finds on the mantelpiece a jewel-encrusted box. Inside it, and within a frame rather than a mirror, Angola discovers a portrait. That portrait, one of the eighteenth century's most cherished fetishes, is of a beautiful young woman.[13] As he inspects that image mirroring an absent woman, Angola finds himself overcome by a force he is unable to understand. As he stares at the portrait he is "astonished and beside himself." To examine it is to "drink deeply of a subtle poison that went straight to his heart" (747). The portrait triggers an immediate infatuation, a longing so intense that it brings with it Angola's first encounter with the dangerous force of passion. In his mind, he and the woman in the portrait may form a couple, but it is an imaginary, unreal couple born of longing, separation, and suffering.

Using questions vague enough to avoid Lumineuse's jealousy, Angola learns that the beautiful young woman in the portrait is Luzéide, the princess of Golconde. Her father, the king, has carefully protected his daughter because, like Angola, her birth was marked by a prediction that "love will be the cause of her unhappiness" (748). Her father has sent the portrait to Lumineuse because, unable to postpone further his daughter's entry into society, he would have her complete her education at Lumineuse's court. Angola, now able to associate the imaginary portrait with an actual person, becomes a changed man. Retiring early, he spends "the entire night thinking about the charms of the incomparable Luzéiade" (749). No longer interested in Zobéide or any other of the willing partners within his reach, Angola's infatuation with the absent Luzéide initiates him to feelings he has never before experienced. "Deeply pondering what he was feeling, he began to understand the difference between the love he now felt and that *fleeting lure* that had heretofore drawn him so swiftly to all the women *who had come within his grasp*" (749). Angola emerges from his all-night reverie only when Almaïr arrives to find out why his friend has so abruptly disappeared. Dismayed at the change that has come over Angola, he warns him that, in choosing the chimeras of desire over the reality of pleasure, "you are all worked up over a love that has no existence, and whose only foundation is a painter's imagination" (751). Watching his friend become "a man who feeds on illusions" (750), Almaïr cautions him that he is dangerously close to playing "the role of some hero out of a novel" (750). The kind of novel whose hero Angola risks becoming has, however, nothing to do with the *brochure* he and Lumineuse read and reenacted together. In turning away from the real, in choosing to long for an absent beloved, Angola becomes instead a hero from the romances of old, in the tradition of Urfé's *L'Astrée*.

Fixated on the inaccessible face mirrored in the portrait, Angola chooses the solitary and the incorporeal. The new object of his desire exists not in the realm of coupling, but within the ethereal idea of "possessing someone's heart" (750). Spurning everything he has discovered with his willing partners, Angola opts instead for the more delicate fare of "a timid love which dared not entertain the slightest hope" (748). The change provoked in him by Luzéide's portrait represents more than a simple migration from one pole to the other of the traditional libertine opposition between *l'esprit* and *le cœur*, between the mind's strategic detachment and the heart's passionate obsession. For Angola, the heart's quest will bring with it the discovery that the word *passion* is rooted in the Latin *patior*, the suffering as patience that was wished upon him at his birth. Luzéide will be invited to court and, after some hesitation, Lumineuse will consent to her marriage to Angola. Their courtship will begin, however, only after a powerful rival has entered the field: Makis, an evil genie allied with Mutine, who will also be smitten with the beautiful Luzéide.

As the instrument of Mutine's curse, Makis confirms Angola's displacement from a novel of coupling's pleasures to what will become a parody of the romance and its heroic quests. Makis, enraged when he learns that Luzéide is to marry Angola, kidnaps the betrothed at the close of a masked ball and carries her off to a distant kingdom. The disconsolate Angola then receives from Queen Lumineuse a magic coach whose axle will break at the exact spot where the languishing Luzéide is being held prisoner. Once there, Angola will use the other charms Lumineuse has given him to neutralize Makis' henchmen. Before he and Luzéide can escape from the stronghold, however, Angola makes the costly mistake of sitting in an armchair which the evil genie has rigged with an amulet whose effect will give its full power to the gift of patience with which Mutine has cursed Angola's birth. Makis' talisman has "a soporific power which will only take effect when the lover, encouraged by his mistress's consent, tries to set a seal upon his happiness. At that very moment, a profound slumber will interrupt his caresses and repeat itself each time he makes the same attempt" (782).

Once back at Lumineuse's court, the couple is married with full pomp. That ceremony, alas, leads directly to the malefic patience with which Angola has been cursed. All his efforts to consummate his marriage end only in yawns and drooping eyelids as he falls fast asleep. Once again, Lumineuse comes to the rescue with her idea that the remedy for his condition is to dispatch Angola and Luzéide to the realm of Moka, the genie who invented the beverage that bears his name. There, the unfortunate groom will be able to avail himself of the coffee that gives all who drink it "a frolicsome and lively air" and allows them "to banish sleep which, for them, was only so much time stolen from pleasure" (790). As fate would have it, Moka is a secret ally of Makis and has told him of the couple's impending visit. Using yet another of his magical powers, a now invisible Makis haunts the bedroom where Moka has insisted that Angola and Luzéide rest for the night before they test the powers of his beverage. Excited at the morrow's happy prospects, Angola suddenly decides he can do without caffeine's help. Just as he proclaims that his troubles are over, however, Makis' spell takes effect: " 'I flatter myself . . . ,' said the prince, who at that instant fell into a deep sleep, '. . . that I shall overcome them,' immediately continued Makis who, taking on a visible body, quite adroitly took the Prince's place as he prepared to consummate his crime" (792).

With Angola in a deep sleep, Makis repeatedly astounds the unsuspecting Luzéide. " 'My dear Prince,' she said to Makis whom she thought was Angola, 'what am I feeling? What superb pleasure!' " (792). When Angola does finally awaken the next morning, Luzéide is more than perplexed at his lament that it now looks as though his only hope for overcoming his syncopated ardor lies in Moka's magic brew: " 'We could have saved ourselves the trouble of this journey,' said Luzéide, 'as the proofs of love I have received from you convince me that it was unnecessary.' 'But how slight they were,' replied Angola, 'compared to those that I am burning to give you!' 'I cannot even imagine,' said the Princess, 'what you could still have in reserve. The ardor you have displayed and which I have been sharing for some hours now makes me incapable of imagining anything greater.' 'I hardly deserve *such cruel mockery* from you,' snapped the Prince, 'and I would never have thought you would hold me responsible for the evils of a cruel destiny' " (792–93).

The Rabelaisian humor of La Morlière's ending underlines the fact that Angola has only himself to blame for what he chooses to see as his cruel fate. It was his surrender, made as he gazed at the face mirrored in her portrait, to the imaginary Luzéide of his passion that set in motion the events that would fulfill Mutine's curse. What is so intolerable for Angola in Luzéide's report on her night at Moka's—that he has in effect been obliged patiently to wait his turn—is no different from the pleasures he quite enjoyed when it was a question of Zobéide and the other mistresses he shared with Almaïr. His doubt, suffering, and humiliation are the fruits of an obsession that led him to opt for the ideal realm of passion's chimeras. Once back at Lumineuse's court, Angola eventually finds the good sense to give up his obsession with being the first and only lover as he learns to take pleasure instead in the tangible reality of "the extreme tenderness Luzéide felt toward him" (795).

By composing his novel as pleasure's mirror, La Morlière recasts the most prevalent stereotypes of the libertine novel. René Démoris, examining what he calls "the esthetics of libertinage," underlines how the listing of conquests so frequent in libertine novels amounts to what he describes as "valuing a series of nonidentical but equivalent units where the paradigmatic clearly overwhelms the syntagmatic."[14] Those juxtapositions without coherence have the effect on the narrative of producing what Démoris calls a "disconnectedness" (*déliaison*): "the objects thus assembled become a collection characterized by a fundamental disconnectedness that inevitably creates the impression of there being too weak a story line" (160). In terms of the novel as a form, the weak story line of the seducer's successive encounters produces both an impression of repetition and a difficulty in ending the list with any effective semblance of closure. Speaking of that same difficulty, Robert Mauzi underlines how the threat of an infinitely extensible list resulted in a nearly unbreachable convention for the libertine novel: the series of conquests would end when the protagonist finally encounters the true virtue and passion that would lead to his renouncing the constant substitutions of serial seduction. This ascent to a higher plane of virtue also had the advantage of generating the apparently moral lesson of a victory of sincerity over deception: "The experience of libertinage occurs as a passing aberration which is always corrected. It takes only an encounter with something true, either love or virtue, and the hero's libertinage miraculously disappears."[15] Translated into plot, this meant that such novels tended to end with the main character's marriage. As to what the frequency of such an ending might tell us about eighteenth-century society, Marie-Hélène Huet notes that the marriage denouement was frequently accompanied by a withdrawal from court and a return to the ancestral estate. The brides, whether young and innocent or older and wiser, tended to be of high birth and devoted to the traditions of aristocracy. On that basis, Huet argues, the libertine novel can be seen as staging an imaginary return to the lost past of the nobility's pre-absolutist and pre-Versailles independence from monarchical control. For Huet, these novels ending in the protagonist's separation from the courtly rituals of libertinage become a summary of "the major tenets of eighteenth-century aristocratic ideology" as well as "the nobility's dying efforts to protect its patrimony."[16]

Understanding the implications of these conventions helps us to appreciate the extent of La Morlière's iconoclasm. *Angola* may end with a marriage, but it is a marriage parodied even before it is consummated. Rather than evoking any lost ideal, the substitution of Makis for the dozing groom reasserts the trope of coupling's infinite mirror as pleasure's polymorphous challenge to marriage as a reestablishment of traditional values. La Morlière mobilizes Epicurean pleasure in a way that cuts a wide swath across the stereotypes of the libertine novel. The lubricious and light-hearted Queen Lumineuse stands as a stark exception to what Nancy K. Miller has called the "law of consequence," which dictated that, even in the amoral world of the libertine novel, to be a woman in the eighteenth century meant that one was obliged to pay dearly for any form of sexual dalliance.[17] As concerns masculine stereotypes, the novel's coda, its brief return to the framing conversation between the Comtesse and the Marquis as they finish their reading of *Angola*, finds both genders unsettled. The Comtesse may be mildly peeved with the portraits of coquettes, but the ending's real caution is addressed to the male reader. Reading as a couple presents challenges for the Marquis which are far more daunting than anything Goulemot's one-handed readers might encounter. "Even if women are not particularly happy with this novel," the Marquis laments, "it places such a heavy burden on us men that we must make every effort to see that it does not become widely known. It is all too easy for these gentlemen authors, safely ensconced in their studies, to rise to the challenge of so much good fortune. But if they were in my place. . . . Really, the whole thing is unbearable, and I am quite upset . . ." (796). With the faltering three dots of the ellipsis as our last image of the Marquis' flagging powers, he becomes a pouting double of the hapless Angola who could only nod off beside the expectant Luzéide. Rather than ending his novel with pieties of marriage and ideological allegory, La Morlière centers it, from beginning to end, on the exhilarating but demanding pleasures of coupling and its infinite mirrors.

Toward the end of his second preface to *Julie, ou la nouvelle Héloïse* (1761), Rousseau too imagines his readers as couples. Speaking of the effect his story of Julie and Saint-Preux might have on such couples, he writes: "I like to picture a husband and wife reading this collection together, finding in it a source of renewed courage to bear their common labors, and perhaps new perspectives to make them useful. How could they behold this tableau of a happy couple without wanting to imitate such an attractive model? How will they be stirred by the charm of conjugal union, even in the absence of love's charm, without their union being reconfirmed and strengthened?"[18]

Rousseau may share La Morlière's hope that couples reading his story will wish "to imitate such an attractive model," but, as he makes clear, what his readers will discover in *Julie* is the charm of a union "in the absence of love's charm." Already in his preface, Rousseau prepared his readers for the final judgment on pleasure and desire that Julie will enunciate on her deathbed. "Woe to him who has nothing left to desire! He loses, as it were, all he possesses. One enjoys less what one obtains than what one hopes for, and one is happy only before happiness is achieved" (693). Rousseau effectively suggests to his reading spouses that the moral value of his novel will depend on their relating to it in exactly the way Almaïr warned Angola he must *not* relate to the fantasies triggered by the portrait of Luzéide. Seeing a virtue where La Morlière saw only a danger, Rousseau tells his readers that they will be morally redeemed only to the extent they choose, to borrow Almaïr's words, "to feed on illusions . . . whose only foundation is a painter's imagination." While things went horribly wrong for Angola once he renounced the pleasure of the tangibly present in favor of what he only imagined, Rousseau's readers are told that they will draw new meaning and purpose for their lives only to the extent that they accept imagination as reality and subscribe to Julie's ethos of renunciation.

Between *Angola* and *Julie,* all valances are reversed and, with them, the very purpose of reading. The *brochure* Angola and Lumineuse read together invites them to mirror the shared pleasures they discover in its pages. *Julie*'s ideal of desexualized virtue enlists instead the intensity of disembodied sentiment as an exaltation that exists only in the reader's imagination. This choice of the imagination over the body and of longing over pleasure would, however, hardly prove to be a caveat to the reader's absorption within the work. Diderot, in his *Éloge de Richardson,* a text roughly contemporary with *Julie,* makes clear how powerful the force of sentimental identification with the characters of an epistolary novel could be in providing the reader with another and better life: "O Richardson! One cannot resist, even if it is impossible, wanting to play a role in your works. We join the conversation, we approve, we condemn, we admire, we get upset, we grow angry. . . . My soul was in a state of perpetual agitation. How good I was! How just I was! How satisfied I was with myself! By the time I set your book down, I felt as one does at the end of a day spent doing good works."[19]

Rousseau takes Diderot's enthusiasm an important step further. When Diderot describes his reaction to reading Richardson, he is fully aware that it is a fiction which has had this effect on him. For Diderot, the proof of a novel's power lies in how real it has made something which is patently unreal. In the second preface to his own novel, however, Rousseau marshals this same effect on the reader in the service of a quite different argument. Rather than acknowledging the letters that make up *Julie* as a novel, a fiction, Rousseau points to the intensity of the sentimental identification they will elicit from his readers as the proof that they are not a fiction at all, that they must in fact be real letters exchanged by real people. Toward the end of that preface, Rousseau's interlocutor, N, clarifies what is at stake in the choice to read this work as fiction or as reality. "Certainly, if it is all just fiction, you have made a bad book; but say that these two women have existed, and I shall reread this collection every year for the rest of my life" (29). In his study of how eighteenth-century readers actually reacted to Rousseau's *Julie*, the historian Robert Darnton leaves no doubt that Rousseau clearly won his bet. His readers wanted passionately to believe that Julie, Claire, Saint-Preux, and Wolmar actually existed. Not only were Rousseau's characters taken to be real, but they were seen as real precisely because their letters functioned as a regenerative mirror of their readers' lives. "They knew his novel was true," as Darnton puts it, "because they had read its message in their lives."[20]

Substituting the imagination for the senses and sentiment for pleasure, Rousseau grounded the novel's power within the very dangers Almaïr identified as concomitant with Angola's choice of imaginary fantasies over mirrored pleasures. No hands, single or paired, would be drawn into play by Rousseau's new dynamics of sentiment and unsatiated desire. The novel of sentiment would, however, accommodate itself to an even more furtive debauchery. Only twenty years after *Julie*, Laclos, one of Rousseau's most assiduous readers, would craft Valmont's initial letter to the virtuous Mme de Tourvel as a transparent pastiche of Saint-Preux's opening letter to Julie. As though responding to the very concerns Rousseau expressed in his preface, Valmont sends that letter to two readers: to Mme de Tourvel, whose deluded imagination will lead her to read it as truth; but also to Mme de Merteuil, who is asked to admire it as the purest fiction.[21] Three-quarters of a century after Laclos, in 1857, the novel's power to goad the imagination toward a frenzied distortion of the real would be the cornerstone of Flaubert's *Madame Bovary*. Within this larger history of the novel as a genre, the mirrored bodies of La Morlière's novel stand out as a monument to the eighteenth century's brief reign of Epicurean pleasure. Parodying any sentiment that would divorce itself from the body and its senses, *Angola* aims the act of reading not at a mimesis of the imagination's angelic virtue, but toward an enactment of the Marquis' suggestion to the Comtesse that "nous devons être *assez joliment ensemble*" (796).

3. Life-Writing as Epicurean Allegory

Thérèse philosophe

During the eighteenth century, pleasure—its genesis, impediments, rewards, and ruses—became a master plot, the most telling story anyone had to tell. Full-fledged autobiography, putting the self into writing, may officially begin with Rousseau's *Confessions*. Well before him, as we saw with Jourdan's *Guerrier philosophe*, the first-person narrative of the memoir novel—a looser, less fervid, and less tortured form of prose fiction—offered countless versions of pleasure's story as a catalyst of identity, the most revealing dimension of exemplary individuality. It is within those narratives that we begin to find evidence of an "Enlightenment self" clearly different from that of classical subjectivity—different because this emerging "self" served to replace a notorious casualty. Materialist philosophy, the signature worldview of the French Enlightenment, proclaimed the death of Christian and Cartesian dualism. More specifically, it refused dualism's hypothesis that consciousness and subjectivity were ultimately grounded in some immaterial soul that served as the bedrock of identity. With the materialist insistence on a single, all-encompassing continuum of matter and consciousness, the "soul" imagined as the apodictic underpinning of subjectivity was suddenly and scandalously gone. The Enlightenment and its philosophies turned on the discursive construction of a new sense of the self that respected the oneness of consciousness and a sensate body moved by the pleasures it experienced and shared with others.

The irony of the Enlightenment's endeavor to elaborate this material self lay in the fact that its articulation could take place only in language, only in writing as an always already abstract representation of any reality tangible to the senses. Be it Rousseau or Diderot, La Mettrie or Helvétius, the century's most militant voices—no matter how different their programs—shared a suspicion that pure constructs of language were obstacles to be overcome, illusions that all too easily occluded a fundamental continuity of matter, perception, consciousness, and thought. Life-writing, representing the self in language, had to be recognized as a trap for the unwary, a negotiation with an always dangerous foe. To represent the sentient body within language was to open the door to all those illusions that existed as a function of language's inevitable remove from matter, from the senses, and from perception.

It is against the background of this dilemma that I would like to examine one of the eighteenth century's most fascinating experiments in life-writing: *Thérèse philosophe*, a first-person memoir novel published anonymously in 1748, and most often attributed to Boyer d'Argens.[1] What makes this novel significant to the genre's ambition of life-writing is the way this psychosexual autobiography draws its narrative structure from the premises of materialist philosophy and physiology. The story its heroine tells, from her first pleasurable contact with her body at age seven to her voluptuous surrender of herself to her lover as the person for whom she writes her memoir at age twenty-five, is structured as the discovery of the period's new understanding of the continuity between the senses and consciousness, between perception and expression, and between experience and writing. *Thérèse philosophe*, in its tone and content, falls squarely within the tradition of the libertine novel. Unlike the bantering humor of La Morlière's fairy tale and its transparent satire of aristocratic sexual practices, *Thérèse philosophe* presents itself as the true story of a real person, the daughter of a shopkeeper, whose misfortunes will lead her to discover a cross-section of eighteenth-century French society that ranges from Provence to the capital. At the same time, its representation of the sexualized body ultimately becomes the vehicle of a far broader reflection on the relation between subjectivity and sociability, between the discovery of the self through the senses and the integration of that self within a community.

Thérèse's earliest memory of herself as a sentient body capable of pleasure is also the memory of her widowed mother's concerted attempt to prohibit any repetition of that pleasure: "What must have been her surprise when one night, thinking I was asleep, she noticed that my hand, placed on that part of the body which distinguishes us from men, was occupied with a gentle rubbing that brought me a pleasure rarely experienced by a girl of seven, but quite common for those of fifteen. . . . She took the measure of tightly binding my hands in such a way that it was impossible for me to continue my nightly amusements."[2] Thérèse's first contact with her sexualized body is remedied with a strand of rope. When, however, four years later, her mother discovers Thérèse's erotic play in an attic with a group of other children, she takes the more radical step of dispatching her to the convent.

It is within that institution so dear to erotic novels of the period that the impressionable adolescent will be subjected to a religious indoctrination demanding that she "avoid at all cost the demon of the flesh" (877). The priest chosen to be her confessor, a close counselor to her mother, structures his guidance of the adolescent by comparing the narrative of the sexually maturing body to the Old Testament narrative of the Fall. Thérèse's sex becomes "the apple that seduced Adam and brought humanity's condemnation by original sin." Denounced as "inhabited by the devil as his home and his throne," this trace of Satan inscribed in woman's flesh becomes something that must never be looked at, let alone touched. Even the physical signs of puberty, the priest insists, will prove his claim as "ugly hair, much like that which covers the skin of ferocious beasts," comes to cover it. Referring to what he knows Thérèse has discovered in her attic games, he defines the male sex as a ferocious serpent endowed with a venom "which will poison your body and soul" (878).

For Thérèse, the cumulative effect of this baroque catechism is the discovery of shame and the vitiation of pleasure: "My face was in a constant blush, and I kept my eyes lowered like a person ashamed and guilty. For the first time, I came to see my pleasure as a crime" (877). Caught between the opposing forces of her maturing body and religious repression, Thérèse's life at the convent alternates between involuntary masturbation recast in terms of the priest's metaphors—"my hand would grasp the apple, my finger took the place of the serpent" (879)—and frantically adopted mortifications of prayer, fasting, and self-flagellation. After fourteen years of such denial, and "in a state of languor which was visibly leading me to the grave" (879), Thérèse finally convinces her mother that she should be allowed to leave the convent.

Soon after returning home, Thérèse's experience of her sexual body will again be recast, not by masturbation's contact with the self but by twinned episodes of voyeurism involving two very different couples. Each of these episodes of watching and touching will mark distinct stages within a larger narrative centered on the transformation of pleasure's meaning. The juxtaposition of these scenes of voyeurism will draw a clear line between an imagination perverted by religious condemnations of the body and an integration of sexual pleasure within consciousness in such a way that it gives birth to a power to think and to reason. Thérèse's allegory will encompass both these options, marking the first as deleterious and the second as beneficent. The first, turning pleasure against the body, draws its force from the delusions of an imagination that enlists consciousness in a battle against the self. The second, presupposing a seamless continuity between the senses and reason, between pleasure and thought, becomes the foundation of a power of judgment reconciling autonomy and community. Both options begin in a voyeurism riveted on the fascinating spectacle of a sexualized couple unaware that they are being observed.[3]

Back home with her widowed mother, Thérèse befriends the intensely pious Eradice, whose spiritual progress toward a total renunciation of the flesh is directed by her religious advisor, Père Dirrag.[4] Eradice, anxious to display her intense spirituality to her new friend, invites Thérèse to assume the position of voyeur: "Hide in this little closet, where you can both see and hear just how far divine mercy will extend itself to save its vile creation through the pious ministrations of our confessor" (884). Instead, what Thérèse finds herself witnessing from that closet is the way that Père Dirrag, manipulating the rhetoric of Quietist asceticism, convinces Eradice that the most eloquent proof of her spiritual progress is a total obliviousness to her physical body—a delusion he does not hesitate to exploit by raping his star pupil. The scene Thérèse watches presupposes a complete break between body and language, between the senses and consciousness. As Dirrag's words exhort Eradice to an ever more complete remove from the baseness of the body, he himself becomes, as Thérèse describes him, an extended textual emblem of animalistic rutting: "Then, all of a sudden, the apparent tranquility of the priest was transformed into a sort of fury! Oh, God! What a countenance! He was like a satyr, his lips frothing, his mouth ajar. Grinding his teeth and snorting like a bull, his nostrils were flared and agitated" (890). Eradice may experience a form of ecstasy, but it is the ecstasy of an imagination so deluded that it cuts itself off from all contact with the body and the senses. Presenting sexual predation and spiritual transport as one and the same, this scene becomes an extended parody of Christian dualism.[5]

Michel Delon has described this scene, as a pornographic extension of Molière's *Tartuffe*, as an explicit satire of "Christian education's foundation in the mortification of the senses."[6] While that satire may be clear to the reader, Thérèse's own reaction emphasizes her confusion and its reshaping of her consciousness. Both deeply affected by and jealous of her friend's climactic beatitude, Thérèse, once back in her room, falls to her knees and begins a hysterical prayer imploring "the grace to be treated" like her friend: "My mind was in an agitation near fury, an inner fire devoured me" (896). What Thérèse beheld as voyeur is no longer simply a perception furnished by vision. It triggers instead the full force of a deluded imagination bent on substituting illusion for reality: "I could not get out of my mind the entry of that rubicund member into Mlle Eradice's parts" (896). Surrendering to that imagination, she herself falls into a trance, what she calls a "deep reverie." Her body and her senses, rather than perceiving reality, become the puppets of an unhinged imagination. With perception yielding to fantasy, her body undertakes a fevered imitation of the remembered scene that transforms what is present into the phantasm of what is absent: "Like a machine, I assumed the same posture as that in which I had seen Eradice, and as though driven by my agitation, I crawled flat on my stomach toward the column at the foot of my bed" (896). Abstracted from reality and volition, Thérèse makes of her bedpost the imaginary equivalent of what so fascinated her during the scene she watched between Eradice and Dirrag: "Never thinking about what I was doing, I proceeded to rock my posterior with an incredible agility, rubbing it back and forth along the salutary column" (896). As she describes this scene, her surrender to fantasy and imagination leaves her incapable of understanding what she has just experienced: "I reflected on all that I had seen in Eradice's room as well as on what I had just felt, *but without being able to draw any reasonable conclusion*" (897; italics mine). At the same time, the orgasmic release she experiences as a result of her trance remains under the sway of a still powerful maternal and religious prohibition that eliminates any possibility of its conscious and less painful reenactment: "Never did I dare touch myself with my hand, as that had been expressly forbidden" (897). Thérèse's involuntary voyeurism, its inflaming of her imagination and the subsequent conflict it generates between bodily appetite and moral prohibition, produces an existential short-circuit. As a consciousness at war with herself, she struggles to reconcile the demands of her senses and the illusions of her imagination. What Thérèse discovered as she watched

Dirrag and Eradice represents the repetition and intensification of the contradiction between nature's dictates and religion's repressions that was first imposed on her during her stay at the convent. In this case, however, the remedy will be found not after fourteen years of suffering but within a matter of days.

Immediately after this episode reinforcing religion's denial of the body, Thérèse is introduced by her mother to her friend, the widowed Mme C. . . . It is during the month she spends as a guest at Mme C . . .'s country estate that voyeurism will again inflect her development—but this time in a very different direction. On two different occasions, once in a sheltered garden and later in Mme C . . .'s bedroom, Thérèse will watch from hiding as her hostess receives her lover, the philosophical Abbé T. . . . Because Thérèse has repressed all acknowledgment of the body's pleasure since her involuntary reaction to Eradice's rape, she finds herself fascinated by what takes place in private between another young woman and the older cleric. The scene of pleasure she discovers as she watches this second couple is, however, distinctly different from that enacted by Eradice and Dirrag. The freely chosen sexual play between Mme C . . . and Abbé T . . . is accompanied by a constant dialogue between them which frankly enunciates all the flows and ebbs of desire as they seek to maximize their own body's pleasure and that of their partner within limits agreed upon by both. Mme C . . . and Abbé T . . . combine language and sexuality, using the first not as an instrument of deception and self-delusion but as the transparent communication of sentient and mutually pleasuring bodies. This choice of a language rooted in and mirroring the experience of the senses will also serve to unblock the repression that, until then, has obliterated for Thérèse any pleasurable experience of her own sexuality.

Sensing that Thérèse is deeply troubled by what has happened to her in the past, Mme C . . . encourages her new friend to share her entire story with the Abbé: "Place your complete confidence in Abbé T. . . . . . . You will not have reason to regret it" (901). The Abbé, a priest distinctly different from those Thérèse has thus far encountered, immediately understands the shame and guilt she has come to associate with what she calls the "excessive tickling" that has so troubled her since her experience with the bedpost. Such feelings are, the Abbé immediately declares, perfectly natural reactions of the senses, reactions which are best addressed with an equally natural remedy: "These instincts are as natural as those of hunger and thirst. . . . If you feel an active pressure to do so, there is nothing wrong with using your hand, or your fingers, to assuage that part of your body with the rubbing necessary for its relief" (902).

Thérèse's time at Mme C . . .'s country estate represents the turning point in her life story, the beginning of her transformation into Thérèse the philosopher. The reader, following the events that occur during Thérèse's stay there, begins to realize that what is distinctive about her narrative voice—the subversive asides with which she has punctuated the stages of her story up to this point—is a result of the couple's example and the Abbé's instruction. It is this middle passage—the period following the convent and preceding Thérèse's move to Paris—that gives this work its particular place within the tradition of the libertine novel. Crébillon's *Les Égarements du cœur et de l'esprit,* for example, is also a memoir novel written in the first person. Like Thérèse, its main character, Meilcour, also tells the story of his youth from a vantage point set in the future. Crébillon's cast of characters even includes a mentor, Versac, the master libertine, who tutors the naïve Meilcour as he sets out to make his way in the world. In spite of these similarities, the two works are completely different. Crébillon's Versac pontificates on the ways of high society in a diction whose combination of the portentous and the elliptical creates the impression that it is constantly on the brink of becoming its own parody. Seeking to dazzle rather than to instruct, Versac has nothing of the carefully pedagogic style that informs the Abbé's Socratic dialogues with Thérèse and Mme C. . . . The lessons Versac would teach concern only the socio-sexual dynamics of *le bon ton,* that combination of witty insouciance and debonair predation that establishes the consummate libertine as the paragon of a style others can only emulate. The Abbé's tutelage, to the contrary, focuses not on the art of social performance but on achieving a personal and private independence from the laws and restrictions society attempts to impose upon sexuality. As in his therapy for Thérèse's shame at her own desires, his guiding principle is that sexual pleasure must be acknowledged as the body's legitimate need.[7] The goal of that pleasure, however, has nothing to do with the libertine's victory over some resisting other. Its real aim is closer to the Stoic ideal of achieving equilibrium within the self. According to the Abbé, the true philosopher is the individual who has achieved a balance of body and mind such that neither impedes nor perverts the work of the other. The needs of the sensate body must not, as in the convent, be denied and, because of that repression, perverted into dangerous passions that threaten both the self and others. The real sinner in Thérèse's sad tale is Dirrag; but his sin has less to do with pleasure than it does with a loss of self-control that establishes him, along with his innocent victims, as more deserving of pity than of punishment. "Father Dirrag is a scoundrel, a poor devil who lets himself be carried away by his passions. He is going to rack and ruin, and he is taking Mlle Eradice with him. However, Mademoiselle, they are more to be pitied than blamed" (902).

As he explained his position to Thérèse, the Abbé, we recall, insisted that sexual pleasure must be seen as a bodily need for which one should feel shame no more than one would for being hungry or thirsty. During his lovemaking with Mme C . . . , the Abbé makes that same point with a vivid comparison that situates pleasure at, so to speak, the other end of hunger and thirst. The Abbé recalls how, during his days as a student in Paris, he was never able to settle down to the hard work of study and abstract thought unless he had first engaged in a bracing sexual workout with a young woman he maintained for just that purpose. Unless he began his day that way, his thoughts, no matter what subject he happened to be studying, would constantly return to the demands of the body. To express that sense of a need so pressing that one can think of nothing else so long as it was unmet, he describes the ministrations of his morning partner as being every bit as necessary as "a chamber pot for peeing" (908). This earthy comparison reduces the entire gamut of religious and social prohibitions placed on sexual pleasure to being no less absurd than an injunction against urination.[8]

For the eighteenth-century reader, the Abbé is a surprising ecclesiastic. Rather than grounding his view of the human condition in the materialists' talisman of "nature," he rejects that buzz word of militant secularism as "a figment of the imagination, a word devoid of sense" (912), insisting that we must imagine the world and all that happens within it as a pantheistic expression of God. "Why can't we admit, once and for all, that nature is a construct of the mind, merely an empty word; that everything comes from God; that the physical evil which strikes down one contributes to the happiness of another; that, from the point of view of the divinity, there is no evil in the world, only good?" (912). The god the Abbé speaks of here has nothing to do with established religion. Positing Christianity and the Church as forces that seek only the destruction of humankind—"It is clear," he states at one point, "that the Christian idea of perfection leads to the destruction of the human race" (920)—his vision of the divine evacuates all moral criteria in a way that establishes him as a spokesperson for what was an eccentric eighteenth-century understanding of Spinoza. "Everything we call good or evil exists only in relation to the interests of society as established by man. . . . A man steals; he does himself good, he does evil to the society whose law he breaks, but he does nothing wrong in the eyes of God" (912). From the perspective of this pantheistic determinism, society's myriad repressions of pleasure amount to a transformation of the divinity into a frenzied monstrosity bent on the unending torture of its creation. "What absurd folly to believe that God has created us as we are . . . but requires that we turn away from sensual satisfaction and our God-given appetites! What more could a tyrant do if he were determined to persecute us from the cradle to the grave?" (921).

The Epicurean premises underlying the Abbé's ideal of a Stoic equilibrium are further confirmed by his frank acknowledgment that the existing laws of church and state produce an unbridgeable gap between private and public morality. During the Abbé's lovemaking and philosophical discussions with Mme C . . . , he clarifies why, for persons like themselves, discretion and secrecy are necessary responses to the hypocrisy of social decorum. "Let us conclude from this, my dear friend, that the pleasures which we enjoy, you and I, are innocent and pure, because they harm neither God nor man, owing to the secrecy and the propriety with which we conduct ourselves. Were it not for these precautions, I agree that we might cause scandal and that we would be guilty of a crime against society" (923). So long as church and state work hand in hand to punish those who transgress a moral code that denies the body and its pleasures, wisdom dictates that true philosophers feign compliance in public while maximizing their pleasures in private. For Thérèse as an unmarried young woman, this also means, he warns her, that the pleasure of sexuality must be separated from the dangers of intromission. Penetration, the Abbé warns, brings with it not only the risk of devaluing herself in the eyes of a future husband, but, should her partner be a man, of exposing her to pregnancy. Harboring no illusions as to the fate of an unmarried mother in eighteenth-century France, the Abbé describes what he sees as Dirrag's most serious crime against Eradice purely in terms of its social implications: "This priest tricked his disciple. He ran the risk of impregnating her. . . . In so doing, he offended against the natural law which teaches us to love our neighbor as ourselves. Is it neighborly love to expose Mlle Eradice, as he did, to the threat of lifelong dishonor and disgrace?" (902).

Thérèse's month in the country—the example of the couple's frank sexuality, her philosophical conversations with the Abbé, and the "torrent of pleasure" she discovers once she has set aside Christianity's condemnation of the body's pleasure—all work together. Correcting the legacy of her mother's binding of her hands and of the convent's exploitation of her imagination, Thérèse's achieves her first contact with the truth of the sentient body. More important, this beneficent harmony between consciousness and the senses initiates her discovery of a new dimension within her subjectivity. No longer at war with herself, she begins to experience the liberating powers of thought and reason. What she has learned about the body from Mme C . . . and Abbé T . . . stands as both the antithesis of and the antidote to the delusional powers of the imagination triggered by Dirrag and Eradice: "The cobwebs in my mind were dissipating little by little, and I was growing accustomed to thinking and to combining things in my reason: no more Father Dirrag, no more Eradice" (904).

Having profited from the couple's example as well as the Abbé's precepts, Thérèse adopts as her own the new vocabulary and understanding that mark her as a *philosophe:* "Precept and example are the greatest teachers in the schooling of the mind and the heart! While admitting that they impart nothing, that each of us has within himself the seeds of his future development, it is nonetheless certain that they help to nurture these seeds. They make us aware of the ideas and the emotions to which we are susceptible, and which, in the absence of teaching or example, would remain buried and enclosed deep within us" (904). This redefinition of the self as part of a predetermined world of matter yet capable of its own agency through thought and reason brings to an end the paralysis of repression and physical illness. Now a reasoning as well as a sentient self, Thérèse is able to situate herself within a cosmic harmony reconciling creation and nature, the divine and the human: "I saw clearly that God and nature were one and the same thing, or at least, that nature acted only through the direct will of God. From this I drew my own little conclusions, and I began to think perhaps for the first time in my life" (914).

Thérèse's allegory of pleasure abruptly changes course when a series of rapid plot twists impoverish her mother, take both of them to Paris, and leave

Thérèse alone and destitute when her mother dies. It is in these dire circumstances that Thérèse will be saved from a return to the convent by Bois-Laurier, a woman who happens to be living in the same *hôtel garni*. In terms of the novel's allegorical structure, Thérèse and Bois-Laurier form a contrasting pair that represents the different yet interlocking dangers that menaced women in eighteenth-century France. Just as Thérèse has been scarred by religion's repression of the body, Bois-Laurier is the victim of society's mercantile exploitation of the female body. Bois-Laurier is a prostitute: "one of those women who in her youth had been forced by necessity to serve the incontinence of a dissolute public" (925). At the time Thérèse makes her acquaintance, she has also managed to become an example of what was a rare phenomenon for the period: a financially independent woman. Orphaned at the age of six, she was literally purchased by a lubricious *président,* who placed her in the care of a notorious Parisian *entremetteuse,* Mme Lefort. This adoptive mother, after raising her to the age of fifteen, made it clear to the young girl that she must begin to earn her keep. Blessed with the physical anomaly of an impenetrable hymen, Bois-Laurier became for Mme Lefort the ideal sexual merchandise. Forever new, she could be sold again and again—finally more than five hundred times—at the top price commanded by a still intact virgin.[9] As Bois-Laurier summarizes her career, "Men of the clergy, the sword, the robe, and finance placed me, one after the other, in the most elaborate positions: all for naught. Either the sacrifice was made at the temple door or the point of the knife turned aside and the victim could not be immolated" (937). Intimately familiar with all strata of Parisian society, Bois-Laurier has acquired not only an encyclopedic knowledge of the ways of the world but the financial security of the *rente* she was able to purchase when she found herself the sole heir to Mme Lefort's considerable fortune. Calming Thérèse's fears as to her future, Bois-Laurier consoles her new friend with a disabused question to which she herself is the most eloquent answer: "Do you think for a moment that, with the distinction, the figure, and the face you have to offer, a girl ever found herself short of funds as long as she exercised a little prudence and know-how?" (925).

The relation between Thérèse and her protectress does not, however, become that of pupil to teacher. *Thérèse philosophe* does not, like Fougeret de Monbron's *Margot la ravaudeuse* (also of 1748), become a picaresque chronicle of the heroine's social ascension within the Parisian demimonde. Instead, Thérèse and Bois-Laurier form a pair that itself allegorizes the complementary roles of body and thought, the senses and consciousness. The protection Bois-Laurier is able to offer Thérèse fosters an exchange of life narratives between the two women from which both will draw different but valuable lessons. Bois-Laurier, thanks to a careful financial exploitation of her physiological anomaly, has risen as high as the body alone can take her. Thérèse, while utterly unschooled as to *les usages du monde* and the commercial value of her body, is able to offer Bois-Laurier the no less important succor of the philosophy she has acquired thanks to her stay with Mme C . . . and Abbé T . . . —what she calls "my understanding of morals, metaphysics, and religion" (931). Her interaction with Bois-Laurier allows Thérèse to move from the passive role she played as the Abbé's studious pupil to the active and altruistic role of a voice capable of remedying the shame and guilt Bois-Laurier feels in relation to her past. As Thérèse shares with her friend her Epicurean vision of the world as a predetermined continuum of matter and motion orchestrated by a universal quest for pleasure Bois-Laurier is led to the point where she can discard the heavy burden of imaginary guilt she feels in relation to her past: "You have opened my eyes to a mystery that has afflicted me my whole life: all those worries about my past left me no peace at all. Who more than me had to fear punishment for crimes—*all of which you have now shown me to be involuntary?*" (932; italics mine).

Part 1 of *Thérèse philosophe* allegorizes in sequential and contrastive registers the relation between body and mind, between senses drawn to pleasure and a negative or positive consciousness of that pleasure. The damage of religious repression and the pathology inflicted on Thérèse by Dirrag and Eradice were evacuated by Mme C . . . and Abbé T. . . . The benefit Thérèse draws from their example becomes in turn the gift she will offer Bois-Laurier. Part 2, consisting of two sections titled "The Story of Mme Bois-Laurier" and the "End of Bois-Laurier's Story and the Continuation of Thérèse's," completes this allegory by narrating Thérèse's subsequent transformation from thinking self to writing self—a transformation that explains the genesis of the novel we are reading. As in Marcel Proust's *À la recherche du temps perdu*, the final pages of this novel complete a circle that brings the reader to the moment when the first-person narrator is able to begin her act of life-writing. From its first explicit mention in the novel, writing functions as the sign of a self overwhelmed and transformed—an activity whose relation to thought parallels that of masturbation to the senses. The first time we see Thérèse engaged in writing is immediately after the morning she spent hidden in Mme C . . .'s bedroom watching the couple make love and listening to the Abbé's disquisition on religion. Once she returns to her own room, she takes up pen and paper to relive and record what she has just heard. "A moment later, a message was brought from Mme C . . . asking me to join her. I sent word in reply that I had not slept the entire night, and begged to be allowed to rest for a few more hours. I used this time to set down in writing all that I had just heard" (924). An important part of what Thérèse transcribes that morning is the Abbé's lesson on pleasure, determinism, and moral responsibility that will later allow her to console the despondent Bois-Laurier.

Thérèse's status as writing subject is, quite literally, the question with which the novel begins. The opening sentence of her narrative expresses to an unidentified *monsieur* her surprise that he should want her to undertake the act of life-writing that we are reading: "What, sir? You seriously want me to write the story of my life? . . . You are asking for an orderly and detailed description from a girl who has never written for anyone before?" (872). The exchanges between Thérèse and this enigmatic instigator of her writing also reveal him to be *mon cher Comte*, someone for whom she herself is *votre tendre Thérèse*. It is only much later, at the close of the novel, that we learn both the identity of that masculine voice and the full stakes of what he is asking her to do. What does become clear in the novel's puzzling opening paragraph is that this act of writing is undertaken as an offering of pleasure and a revelation of truth intended for an audience that may begin as a single reader but that will extend to the far broader public: "But, you say, if their example [that of Mme C . . . and the Abbé] and their argument have brought me happiness, why wouldn't I try to bring happiness to others in the same way—by example and by argument? Why be afraid to write truths useful for the good of society?" (873).

As presented in this opening paragraph, writing exists as part of an exchange between Thérèse and her unnamed reader: "Well, my dear benefactor, I will resist no longer: I will write. . . . No, you will be denied nothing by your dear Thérèse" (873). Similarly, if what Thérèse sets out to write will be characterized by complete frankness and unblushing realism, it is in repayment for the help she has received from this single unnamed reader in completing an itinerary that has led her to pleasure in its most complete form: "You will know all the secret places of her heart and from her earliest days. Her soul will be completely revealed through the little adventures which have led her, despite herself, step by step, to the height of sensual delight" (873).

Like a secular version of the Catholic mass, *Thérèse philosophe* is constructed as a loose narrative linking together scenes and situations that illustrate the central tenets of Epicurean philosophy. The heroine's childhood and her time in the convent are a period of pleasure refused and perverted by repression and deluded imagination. During her stay at Mme C . . .'s country house the heroine corrects that past by learning to accept the sexual body, in turn transforming the sentient self into a thinking and reasoning self. This development prepares the heroine's subsequent progress from thinking self to writing self, from a self who acts in her own interest to a self who acts in the interest of others. The novel's beginning and ending, Thérèse's first step toward her life-writing and the "continuation," or epilogue, that focuses on her relation to the man who has encouraged her to write, enclose and complete the lessons of those other episodes. The prologue and coda establish Thérèse's story as the passage from a consciousness still limited in its pleasure by fear, to a consciousness finally able to participate in the full and voluptuous exchange of pleasure with another. Thérèse's final trajectory, taking her from masturbation to coitus, becomes a sexualized allegory of the self's opening to the other, of a pleasure that becomes *volupté* by responding to the desire of the other.

Bois-Laurier's narrative of the many bizarre encounters that punctuated her life as a Parisian prostitute is followed by an evening at the opera where she and Thérèse meet the man who will set Thérèse's final evolution in motion. As Thérèse describes that moment, even their first fleeting awareness of each other triggered an immediate melding of body and mind, of eyes that meet by chance but linger by choice: "If our eyes met by chance, they remained locked by reflection" (955). When the Count approaches the two women after the performance, what had begun with a glance consolidates itself as a second apprenticeship of pleasure that lifts Thérèse to a new intensity of consciousness and feeling: "I listened to you and I watched you with a pleasure until then unknown to me. The sharpness of that pleasure enlivened me, made me witty, and brought feelings I had never before experienced" (956). Drawn together by what she calls an "accord of hearts," Thérèse discovers over the following three weeks that, to her great surprise, "the modesty of your language and the moderation of your demeanor" (958) mark the Count as a suitor unlike the long list of Parisian partners described by Bois-Laurier as demanding immediate satisfaction of their sexual desires. For Thérèse, the Count's unfailing discretion becomes the proof that "reasonable people love in a reasonable way, and the rash are rash in everything they do" (958).

What the Count finally proposes to Thérèse is a relationship that will create for both the Epicurean utopia of pleasure redoubled by its reciprocal exchange: "The strongest passion I feel," the Count explains, "is the passion to make you happy" (958). Their future, he insists, will depend on how Thérèse's pleasure will respond to his own, on what he describes as "the pleasure you will have in giving me pleasure" (959). Suggesting that they leave behind the world of Parisian distractions, the Count offers Thérèse both the financial independence of a *rente* that will allow her to live as she wishes and an invitation to accompany him to his country estate—but only if she decides she can share his commitment to their reciprocal happiness. True felicity, he explains, can never be achieved in isolation, as an idiosyncratic state of mind. It must extend beyond the self and be secured by a careful regimen allowing each independent subject, motivated by his or her individual pleasures, to discover whether each can share and complete the pleasure of the other: "'It is a folly,' you added, 'to believe that you can make yourself happy by the way you think. It has been proved that one cannot think as one would like. In order to achieve happiness, one must seize the pleasure which is peculiar to oneself, which suits the passions with which one is endowed. . . . Man, because of the multiplicity of his needs, cannot achieve happiness without the help of other persons, and he must be careful to do nothing to diminish his neighbor's happiness. Anyone who holds himself aloof from this system flees from the very happiness he is seeking'" (959). The one question Thérèse must ask, as the Count puts it, is "if you can be happy by making me happy" (959).[10]

Faced with that choice, Thérèse is uncertain as to what her course should be. On the one hand, the Count's proposition would make her a kept woman—but that would certainly be a fate less unpleasant than the lucrative prostitution offered by Bois-Laurier. On the other hand, her vivid memory of how her mother renounced sexuality after nearly dying in childbirth has left Thérèse with a morbid fear of pregnancy. A possible solution, she remembers from Abbé T . . .'s lesson on masturbation, would be to propose to the Count that their sexuality be limited to mutual caresses. After much reflection, Thérèse tells the Count she will accept his proposal, but on the condition that their lovemaking exclude coitus and the risk of pregnancy: "Yes, Monsieur, I am yours. . . . Deal kindly with the heart of a young woman who adores you. Your feelings lead me to believe that you would never force my own. You know my fears, my weaknesses, and my habits" (960).

Once in the country, two months go by during which, respecting Thérèse's conditions, the couple practice only mutual masturbation. Thérèse, however, cannot help but notice that her own contentment with this arrangement is hardly matched by the Count's. Time and again, "once the goad of desire had been blunted" (961), he would reiterate, but only as an abstract philosophical argument, his contention that the reciprocity of their pleasures could become even more complete. So long as his request is expressed only in words, however, no progress is made toward resolving their dilemma.

Finally, remembering the fundamental Epicurean tenet that "either the mind is a chimera, or it is part of matter" (962), the Count finds a way to replace the abstractions of philosophical argument with a direct appeal to the body and its senses. Recalling how taken Thérèse had been with his collection of erotic novels and paintings when he showed it to her in Paris, it occurs to the Count that they might provide a way out of their impasse. As esthetic objects, these novels and paintings may be able to move Thérèse in a way that implies no coercion on his part. The Count carefully considers how he might proceed. He knows it would be self-defeating to offer the collection to Thérèse as a gift. For her, his gifts become painful reminders of the disparity between their desires, of the fact that she is not willing to offer him as a gift what she knows he most desires: "Is it not true that every time I give you a present, your pride is wounded because you are receiving it from a man whom you are not making as happy as he could be?" (964). To avoid that dilemma, he proposes the collection to Thérèse not as a gift but as the stake he will put up in a wager between them. The entire collection will be brought from Paris and placed in Thérèse's apartments for her private delectation. As her part of the bet, she must resolve to refrain, for a full two weeks, from all solitary consolations of what he calls her *manuélisme*. If she is able to do that, she will have won their bet and the collection will be hers. Should she, however, succumb to the collection's charms, she will drop the restriction that defines their sexuality.

Certain of her self-mastery, Thérèse not only accepts the bet, but proclaims that she will spend each morning savoring the delights of the books and paintings. Over the days that follow, the novel's allegory comes full circle. In forsaking philosophical argument and addressing instead the more fundamental reality of the sensate body, the Count has found a way, with no coercion on his part, to overcome the limit that her fear of pregnancy has placed on Thérèse's pleasure. During her first four days in the collection's company Thérèse reads all the classics of seventeenth- and eighteenth-century pornography while regaling herself with paintings that send fire coursing through her veins (964).[11] On the morning of the fifth day she happens to come upon two paintings she had not seen before: *The Feasts of Priapus* and *The Loves of Mars and Venus*. As she examines the first of them, Thérèse finds herself drawn to a female figure placed off to the side and depicted as being manually caressed by two impressive male figures. Involuntarily, her hand begins to imitate those of the two males who caress their willing partner. Remembering the terms of her wager, she stops short. No sooner, however, does she manage to overcome the effect of that first painting than she falls even more completely under the sway of the second, that of Mars poised to penetrate the willing Venus. Overcome by the painting's appeal, her writhing body and inflamed consciousness become themselves the canvas on which the summit of pleasure depicted in the image begins to inscribe itself: "What sensuality in Venus's posture! Like her, I lasciviously stretched out. With my thighs slightly apart and my arms voluptuously open, I admired the striking attitude of the god Mars. The fire of his eyes, and especially of his lance, passed directly to my heart. I stretched out on the sheets. My buttocks thrust lustfully forward as though to bear onward the crown destined for their conqueror" (965). Enraptured within her bodily mimesis, becoming herself an animated version of the painting, her excited senses lead her to entirely reconsider the restrictions she has placed on the Count: "My god, how foolish I have been to resist so inexpressible a pleasure! Such are the effects of prejudice: they are our tyrants" (965). Finally overcoming her fear of pregnancy, Thérèse combines the gesture of placing her finger where it will confirm her now joyful loss of the bet with her calling out to the Count—whom she now addresses for the first time as *tu*—to join her in a shared reenactment of the image she beholds: "Ah, dear love! I can resist no longer. Come forward, Count, I am no longer afraid of your lance" (965).

The Count, needless to say, appears immediately. But even as he reveals himself to be "more proud and more brilliant than Mars in the painting" (965), he pauses, draws back, and asks Thérèse: "Have you made a decision?" Her immediate response, "Yes, dear love, I am entirely yours"

(966), prefaces her discovery of a pleasure so complete that she takes no notice of the pain that accompanies her accommodation to the count's prodigious gifts: "At that very moment you fell into my arms. I seized without hesitation the shaft which, until then, had appeared so fearsome to me, and I myself placed it at the opening which it was threatening. You drove it in; your redoubled thrusts did not wrest from me the smallest cry. My attention, fixed on the idea of pleasure, did not allow me any feeling of pain" (966). Even within the intensity of their first full union, the Count maintains his infinite solicitousness, withdrawing at a moment which precludes any danger of pregnancy. At one level, this scene can be read as the repetition and reversal of the earlier episode of voyeurism during which Thérèse found herself a spectator of Dirrag's exploitation of Eradice. There, it was the sight of real bodies engaged in a sexual act that triggered Thérèse's sad attempt to simulate penetration with the help of her bedpost. In this closing scene, it is not real bodies but bodies represented on canvas that prepare what will be her complete and completely satisfying sexual exchange with the Count. The paintings are not less powerful because they are unreal esthetic representations; rather, they are more powerful. As Thérèse describes this moment of fear vanquished and pleasure maximized, her narrative unexpectedly extends its temporal frame to include within a single sentence, not only her immediately making love once again with the Count, but the expanse of the ten perfect years that now separate that delicious morning of pleasure from the moment when she would begin to write the story of her life that we have now finished reading: "Afterward we began again, and have continued to renew our pleasures in the same manner for ten years, without a problem, without children, without a worry" (966).

Abruptly projecting the reader across a period of ten years, Thérèse's coda designates that interval as the repetition of perfect pleasure. *Thérèse philosophe* is both the narrative of its heroine's first twenty-six years and the marker of an already lived future encapsulated within a single phrase. It is only after that decade of pleasure's repetition that Thérèse grants her lover's request that she write the story we have now finished reading. In so doing, this narrative taking her from pleasure discovered to pleasure repressed, and from pleasure deluded to pleasure shared, finally coincides with the promise made in the novel's opening paragraph that it would offer "truths useful to the good of society" (873).

Thérèse philosophe is the explication of a paradox. Begun as a voice agreeing to provoke the Count's pleasurable reminiscence, Thérèse's story is able to address itself to a larger community of readers only as it becomes a printed text. So transformed, it shares with its readers the full benefit of the verbatim transcription of Abbé T . . .'s careful exposition of Epicurean pedagogy. The lesson the Abbé would teach, however, is not only that pleasure is natural and innocent, but also that it is everywhere repressed by a hypocritical social order built on idealist illusions that have no substance beyond that of empty words. In the same way that the Count's purely philosophical arguments in favor of coitus needed to be consolidated by esthetic images speaking directly to Thérèse's senses, so also the final moment of her life-writing completes the Abbé's disquisitions with an experience of pleasure as the ultimate arbiter of consciousness. The novel's closing scene stages the power of the senses excited not by language but by the full force of an erotic image. It is as those images impose their mimetic reenactment upon their enchanted beholder that Thérèse's allegory of Epicurean physiology is able to come to a close. Staging pleasure as a dialogue between the mind and the senses, the novel's crucial message is the grounding of consciousness within the reality of the body and its pleasures. Once her delighted senses have fully prevailed, and once Thérèse has overcome the last traces of pleasure's repression, there is nothing left to say.

4. The Esthetics of Pleasure

Du Bos and Boucher

Paintings have a curious way of moving to center stage in each of the novels we have examined. For Sophie in Jourdan's *Guerrier philosophe*, her aunt's gallery of departure scenes from antiquity speaks of men's faithlessness with a force that Lafayette's *La Princesse de Clèves* simply cannot achieve. Yet those same images speak to the Chevalier of the true hero's higher duty to his destiny. For Angola, it is the enchantment born of his fascination with the minipainting of Luzéide's portrait that leads him onto the dangerous path of preferring charms that exist only in the imagination over those of real bodies. For Thérèse, things are even more complex. Her mission as the philosopher of pleasure can be achieved only when the esthetic yet intangible power of the Comte's erotic paintings proves stronger than his caresses and more persuasive than even his most carefully reasoned arguments. These paintings—unreal yet changing what is real—allow Thérèse to achieve her Epicurean ideal thanks to the esthetic object's Stoic distance from what is real.

    How did eighteenth-century artists and those who propounded theories of the arts address the question of the role of pleasure in the visual arts? How did it happen that François Boucher would become the signature artist of that period by placing his viewers' pleasure firmly at the center of his art? Boucher's celebrations of pleasure encompassed all forms of the visual arts. As a painter, he was revered for his landscapes and pastorals as well as for his historical and genre scenes. He designed costumes and sets for the Opéra, the Théâtre de la foire, and the Opéra-Comique. He sketched tapestry cartoons for the weavers at Beauvais and les Gobelins. He provided models for the porcelain manufactory at Vincennes-Sèvres and inspired a steady stream of sculpted works by Étienne Falconet. The breadth and diversity of his monuments to pleasure set a style that spread to all corners of Europe. Every year during the middle third of the eighteenth century saw the publication of at least one new edition of prints and engravings inspired by his works. During his lifetime, over fifteen hundred engravings based on his paintings were produced by more than one hundred engravers, among them not only revered professionals but Mme de Pompadour, Louis XV's mistress and Boucher's protector.

The beginnings of an answer to the question of pleasure's new place within the arts of the eighteenth century can be found in an influential treatise on painting and poetry that first appeared when Boucher was an apprentice of sixteen. Jean-Baptiste Du Bos, its author, was himself forty-nine when, at the height of the Regency, he published his *Réflexions critiques sur la poésie et sur la peinture*. The son of a Beauvais merchant, Du Bos was schooled for the clergy and, at the age of twenty-five, his ecclesiastical career seemed settled when he was named to succeed an uncle who because of poor health was about to resign his position as canon of the Beauvais cathedral. When, however, that uncle recovered and withdrew his resignation, Du Bos took his first steps toward a very different career. Moving to Paris and entering the service first of the Maréchal d'Huxelles and then of Monsieur de Torcy, the minister of foreign affairs, Du Bos began a diplomatic career that would lead to extended stays in England and Holland over the course of the negotiations that accompanied the War of the Spanish Succession.[1] During this same period he also established himself as an authority in the field of historical numismatics, publishing in 1695 his *Histoire des quatre Gordiens*, which attempted to prove, on the basis of surviving medals and coins, that there had been not three but four Roman emperors by the name of Gordian. The full flower of his career as a gentleman esthetician came, however, some twenty-four years later with the appearance of his *Réflexions critiques*. Du Bos brought to his attempt to establish a comparative analysis of poetry and painting a broad knowledge of literary and pictorial works ranging from Homer and Aristotle to the major dramatic poets and painters of French classicism. In 1720, less than a year after publishing what would become the most influential esthetic treatise of eighteenth-century France, Du Bos was elected by unanimous vote to the Académie française. Three years after that, he was named its *secrétaire perpetual*, a post he held, along with the abbacy of Ressons given him in 1723 by Cardinal Dubois, until his death some twenty years later, in 1742.

Du Bos' two-volume treatise, a work with which Boucher was surely familiar, set as its goal to offer the reader a considered exploration of "what might be the principal components of beauty in a painting or a poem."[2] What, however, was revolutionary in Du Bos' approach was the way he defined the measure of the beauty he undertook to explain. Rather than looking for the proof of beauty in the work itself and its conformity with established esthetic rules, Du Bos, from the opening line of his first chapter, proposed that the real measure of beauty lies elsewhere. It is to be found not in the objectivity of the work as text or image but in the reaction of the work's reader or spectator. Approached in those terms, the real object of his study became the understanding of pleasure: "Every day we experience real pleasure from poetry and from paintings, but how difficult it is to explain what makes up that pleasure" (1). Du Bos was willing, in other words, to confront directly the conundrum of subjectivity—the individual nature of esthetic perception and taste. "I undertake to elucidate and explain the origin of the pleasure we experience from verse and from paintings. So bold an endeavor could pass as foolhardy, since to do so amounts to accounting to each individual for his tastes and distastes, to instructing others as to how their sentiments come to be born" (1). It is difficult to exaggerate the effect this reversal of perspective must have had on a young apprentice like Boucher. The measure of a painting's beauty and value lies, not in its conformity to some set of rules a pupil might learn from his master, but in the reaction it elicits from its spectator, in the sensory pleasure it provokes as it is viewed.

During his visits to England Du Bos learned the language well, became an admirer of Addison (whom he frequently quotes in his *Réflexions*), and was a reader and friend of John Locke. His familiarity with the philosophy of the English empiricists and their privileging of the five senses as the bedrock of all knowledge played an important role in his decision to establish the experience of pleasure as the foundation of his esthetic theory.[3] For young artists struggling to understand and observe the strict rules of the academy, there can only have been something liberating in this new way of understanding beauty and its representation.

Toward the end of the *Réflexions*' first volume there is a section titled: "Why it is useless to argue over whether the work of line or the work of color is to be preferred." In choosing that title, Du Bos explicitly addresses the controversy which had preoccupied the Académie royale de peinture et de sculpture for more than half a century after its foundation by Mazarin in 1648. Continuing the sixteenth-century Italian debate between the line-oriented school of Rome and the colorists of Lombardy, the academy was defined by the successive ascendancies of two contrary doctrines during the second half of the seventeenth century. During the first phase, Charles Le Brun explicated and championed Poussin's primacy of line as the foundation of painting's power to express the work's all-important signified meaning as story. By the end of the century, however, the shift in favor of Roger de Piles confirmed the victory of color, *le coloris*, which defined painting as an art of fascinating surfaces.[4] This complex and protracted controversy—one that would still be very much alive when Rousseau wrote his *Essai sur l'origine des langues*—is suddenly, from the perspective of Du Bos' new primacy of pleasure, dismissed as irrelevant: "But for such questions as whether Le Brun is preferable to Titian, whether composition and expression are preferable to color, and which is superior to the other, *I hold it pointless even to raise them*" (164; italics mine).

For a young artist finding his way among quarreling teachers, Du Bos' position amounted to striking from the syllabus all reference to what had been the curriculum's most heated debate. If Du Bos takes that radical a step, it is because, as he sees it, the fundamentally subjective nature of pleasure implies that any exclusive choice in favor of line or color can only be the result of confusing opinion and truth, taste and rule.[5] "Everyone finally adopts the opinion, as though the question were closed, that the aspect of painting that pleases him most is the one that should have precedence over all others. And it is in following this principle that people find themselves in disagreement.... Everyone naturally believes that his taste is good taste.... It is never the case that people of different opinions manage to agree about preferences that are decided on a personal basis [*par rapport à soi-même*]. For each of us, the greatest painter is the one who gives us the most pleasure" (164).

Putting the viewer's pleasure first set the stage not only for Boucher but for the entire school and style we now refer to as the rococo. Du Bos' deft stepping away from esthetic dogma amounted to a dismissal of the academy as a forum empowered to legislate on such questions. Rather than looking to some royal institution for a sense of what was beautiful, Du Bos' readers—an educated, upwardly mobile, and moneyed bourgeoisie that would become less and less distinguishable from the nobility—were told to have confidence in, and direct their purchases toward, what gave them the most pleasure. Not only Boucher, but Nicolas Lancret, Carle Van Loo, and Jean-Honoré Fragonard would all build their reputations, not on the canonical history paintings that were given precedence by the academy, but on the genre scenes, *fêtes galantes*, and decorative pieces that their clients could not get enough of. Rethought from the perspective of pleasure, Du Bos' esthetic theory ushered in the new age of the market and of fashion, as private purchasers, unconcerned with academic dictates, became a clientele willing to reward lavishly those artists who provided them pleasure.[6]

Du Bos' comparative approach to poetry and painting as distinct yet similar vehicles of pleasure led him to adopt what we would call a semiological approach to the work of art. How, Du Bos asks, do poetry's words and painting's images actually work as signs? How do they produce pleasure? Does one of them do so more effectively than the other? In addressing these questions, Du Bos looks to what he sees as the most tangible physical differences between painting and poetry. While painting relies on what he calls the "natural signs" of the figures, objects, and places the viewer recognizes on the canvas, poetry has only the "artificial signs" of words printed on a page or spoken by the poet. If Du Bos takes the position that "the power of painting is greater than that of poetry" (133), it is because painting's iconic signs rely on a direct resemblance between sign and meaning whereas poetry's words presuppose the learning of an arbitrary code linking sounds and letters in ways that produce meaning. Images and words differ not only because the first are motivated and natural while the second are arbitrary and artificial, but because their creation of meaning is distinguished by different temporalities. Poetry's words produce their meaning only as a sequential and cumulative process: "Even the most touching verses are able to move us only by degrees, and by putting the springs of our machine into play one after the other. Words must first awaken in us the ideas for which they are arbitrary signs. After that, these ideas must be arranged in our imagination, forming tableaux that move us" (134). As readers or listeners, we first understand one word after the other and only then integrate them into the synthesis that is their meaning. Given that difference, painting's images, relying on immediately recognized resemblances, produce an "impression that is stronger than that which verses can achieve" (134).

As obvious as these claims may appear, their limits when applied to the specific case of what we now call rococo painting bring into focus what are the distinctive characteristics of Boucher's art. Is it enough to say of the rococo's frequent scenes of sensuality and sexual pleasure that they act as signs for which the viewer needs no code—as signs "whose energy," as Du Bos puts it, "does not depend on an education" (133)? In fact, the visual style of the rococo frequently presupposes a kind of worldly connoisseurship, an ability on the viewers' part to read the images they see in terms of sometimes quite sophisticated codes. The celebrations of nature, desire, and pleasure central to the rococo often rely, in spite of their apparent immediacy, on the informed viewer's ability to read a second level of meaning based on associations specific to their culture. In so doing, the rococo image often functions, pace Du Bos, as an "artificial" sign, a sign that produces meaning to the extent that its viewer makes a connection in a way not unlike what is involved in recognizing an allusion or catching a joke. In the case of the rococo, two different kinds of such secondary codes tend to be at work, one *cultural* and the other *narrative*. The *cultural* code relies on associations that can be assumed to be familiar to the savvy viewer, while the *narrative* code is specific to the image as a whole and the way it deploys its constituent elements.

I describe the first of these semiotic strategies as cultural because it depends on the viewer's ability to recognize symbolic objects, configurations, and allusions that inscribe a second, often ironic level of commentary within the image. In a work like Boucher's painting *The Pretty Cook* (fig. 1), the growing erotic tension between the boy and girl is reinforced by both the ruddy glow of the wood burning in the fireplace and the pot it brings to a boil. The fire's crimson warmth is transferred to the couple by the bright red of the girl's skirt. That skirt, as though calling attention to the area of the floor in front of the figure, directs the viewer's attention to the single broken egg as an emblem of lost virginity. To the right, and still on the floor, phallic cucumbers are arrayed in front of an oval cooking pot that lies gapingly open on its side. At the lower far right, inflecting the apparent sweetness of the scene, a predatory cat is about to devour the bird it holds captive in its mouth.

Reading rococo images in this way does little more than make explicit a set of emblems, an iconographic code, which the conventions of early-modern northern genre painting had firmly established and which were familiar to Boucher's educated audience.[7] This cultural semiotics works by arraying

Fig. 1. François Boucher, *The Pretty Cook* (1733–34), oil on canvas, 54×46 cm. Musée Cognacq-Jay, Paris.

objects, shapes, and colors in such a way that they play off of and comment on the immediate theme of the image. The complexity of what Du Bos refers to as the "education" on which appreciating these signs depends can range from the obviousness of the boiling pot and cucumbers to references that are far more culture-specific. In *The Pretty Cook*, for instance, a head of cabbage is prominently placed on the barrel to the right of the couple. While the labial quality of the cabbage's parted yet enfolding exterior leaves establishes it as a variation on the copper cooking pot below it, the cabbage also evoked for eighteenth-century French viewers such associations as the practice at country weddings of serving a bowl of cabbage soup to the newlyweds as their first dish after the marriage ceremony—a dish reputed since antiquity to have aphrodisiac powers. Even today, when French children ask where babies came from, they are told, not that the stork brings them, but that boys are found "in a cabbage"—while girls are found "in a rose."[8]

Unlike the blatant cucumbers, the elements of such cultural semiosis can be erased as history separates the viewer from the work's cultural context. A good example of this erosion of reference over time can be found in Boucher's title, *Of Three Things, Will You Do One of Them?* (fig. 2), for one of his works. His title for this image of a boy and girl facing each other with the girl seated and the boy kneeling before her has long puzzled critics. Why, with one hand, is each of them holding the other's wrist while one finger mysteriously points at the upper hand? And what might be the "three things" to be associated with this image of childhood innocence? As Jennifer Milam has shown, the answers to these questions lie in the popular children's game of the seventeenth and eighteenth centuries, then called *pied-de-bœuf*. Usually played by a boy and girl, this simple game involved both using their hands to grab, successively one after the other, the uppermost wrist of the other player as they counted from one to nine. The player holding the wrist of the other when the count reached nine would then exclaim, "Neuf! J'ai mon pied-de-bœuf"; as the winner, he or she would then have the privilege of asking the other, "Cow foot, of three things, will you do one?" The loser would then respond: "Yes, but what are they?" To that, the winner would offer some version of a decidedly loaded choice: "Will you go to the moon? Will you move our village to the other side of the mountain? Will you give me a kiss?"[9]

The other secondary code, what I am calling the narrative code, likewise qualifies Du Bos' claim as to the *suddenness* of the way paintings mean: their power, unlike the sequential words of poetry, to state their meaning in the single moment of perception. The rococo frequently works by deploying within the image disparate elements which, when brought together as narrative, inflect the meaning of what we see. They tell, in other words, a story that emerges only from a cumulative reading. At the center of Nicolas Lancret's *Young Lady on a Sofa* (fig. 3), a fashionably dressed young woman is seated in a richly furnished salon whose dominant color is a sensuous red. Using the small mirror in her left hand, she admires or adjusts her impressive décolleté. To the far left of the image, hidden in shadow, we see an older male figure who appears quite startled by what he beholds as he enters the room. As the

Fig. 2. François Boucher, *Of Three Things, Will You Do One of Them?* (1733–34), oil on canvas, 105 × 85 cm. Villa Ephrussi de Rothchild, Saint-Jean-Cap-Ferrat, France.

viewer brings these elements together, two different readings—two different narratives—become possible. For some critics, the older male figure is the woman's husband. His unexpected arrival disturbs his wife's preparations for the arrival of her music instructor, a younger man whose lesson will certainly extend beyond a mastering of the viola that lies against the side of the sofa. A second and different narrative is postulated by those critics who call attention to the lace collar, or rabat, worn by the older male figure. That collar, as they see it, marks him not as the young woman's husband but as an elderly prelate, a man of the Church, who has happened upon this unexpected and disconcerting scene. According to this second narrative, the woman can be seen as using her mirror not to stage or admire her charms, but to glimpse her watcher, to amuse herself at the sight of the elderly gentleman's dignified public persona being upset.[10] Depending on the meaning the viewer gives to the lace collar, this scene is either a droll commentary on the dangers of marriages forced on dutiful daughters or a softer vignette highlighting the fragility of the pomposities that come with rank and age. Whichever option one chooses, this painting's meaning depends on the way its elements are brought together within a narrative, a before and after generated by the image and read by the viewer.

This use of what I have called cultural and narrative codes is, of course, hardly specific to the rococo. If anything, this overlapping of writerly and painterly semiosis was far more central to the more exalted genre of history painting and its careful deploying of historical, biblical, and mythological references. If I have used examples from the rococo to underline where Du Bos' distinctions between poetry and painting break down, it is because the fragility of that boundary takes us to the essence both of Boucher's way of painting and

Fig. 3. Nicolas Lancret, *Young Lady on a Sofa* (1735–40), oil on panel, 23 × 31 cm. Collection of Mr. and Mrs. Stewart Resnick, Los Angeles.

of the fraught reactions his work continues to provoke from critics and art historians. My contention is that Boucher, taking seriously Du Bos' centrality of pleasure, had as his defining ambition to establish the painted image as a sensual pleasure so direct and so intense that it beguiles the eye with an immediacy of effect that is independent of such "artificial" codes.

Boucher is often described as the most accomplished painter of the female form between Rubens and Renoir. That claim, true or false, does little to dissipate the aura, faint or lurid depending on the critic, of prurience that hangs over his work. One rarely senses, in art historical discussions of Rubens or Renoir, anything like the discomfort and even outrage that can characterize Boucher criticism. At one level, this may be because those other painters practice an overt stylization of the body, be it toward the contorted rotundity of Rubens's northern baroque or toward the dreamlike elusiveness of Renoir's impressionism. Boucher, to the contrary, depicts the curves and textures of the human form in a way that far more tangibly evokes the carnal presence of the body. Looking at the figures depicted in Boucher's canvases, one senses, pace Diderot, a distinct "truth" of corporality.[11] Boucher's images are often distinguished by the strong contrast between a central figure of almost naturalistic appearance and a surrounding context set apart from the real by an elaborate use of mythological and pastoral emblems.

However we explain the discomfort that can result from an encounter with Boucher's work, the prominence in his art of alluring female forms has, from their initial displays in the biennial Salons, been at the center of the reception of his paintings. For Diderot, the inevitable baseline for Boucher criticism, he is a painter "who takes up his brush only to show me breasts and buttocks" (4:312). In his *Salon de 1765*, Diderot wrote the most scathing of his many diatribes against Boucher. Reaching to include in his indictment of Boucher's nefarious influence every conceivable aspect of painting, Diderot designates him as single-handedly responsible for the "degradation of taste, color, composition, character, and design" (4:308). To Diderot's censorious eye, Boucher is suspect not only as an artist but as a moral person. His choice of subjects, for Diderot, leaves no doubt that he is the consort of "prostitutes of the lowest class" (4:308). Vicious anecdotes abounded that Boucher had painted the Irish prostitute O'Murphy at the specific request of Mme de Pompadour to stimulate the king's flagging libido and that, as an artist who made a practice of seducing his models, a sitting by the Duchesse de Chartres made him the biological father of the ill-fated Philippe-Égalité.

After the Revolution, Diderot's brand of ad hominem gave way to a different but equally negative discourse presenting Boucher as the perfect product and revealing mirror of a corrupt age and a degenerate class. Louis-Charles Soyer, very much in the tone of Diderot, claimed in the *Encyclopédie des gens du monde* of 1843 that, "as a man and as a painter, François Boucher is the very image of his century. The depravity of his morals, the decadence of his taste, the artificiality of his palette, the speciousness of his compositions, the affected character of his heads ... all followed step by step the licentious and degenerate course of society under the Regency and the reign of Louis XV."[12] Closer to our own time, Daniel Wildenstein wrote that "François Boucher could achieve his full flowering only in the eighteenth century. He is so perfect an incarnation of it that one is tempted to see in him a synthesis, almost a symbol, which can stand alone in our minds as a summary of all the painters of his kind."[13] For Georges Brunel, "[Boucher's] genius lies in having invented simultaneously a style, a subject matter and a means of working which were perfectly adapted to the spirit of his age. . . . No other artist represents so well the diversity and even the contradictions of French society in the eighteenth century."[14] Behind Brunel's suave reference to "contradictions" lies the charge that Boucher's talent was fatally circumscribed by his status as pander to a degenerate class that would be deservedly swept away in the fury of the Revolution. Earlier in the twentieth century, Haldane Macfall minced no words in delivering his verdict on Boucher's place in the conflicts of ancien régime France: "Boucher's art holds the significance of his age in astounding fashion. Nothing could more closely define the vast gulf that lay between the outworn, weary, and decaying aristocracy of France allied with a reactionary, narrow, and selfish church, and wedded to an unscrupulous wealth-seeking plutocracy on the one hand, and the real France of dogged self-respecting toil, supported and championed by intellect and sincerity on the other."[15]

While contemporary art historians would hardly feel comfortable with such direct conflations of class affiliation and painterly style, Boucher nonetheless remains under a cloud of political incorrectness no less somber than the one that descended on his work in the last third of the eighteenth century. Denounced as near pornography, his images of the naked female form still find themselves charged with purveying dubious pleasures. Today, however, that charge involves not the pleasure of an aristocracy long absent from the scene but the noxious "male gaze" that seeks to luxuriate in a patriarchal debasement of woman to the status of pure object. Boucher's female figures become consumable bodies prettied up for the prurient tastes of an aggressively gendered and domineering male spectator. Even the most innovative perspectives on Boucher's work from the 1970s until the recent past too often feel obliged to castigate Boucher for his congruence with a fundamentally patriarchal age.[16] The cultural conflicts generating Boucher's expulsion to the realm of the unacceptable may have changed over the last two centuries, but their result is a taboo that has remained singularly tenacious.

Faced with the continuities of this critical tradition, approaching Boucher through Du Bos' insistence on the primacy of the viewer's pleasure offers the possibility of reconstructing, tentatively and hypothetically, certain aspects of his cultural context that help us to see him differently. To get at that context, I will begin by examining a work marked by a surprising dissonance between its explicit subject matter and its strategies of composition and execution. That dissonance not only sets this work apart from what we think of as Boucher's signature style but also establishes it as a retrospective commentary on how the cultural premises of the seventeenth century—the source of its subject matter—differed from those of the eighteenth century. In the Salon of 1742 Boucher exhibited an oil painting on canvas, most probably commissioned by Baron Crozat de Thiers, titled *Landscape with Hermit* (fig. 4).[17] This painting illustrates a scene from one of the tales in Jean de La Fontaine's *Contes et nouvelles en vers*, a work first published in 1666 and which immediately became a source of considerable scandal. Borrowed from Boccaccio's *Decameron* (1380) and the anonymous *Les Cent nouvelles nouvelles* (ca. 1465, published in 1486), this tale has as its main character Frère Luce, the hermit of Boucher's title. La Fontaine's verse narrative begins by stating the moral lesson the story is intended to illustrate: "Lady Venus and Lady Hypocrisy, / Sometimes pull off good tricks together."[18] In a forest far from any town there lives a hermit revered for his holiness. His only neighbors are a widow and her daughter, a young woman described in three verses that qualify her for a place of honor in Boucher's repertoire: "Young, ingenuous, pleasing, and sweet; / A maiden still, but, in truth, / Less by virtue than by innocence" (139). The hermit, far from indifferent to the young woman's charms, must nonetheless preserve his mask of austere self-denial. Using a horn to deepen and disguise his voice, he sneaks close to the widow's hut

Fig. 4. François Boucher, *Landscape with Hermit* (1742), oil on canvas, 67×55 cm. Pushkin Museum of Fine Arts, Moscow, Russia.

and, in the dark of night, delivers his own version of the Annunciation. Speaking as the voice of God from his heaven, he intones:

> Luce is benign. You, widow, must see to it
> That of your daughter he becomes the companion;
> For from them will be born a pope, whose life
> Will reform all Christian peoples. (140)

The pious widow dutifully accompanies her daughter to numerous repetitions of her divinely appointed mission, each time finding the hermit pretending to flagellate himself. As time passes and as the daughter becomes visibly pregnant, the hermit loses interest in continuing his ruse. Resorting once again to the horn, the voice from heaven now tells the widow her mission is complete. The mother and daughter must refrain from future visits and await the birth of the pope-to-be who will also make them rich and powerful. And so they do—until the dutiful daughter gives birth to a girl.

What is most striking about the way Boucher chose to illustrate this tale is how little his decision to treat it more as a landscape than as a vignette corresponds to the style we associate with his depictions of sexualized desire. An underarticulated but basically realistic sky sets off a scene rendered in careful perspective. The tone becomes darker and more forbidding as the eye moves from the washed-out sky to the human figures, the two women at the left and the hermit to the right who stands in front of the dark entrance to his cavern. The male and female figures are separated from each other, with the hermit and mother portrayed as older figures either hypocritically or naïvely exploiting youthful innocence. The sexual tension animating the scene is hidden and muted, present only in the innocent gait of the young girl and the surreptitiously turned head of the hermit.

Two well-known later illustrations of the same tale, one by Charles Eisen and the other by Jean-Honoré Fragonard, highlight eloquently what is most surprising about the way Boucher chose to treat this subject. Eisen's *Hermit* (fig. 5) brings the three figures close together within a shared space just outside the monk's dwelling. The mother, placed between the daughter who stands to her left and the monk who kneels to her right, attempts to close the gap between the rigidly posed girl and the contorted monk. The mother's left hand, placed on the daughter's shoulder, encourages her toward the monk. Her right hand, placed in front of the monk, beckons him toward the girl. The monk's elongated right arm, extended toward the girl, ends in a hand whose gesture hovers between grabbing at the prize offered him and feigning pushing her away.

Fragonard's *Hermit* (fig. 6) chooses as the focus for its illustration a later and more intimate moment in La Fontaine's narrative. With the mother now absent from the scene, the monk, in the space of his covered sleeping area, assists the timid young woman as she lifts over her head the last garment covering her body from his concupiscent gaze. Both these illustrations, in

Fig. 5. Charles Eisen, *The Hermit* (1762), engraving, 10.5 × 6.5 cm. From Jean de La Fontaine, *Tales and Novels in Verse with One Hundred and Twenty-Three Engravings by and after Eisen, Lancret, Boucher, Pater, etc., Printed from the Original Copper-Plates*, 2 vols. (London: Society of English Bibliophilists, 1888), vol. 2, facing 19.

terms of the scale and placement of their central figures, are much closer to the style we associate with Boucher than is the image he himself produced.

Precisely because of these choices, Boucher's eccentric strategy for illustrating La Fontaine's tale is revealing. When contrasted with his signature style as seen in a work like the kitchen seduction of *The Pretty Cook*, significant differences emerge between the visual and cultural premises that sustain these two very different representations of desire. In *The Pretty Cook*, the de-

THE ESTHETICS OF PLEASURE 87

Fig. 6. Jean-Honoré Fragonard, *The Hermit* (1762), engraving, 19.6×13.3 cm. From Jean de La Fontaine, *Tales and Novels in Verse with One Hundred and Twenty-Three Engravings by and after Eisen, Lancret, Boucher, Pater, etc., Printed from the Original Copper-Plates*, 2 vols. (London: Society of English Bibliophilists, 1888), vol. 2, facing 24.

siring yet hesitant bodies of the young man and woman dominate and become the center of the image. In *Landscape with Hermit*, the three human figures are dwarfed by the landscape that surrounds and engulfs them even though they are the focus of the story's narrative intent. Boucher's emphasis here on separation rather than proximity, on a careful maneuvering of prey toward predator, refers to an earlier tradition. It was not by accident that La Fontaine's tale of a hypocritically lustful hermit appeared and was thunderously denounced at the height of the scandal provoked by the other great work of 1666—Molière's *Tartuffe*.

Landscape with Hermit depicts a sexual extortion carried out under the cover of religious devotion. It is an emblem not of bold display but of furtive hypocrisy. It relies for its meaning, for the force of its anticlerical statement, on a feigned refusal of the senses—on sensual pleasure as it was portrayed in those edifying seventeenth-century variants of the *nature morte* called *vanités*. In those images, the devaluation of the senses' fleeting pleasures was emblematized by juxtaposing an array of objects—a book for sight, a musical instrument for sound, a flower for smell, a fruit for taste, and cards or dice for touch and its unleashed passions—with the timeless truth of death represented by a stark skull.[19] While the dark tonalities of *Landscape with Hermit* evoke the value system summarized in those seventeenth-century moralities, Boucher's signature style lies at the antipodes of that paradigm.

The canonical Boucher revels in direct and forceful appeals to the viewer's senses. A work of his like *The Cage* (fig. 7) reconfigures entirely the austere countryside of *Landscape with Hermit*, rejecting everything that painting presupposes about the danger of what is experienced through the senses. In *The Cage*'s image of a young woman being courted by the bird catcher seated at her side, separation, duplicity, and denial are replaced by proximity, anticipation, and a luxuriance in sensation that extends even to the feel of the bird's wing as it flutters against the woman's cheek.

If I insist on the contrast between *Landscape with Hermit* and the canonical Boucher, it is because their comparison helps to identify an opposition that lies at the core of his work. The images we think of as most typical of Boucher—such as his *Birth and Triumph of Venus* (fig. 8)—rely on a tension between two distinct components. On the one hand, his settings, the peripheries surrounding his central subject, are explicitly unrealistic. Rejecting perspectival construction, their lack of realism short-circuits any easy integration of the image within a unifying narrative coherence. Boucher's backgrounds within such mythological pieces tend toward billowing clouds, floating putti, swirling fabrics, turbulent oceans, gossamer mists, and elusive countryside. In all their variants, these peripheries exult in an indifference to the laws of verisimilitude and realism. On the other hand, the central figures within Boucher's mythological images are marked by a careful and naturalistic evocation of carnal presence. Taking human shape, these exercises in

Fig. 7. François Boucher, *The Cage* (1763), oil on canvas, 93 × 73 cm. Musée du Louvre, Paris.

color and form speak directly to the eye. They address vision as a sense able to trigger a synesthesia that extends the phantasmatic appeal of the body beheld to consciousness and the other bodily senses.

In the same way that Du Bos invoked the viewer's pleasure as a goal that renders pointless any academic dispute as to whether one should opt for *either* narrative line *or* sensuous color, so also Boucher's signature style brings together within his esthetic of pleasure *both* the carefully rendered bodily details of his central figures *and* the fantastical unreality of his peripheries. Rather than choosing between Poussin and Rubens, between Le Brun and de Piles, between narrative and chromatics, Boucher, both an accomplished draftsman and an exquisite colorist, elaborated a new way of painting directly

Fig. 8. François Boucher, *The Birth and Triumph of Venus* (1743), black chalk and gouache, 39×31 cm. The J. Paul Getty Museum, Los Angeles.

for the senses. In so doing, his esthetic of pleasure addresses the enchanted spectator not as Cartesian mind but as sensate body.

This painting for the senses—precisely what his anomalous execution of *Landscape with Hermit* highlights by its elision—represents Boucher's espousal within his signature style of what I am calling Epicurean Stoicism. An important part of Boucher's cultural milieu, and often referred to as *libertinage,* Epicurean Stoicism is a juxtaposition of apparent contraries not unlike the tension between center and periphery so important to the construction of Boucher's mythological images. To speak of Epicurean Stoicism as an alternative to the more familiar *libertinage* has two advantages. On the one hand, that term's now negative connotations reinforce too easily the prim disapproval that has exercised so distorting a force in Boucher criticism. On the other hand, rethinking *libertinage* as Epicurean Stoicism offers a clearer vision of how Boucher's esthetic corresponds to premises of eighteenth-century French culture that extend far beyond the protocols of sexual conduct.

Libertinage was, as the word indicates, a praxis of liberty. The liberty it posited was not, however, the natural freedom that Rousseau projected onto his vision of humankind at a time before history and society when all were free in their forest world. It was instead a liberty wrenched from enslavement, a modernized form of Epicurean *ataraxia* as a freedom from the disturbances of the mind and its passions. The *Encyclopédie*'s short entry for *libertins* reminds the reader that the term comes from the Latin *libertini*, designating a slave who has been granted freedom (2:637). *Libertinage* implies a vision of the human condition and a regimen of conduct both of which are intended to achieve a maximum of individual autonomy within a structured and hierarchical society. As a philosophy, eighteenth-century *libertinage* relied on a physiology and a psychology that were distinctly its own. Based in the sensationism resurrected from Ovid and Lucretius by Gassendi and articulated by Thomas Hobbes, John Locke, Julien Offrai de La Mettrie, and Étienne Bonnot de Condillac, the *libertinage* that is part of Epicurean Stoicism posits the individual as a perceiving body whose awareness of the exterior world depends entirely on the data supplied by the senses. It is through the senses that the individual is able to perceive objects distinct from the self that inspire either attraction or repulsion. In the case of attraction, sense perception produces desire which itself becomes a prelude either to freedom or to enslavement. Whether desire's force leads to liberty or to subjection depends on to which of two distinct agencies it is referred. A desire consonant with freedom is a desire subsumed within *l'esprit,* understood as a faculty of estheticized appreciation and strategic control that allows for a distance from and domination of the desired object perceived by the senses. A desire leading to subjection, desire in its most virulent form, is one subsumed by *le cœur,* the heart understood as the agency of imagination, passion, and even madness. *Le cœur* is a faculty that provokes a hypertrophy of desire transforming the longed-for object into an alluring and enslaving illusion. Born in vision, desire compromises liberty when *le cœur* and its triggering of imagination make of the object a prize that can never be won for the simple reason that the object never exists as what the imagination has led it to become.

Novels of the period are rife with permutations of this model. First encounters between the sexes are regularly portrayed as beginning with an unexpected vision. Usually adopting the point of view of a central male character, these novels portray a hero who finds himself smitten with a beautiful woman in much the same way as Angola reacted to the portrait of Luzéide. In Prévost's *Manon Lescaut*, des Grieux describes his first reaction upon seeing Manon as she steps from the public coach that has just arrived in Amiens: "She appeared so charming that . . . I found myself suddenly enflamed as though in a transport."[20] In Crébillon's *Les Égarements du cœur et de l'esprit*, Meilcour—not unlike Thérèse as she first encountered the Count at the Opéra—develops even more explicitly the stakes of the first sight when he describes the effect on him of his seeing Hortense for the first time in the loge next to his at the Opéra. "Curious to see who was occupying it, I turned my eyes toward it, and the object that appeared there held them spellbound. . . . I cannot express the singular and sudden feeling that overwhelmed me at that sight: struck by such exquisite beauty, I felt overcome. My surprise became a kind of transport. I could feel in my heart a disorder that flowed through all my senses."[21]

The other option within the libertine model, the one that prevails when the data provided by the senses are referred not to *le cœur* but to *l'esprit*, tends to be the hallmark of older, more predatory characters such as Crébillon's preening Versac and Laclos' Valmont. When Valmont claims that he is at every moment the master of his feelings, he captures in a single sentence the guiding rule of the libertine model: "But, let me make it clear, this intoxication of the senses, perhaps even this delirium of vanity, has in no way penetrated *to my heart*" (italics mine).[22] Laclos' reliance on the libertine paradigm extended even to his choice to portray each of the main female characters in *Les Liaisons dangereuses* as contrasted incarnations of three distinct registers: the naïve Cécile acts only on the immediate urges of her senses; the passionate Tourvel on those of her self-deceiving heart; and the calculating

Merteuil on those of her always manipulating mind. The protective calculations of *l'esprit* are, however, by no means the sure winner. Marivaux's theater offers countless variations on how *l'esprit* eventually finds itself tripped up by *le cœur*, on how masters and mistresses who have cleverly disguised themselves as servants find themselves falling in love with someone they believe to be a servant.

Boucher's Epicurean Stoicism accommodates the premises of *libertinage* in a way distinctly his own. The tension in his works between center and setting, between carnal allure and peripheral illusionism, establishes his images as signs that speak to the senses but that, as purely esthetic stimuli, short-circuit any subsequent referral to the psychological agencies of ensnarement and enslavement. The pleasure offered by Boucher's images, the core of his style, is a self-enclosed and self-sustaining sense experience held safe from absorption within the twin dilemmas of domination and subjection. Boucher's spectators, scrutinizing his images, are offered the intense pleasure of a desire born in sight but impervious to the anguish of referral. As painted surfaces simulating desire's pleasure with none of its dangers, Boucher's images open the way to a utopia of visual perception impossible within the real. In so doing Boucher articulates within his art the inspiration he drew from Du Bos' doctrine of pleasure as the criterion of esthetic experience. In section 3 of his *Réflexions critiques*, Du Bos describes "the pleasure which painters and poets are able to impart to objects" as distinctly different from the pleasure provoked by real objects, because, "had they been real, they would have excited in us passions which become burdensome." For Du Bos, it is only this pleasure without burden that can become "a pure pleasure" (10). The essence of art lies in its power to create what he calls "phantom pleasures." "Could not art," he asks, "find ways of separating what is agreeable about the passions from the painful consequences so often associated with them? . . . Could not art produce objects capable of stimulating us at the moment we perceive them, yet incapable of bringing with them real suffering and true affliction?" (9). While Du Bos is referring here to the power of history paintings and verse tragedies to produce an Aristotelian catharsis, the economy of the esthetic experience as he describes it is the same as that at work in Boucher's direct appeal to the eye and the pleasure it might take in the perception of distinctly bodily *grâces*.

Approached in terms of Epicurean Stoicism, Boucher's images can be described as beginning with a careful attention to what I would call sensory trigger points. As we know from his preliminary sketches, Boucher's finished paintings often begin from a fixing of attention on a tightly focused physical detail. His sketch titled "Head of a Young Girl" (fig. 9) is a highly charged foregrounding of the sensuous curve of a woman's neck seen from the rear as her head is turned slightly to the left. The careful play of pencil strokes delineating fabric, hair, and flesh animated by a pensive downward glance establishes this constellation of shoulders, neck, and head as a potent visual stimulus that could be incorporated into such fuller depictions as the sketch titled "Young Girl Seen from Behind" (fig. 10), or even, with a shift to

Fig. 9. François Boucher, "Head of a Young Girl" (sketch, 1733), trois crayons, 22 × 18 cm. From *Catalogue de dessins et aquarelles du XVIIIe siècle* (Hôtel Drouot, Paris, March 6, 1899).

THE ESTHETICS OF PLEASURE 95

Fig. 10. François Boucher, "Young Girl Seen from Behind" (sketch, 1733), black chalk, 174×125 cm. The Ashmolean Museum, Oxford, England.

a more lateral angle, the neck of the young girl who accompanies her mother in *Landscape with Hermit*.

Even more frequently, as in his preliminary sketch (fig. 11) for *Aurora and Cephalus* (fig. 12), it is the entire body as an extended syntagma of signs speaking to the senses which will find its way into the finished work. Reacting to that body, the viewer is invited to become a version of the faithful Cephalus as his hunt ends with the apparition of the beautiful Aurora. Boucher's contemporaries frequently underlined the workings of these trigger points. Jean-Bernard Leblanc, describing his reaction to *The Abduction of Europa*, claims that "there is in Boucher's paintings much science and poetry, along with a

96 THE ESTHETICS OF PLEASURE

Fig. 11. François Boucher, sketch for *Aurora and Cephalus* (1733), red and white chalk, 37×23.5 cm. National Gallery of Art, Washington, DC.

spirit which is his alone."[23] As an example of Boucher's potent syntheses of science and poetry, Leblanc recalls the way his depiction of Europa's longing gaze as she is carried off by Zeus in the form of a bull provoked for him a visual experience so intense that it passed immediately from eye to heart, even while remaining obviously unreal: "And soon the warmth of that look made flow to my heart all the love that animates it" (54). The force of Boucher's images as arrays of sensory triggers even became the subject of the short verse legends that were often appended to print versions of his works. In Michel Aubert's 1735 print of Boucher's *Venus Asleep*, the engraver François-Bernard Lépicié added a legend that underlines Boucher's ability to trans-

Fig. 12. François Boucher, *Aurora and Cephalus* (1733), oil on canvas, 250×175 cm. Musée des Beaux-Arts, Nancy, France.

form even the abstracted state of sleep into an array of eloquent sensual stimuli:

> Ne cessons de craindre une belle;
> Son repos même a des appas.
> L'Amour fait toujours sentinelle
> Et ce Dieu ne sommeille pas.[24]

> [Let us never cease to fear such a beauty;
> Even in sleep her charms enchant.
> Love is always on the watch
> And that God never sleeps.]

As though illustrating the arresting potency of the sense perceptions his images offer, Boucher often includes within his scenes of sleeping shepherdesses or goddesses a second figure who, transfixed by the body beheld, becomes a surrogate for the enchanted spectator.

In terms of Boucher's sensationist paradigm, the alluring body perceived by the senses exercises a far greater power than any idea, than any already processed residue within consciousness of earlier but now absent sense impressions. As the *Encyclopédie* entry titled "sensation" puts it: "We are masters of the attention we give to our ideas.... We control them with a power every bit as sovereign as that of a collector deciding how he will display his paintings. It is not at all the same with our sensations. The attention we give them is involuntary; we are forced to give in to them. Our mind is possessed by them, sometimes more, sometimes less, in proportion to how strong or weak the sensation itself happens to be" (3:495). What makes this entry useful for understanding Boucher's artistic practice is the way Diderot brings painting into the discussion. The calm control we exercise over ideas is, as he sees it, the same mental state as that of the connoisseur contemplating his collection of paintings. That coupling of painting with the idea clarifies why Diderot so much preferred the explicit moralizing of Jean-Baptiste Greuze—whose vignettes he delighted in explicating—to Boucher's sensationism, his exaltation of painting's ability to provoke the surprises of pleasure. Boucher, so distant from Diderot's call for a new classicism, was a painter who sought far more to delight the eye than to instruct the mind.[25]

Charles-Nicolas Cochin, historiographer of the Académie royale de peinture and Boucher's faithful defender, argued that the sensual pleasure provoked by Boucher's works was so intense that the absence of a reaction to its stimulus could only be taken as a proof of the spectator's brute insensibility. Replying to a critic who had spoken harshly of the twinned images of Apollo and Tethys that Boucher produced for Mme de Pompadour in the early 1750s under the titles *The Rising of the Sun* and *The Setting of the Sun*, Cochin left no doubt as to where the fault lie. "If they [Boucher's two paintings] do not produce the same effect on a person who esteems himself so enlightened, should we not assume that the fault is his, and that only he is afflicted with this degree of insensibility?" Cochin ridicules the conventionality of such a critic as a viewer who looks only for, as he puts it in derisive italics, "*decisive action rendered with force*," while it is obvious that Boucher's true genius is to be found elsewhere: in "the flesh of Apollo and of these women in all their tenderness and delicacy" as stimuli that produce the most refined "sentiments of pleasure."[26] It is significant that Cochin articulates his argument on the basis of two mythological paintings in which the male body, "the flesh of Apollo," is even more prominent as a syntagma of sensory trigger points than are the female figures of Thetis and her attendants. Although Boucher is most often discussed in terms of his female figures, his male figures are equally marked by a rendition of the body as signs that speak directly to the senses.[27] Boucher's male figures tend toward two distinct types. In one register there are the bodies of such male figures as the supplicant Cephalus and the smoothly epicene bodies of the two versions of Apollo which Cochin praises.[28] In the other register, his subordinate male figures of the gods' attendants are marked by the rough, sinewy, and hypermuscular traits of distinctly less epicene characters. Boucher's gestalts of masculinity and femininity may be varied, but they all rely on a careful deployment of carnal trigger points.[29]

If Boucher's celebration of a pleasure that beguiles the eye yet remains cut off from the dangers of referral had so short a future, it is because the sensationist premises of his art never survived the rise of sentimentalism. Diderot's conviction that painting must provide a didactic illustration of familial or civic virtue could only set him against what he found, or failed to find, in Boucher's works. Diderot, in his *Salon de 1761*, may find much to admire in Boucher's work, but, for him, something essential is missing. "What colors! What variety! What a wealth of subjects and ideas! This man has everything, except truth" (4:205). The truth Diderot finds so singularly lacking in Boucher's work has nothing to do with the verisimilitude of his figures, with the idea that a painting should provide a convincing representation of reality. To the contrary, the truth Diderot sees Boucher as incapable of portraying is the moral truth of an image that sets out to instruct its viewers at the same time that it pleases them. If Boucher became for Diderot the antithesis of truth, it was because his paintings made no attempt to articulate the secular pieties that Diderot so admired in Greuze's scenes of dramatized virtue. In the broader culture, it was Rousseau's *Julie* of 1761 that quickly became the crucial work in this new valorization of sentiment and feeling. Rousseau's celebration of sentiment's transformative power as the foundation of truth, virtue, and sincerity redefined Boucher's short-circuiting of referral as an espousal of the corrupt, the jaded, and the inhuman. Speaking very much in Rousseau's wake, even

Laclos' Valmont, the prototypical rake, finds himself forced to admit that an imperviousness to sentiment's subjection and infatuation carries a heavy price. "Let us be frank. With our intimacies as cold as they are shallow, what we call happiness is scarcely a pleasure. But shall I tell you something? I thought my heart had withered away, and, finding nothing left to me but my senses, I lamented my premature old age" (18–19).

For us today, it is hardly an allegiance to Greuzian or Rousseauian sentimentality that gets in the way of our appreciating the premises that sustain Boucher's esthetics of pleasure. Quite different reasons place Boucher's attempt to provide a sensory pleasure prior to and independent of mediation by the mental processes of imagination outside the realm of the conceivable. Within the Freudian paradigm that is still very much our own, the senses are assumed to perceive the world only as mediated by an unconscious that is always already structured by the trauma of its integration within the constraints of the symbolic order. Perception, in our post-Freudian age, is never innocent or unmediated. Accessible only as filtered through the drives of the unconscious, figurative images are perceived not as clusters of pleasurable signifiers but as stimuli to be processed by an unconscious already bent on appropriation and consumption. Seen through the prism of the Freudian id, Boucher's central figures all too easily become emblems of danger, exploitation, and prurience.

For less censorious reactions to Boucher's esthetics of pleasure, we must turn to voices speaking outside both the religion of sentimentality and the hegemony of psychoanalysis. Edmond and Jules de Goncourt, for instance, described Boucher as capturing a "voluptuousness without torment," claiming that "voluptuousness is the whole of Boucher's ideal: it is everything his painting has as its soul."[30] Closer to us, a critic like Daniel Wildenstein says much the same thing when he speaks of Boucher as proposing a "constantly aroused sensuality" achieved by "a way of drawing that translates the trembling of life and of pleasure." As if sensing his readers' discomfort with that claim, Wildenstein quickly adds the proviso that Boucher, unlike modern artists, "presents as games what we take to be problems."[31]

Boucher's way of playing the painter's game assumed that his only opponent, yet also the stimulus for his most important achievements, was nature itself. In the 1743 version of *The Toilette of Venus* (fig. 13), Boucher explicitly allegorizes painting's rivalry with nature in its power to address the senses. Below and to the left of the recumbent Venus a putto holds up an

Fig. 13. François Boucher, *The Toilette of Venus* (1743), oil on canvas, 101 × 86.7 cm. Hermitage, St. Petersburg, Russia.

oval mirror to the goddess. That mirror—the site of nature's reflection, yet also a metaphor of the artist's attempts to emulate nature—is positioned in such a way that it captures in profile the face of the central figure. The image within the mirror, however, has nothing of the vivacity, line, or arresting force of the face produced by the painter's brush.

My point in underlining this conflation of art and nature within their shared status as stimuli speaking to the senses is not that Boucher painted as a Pavlovian pornographer. To the contrary, Boucher, as we have seen, consistently encloses the appetitious realism of his central figures within the formal, chromatic, and thematic unreality of his peripheries. That highlighting of the frame as limit and as boundary insures that the spectator draws from his work an intense awareness that the *plaisir pur* his works provide is first and always an artistic manipulation of color and form. Understood in terms of the Epicurean Stoicism that sustains them, Boucher's images become an instance of what Thomas Crow has called "the autonomy thesis in visual aesthetics." For Crow, the "authenticity" of a work of art depends on whether it manifests a choice to dramatize "the material possibilities and limitations of its unique medium."[32] Put differently, and in the language of Boucher's period, Claude-Augustin-Pierre Duflos pointed precisely to this aspect of Boucher's work in the last strophe of the verse legend he appended to his engraving of the *Toilette pastorale* of 1745:

> C'est ainsi que semant des fleurs toujours nouvelles,
> Agréable Boucher, Peintre chéri des Belles,
> Tu nous fais admirer dans ce charmant Tableau,
> Les attraits séduisants de ton brillant pinceau.[33]

> [Thus as you sow flowers always new,
> Pleasing Boucher, beloved painter of beautiful women,
> You make us admire in your charming tableaux,
> The seductive charms of your brilliant brush.]

The pleasure offered by Boucher's images of the body remains as strong today as it was when his paintings were first presented to his contemporaries. What has changed entirely, however, is the way our own culture, neither Epicurean nor Stoic, chooses to react to and interpret that pleasure.

5. Rousseau's Eudemony of Liberty

Boucher's celebration of *les grâces* in their most alluringly bodily form eloquently illustrates how the eighteenth century's esthetics of pleasure challenged Christianity's contempt for the senses. His art, working in a different register, can be seen as another version of *Thérèse philosophe*'s insurgency against the Church's demonizing of the flesh. The Enlightenment certainly included Kant's daring to know; but it also extended to a daring to feel, to experience, and to relish the pleasures that feeling brought. In the same way that the Enlightenment based its epistemology on the senses and their ability to know the world, it recast its ethics as an Epicurean recognition of the body and its right to take pleasure from the world.

As the Church's horror of the flesh found itself ridiculed by a broad spectrum of materialists and *philosophes,* there emerged one figure, Jean-Jacques Rousseau, whose political, literary, and autobiographical writings would articulate a deeply paradoxical challenge to the new legitimacy of pleasure. While Rousseau's anthropology of nature left no room for any Christian version of history, his challenge to the Enlightenment's new values of the sciences and the arts prepared the way for a return of the religious in another form. As civic community replaced mystical body, as sensation became the docile acolyte of sentiment, and as complicity with modernity became the most grievous sin, Rousseau's religion of liberty set the stage for a new shaming of pleasure. Civic rather than Christian, Rousseau's critique of pleasure in the name of liberty remains very much with us today. The enigma of his legacy lies in the fact that, while Rousseau articulated a vision of history as an apprenticeship of servitude which few can deny, that vision also posed a challenge to his readers which finally neither they nor he could meet. Rejecting the secular optimism of the *philosophes*, Rousseau articulated a new version of the Fall. His religion postulated an Eden not of innocence but of a primordial liberty whose respect and restitution within the present became the defining duty of a refashioned state. When, as Rousseau came to see it, all his attempts to show the path to true liberty were rejected by his fellows, when civic salvation receded hopelessly beyond reach, Rousseau would finally be left to draw his only consolation from an ecstasy of memory that relegated sensation and pleasure to a realm of remembered phantoms.

Let me, as a way of giving shape to my analysis of the trajectory that Rousseau's ultimately tragic vision would follow, begin by looking at two eighteenth-century prints which were important to Rousseau but for very different reasons and at very different moments. This first, the frontispiece to his *Discourse on the Sciences and Arts* (fig. 14), accompanied Rousseau's first published appearance within the Republic of Letters.[1] It is an allegorical image whose stark figures tell a monitory tale. Rousseau summarized what it was intended to mean in a quotation from Plutarch which he placed in one of his footnotes to the *Discourse:* "The satyr, an ancient fable relates, wanted to kiss and embrace the fire the first time he saw it; but Prometheus cried out to him: satyr, you will mourn the beard on your chin, for fire burns when one touches it."[2] The second print is an engraving done by Barthélemy Augustin Blondel d'Azaincourt titled *Woman with Bird Cage* (fig. 15) and based on a now lost painting by Boucher.[3] This self-enclosed, almost dreamlike image was the most cherished of the small collection of inexpensive prints that Rousseau kept in his baggage even during his darkest days. In December 1764, when he was a fugitive beset by enemies on all sides, Rousseau nonetheless wrote to François Coindet to ask his help in finding additional copies of this print so that he could offer them to friends as gifts. "I am," as he put it, "madly in love with that charming print."[4] The clashing dissimilarity of these two images—the frontispiece's masculine allegory of danger and the Boucher print's evocation of feminine reverie—emblematizes the chasm that, both through Rousseau and for Rousseau, would come to separate allegiance to the civic ideal of liberty from any experience of pleasure other than as part of a remembered past.

Within the Western tradition, Rousseau stands at the center of how we conceive of liberty and of how we see that liberty affecting the possibility of in-

Fig. 14. Jean-Baptiste Pierre, frontispiece to *Discours sur les Sciences et les Arts* (1750), engraving, 13.5 × 8.3 cm. In Jean-Jacques Rousseau, *Discours qui a remporté le prix de l'Académie de Dijon, en l'année 1750* . . . (London [i.e., Paris]: Chez Edouard Kelmarneck, 1751), 3.

dividual pleasure and happiness. If, to our twenty-first-century ears, invoking pleasure and happiness in tandem with liberty seems incongruous, it is in large part because of what Rousseau taught his readers about liberty and equality as two faces of the same coin. I have chosen the word *eudemony*—a combination of *eu*, meaning good, and *daimon*, designating the minor deity who provides it—to speak of Rousseau's new ethos of liberty because that little-used Greek term retains a strangeness that suits it well to a conceptual landscape in which pleasure and happiness were less uncomfortable in each other's presence, when pleasure had not yet acquired its strong coloration of

Fig. 15. Barthélemy Augustin Blondel d'Azaincourt, *Woman with Bird Cage* (1759), crayon manner, 24.7 × 19.1 cm. Musée du Louvre, Paris.

the egotistical and the tawdry.[5] The Greek notion of eudemony also predates Christianity's strict separation of happiness as positive because it is spiritual from pleasure as negative because it is grounded in the body and its senses. More important, a return to the eudemony of the classical heritage allows that term to stand as a concept uninflected by Rousseau's different separation of happiness as a state that is shared, communal, and civic from the experience of pleasure which is solitary, solipsistic, and selfish.

To approach Rousseau's rewriting of history from the perspective of eudemony also clarifies how much his challenge to the Enlightenment reconfigures the classical opposition between Stoicism as the quest for a virtue to be practiced within the community and Epicureanism as a personal regimen aimed at maximizing pleasure and minimizing pain. The eudemonic, I am arguing, lies upstream of what separates the social from the personal, the Stoic from the Epicurean, and happiness from pleasure. English translators of Plato's *Republic* and Aristotle's *Nicomachean Ethics* most often opt for the term *well-being* to translate the eudemony which both authors present as the reward of those who achieve a balance of the individual's constituent dimensions: the rational, the imaginative, and the appetitive. It is no accident that the French tradition of *libertinage*—itself an understanding of liberty born in the Renaissance's return to the classical texts and reaching its full flower in the eighteenth century—resurrected that heritage of the rational, the imaginative, and the appetitive in its own insistence on a tripartite human psychology made up, as we saw, of *l'esprit, le cœur*, and *les sens*. In returning to the topology of the classical model, the aggressively materialist ideology of *libertinage* rejected the Christian tradition which—from Augustine's translation of eudemony as "beatitude" to Aquinas's definition of salvation as the soul's ecstasy within its "beatific vision" of God—dismissed the pleasures of the senses as but pale anticipations of what the soul alone would experience once death had purged it of the body's dross.

The French tradition of *libertinage*, as we saw in the previous chapter, established liberty as a complex, Janus-faced concept whose positive value depends upon a prior and more fundamental negativity. The word *libertin*'s derivation from the Latin *libertinus*, designating a slave who had been freed, underlines how liberty presupposed a servitude which it has overcome. This understanding was at the heart of Étienne de La Boétie's choice of the title *A Discourse of Voluntary Servitude* for his foundational mid-sixteenth-century essay on civil disobedience and nonviolent resistance to the state.[6] For La Boétie, understanding liberty meant recognizing that it was the function of a more fundamental servitude from which it had to be wrested. Imagined in the abstract, liberty may be a worthy aspiration. It is, however, only when some precise shape is given to liberty's enemy twin of servitude that it acquires the tangible delineation of a goal that might actually be achieved. The cry for liberty, as La Boétie saw it, always arises as the slave's response to his sufferings, to the tyranny exercised by a master over a debased collectivity. The slave may suffer as an individual, but it is only when the suffering of each recognizes itself in the tribulations of all that a vision of liberty emerges from what before existed only as an individual experience. If we speak readily of "life, liberty, and the pursuit of *happiness*"—but only grotesquely of "life, liberty, and the pursuit of *pleasure*"—it is because the very notion of pleasure assumes a self-enclosure separating it from the collective servitude that always lies behind the articulation of liberty. Rousseau stands at the beginning of the modern genealogy of liberty because he articulated, more cogently than anyone before him, a new understanding of servitude. His vision of enslavement as a condition intricately interwoven with our very sociability implied for all who would enlist under his banner—and for no one more acutely than himself—that the liberty of the many must be severed from the pleasure of the individual. Liberty, as Rousseau refashioned it, had as its most paradoxical result the fact that he would find his own final refuge in pleasures that, divorced from any possibility of shared happiness, became the solipsistic ecstasies of his final work, *The Reveries of the Solitary Walker*.

Leo Strauss, in the chapter he devotes to Rousseau in his *Natural Right and History*, writes that Rousseau's struggle against the status quo presupposes a separation between two distinct concepts: "Rousseau attacked modernity in the name of two classical ideas: the city and virtue, on one hand, and nature, on the other."[7] Strauss's analysis is concerned less with the history of those two ideas than with how their irreconcilability became the driving motor of Rousseau's thought: "There is an obvious tension between the return to the city and the return to the state of nature. This tension is the substance of Rousseau's thought. . . . At one moment he ardently defends the rights of the individual or the rights of the heart against all restraint and authority; at the next moment he demands with equal ardor the complete submission of the individual to society or the state and favors the most rigorous moral or social discipline" (254). For Strauss, Rousseau's importance for our modernity derives, not from his having opted for one or the other of these ideas, but from the way his works chronicle the impossibility of making any such choice: "The question is not how he solved the conflict between the individual and society but rather how he conceived of that insoluble conflict" (255).

Strauss's approach to Rousseau in terms of the tension between nature and virtue parallels Rousseau's own explicit opposition between the primordial eudemony that is characteristic of the lone primitive as he passes almost mechanically from one occasion of pleasure to the next and the civic eudemony that is the hallmark of the citizen's virtuous congruence with the common good. If, in the early 1750s, Rousseau became Rousseau, it is because, within the arguments of his two *Discourses*, he changed forever the eudemonics of modernity. The question posed by the Academy of Dijon in the fall of 1749—"whether the restoration of the sciences and arts has served to purify morals"—became, from the moment Rousseau discovered it in the October issue of the *Mercure de France*, the occasion of a personal epiphany. Some twelve years later, in his second letter to Malesherbes, Rousseau explained how that question provoked for him a vision so overwhelming that he would spend the rest of his life struggling to express what at best would be only a small part of it.[8] As posed by the Dijon academy, the wording of the question implicitly took the side of those who championed modernity. The very pairing of the two domains to be examined suggested that what distinguishes the present century from the past is its bringing together in beneficent harmony two options which antiquity had conceived of as mutually exclusive. The advances and practical applications of the sciences fulfill the Stoic imperative that virtuous individuals contribute to reason's potential mastery of the world through endeavors that benefit the community as a whole. The practice and appreciation of the arts, on the other hand, evoke the Epicurean dictum that individuals ask from the world that maximizing of pleasure concomitant with the creation and contemplation of beauty in all its forms. In a very real sense, the Enlightenment's defining ambition could be described as an attempt to surpass antiquity by bringing together and satisfying simultaneously what before had been the opposing ideals of the Stoic and the Epicurean, of those for whom life's goal was reason's contribution to collective happiness and of those who saw that goal as the maximizing of pleasures experienced by the individual.

Rousseau's *First Discourse* is a frontal attack on the premises and comforts of that eighteenth-century ambition. The sciences, born in and extending our vices—astronomy in superstition, physics in vain curiosity, and so on—foster indolence and intellectual pride, setting each against all in ways that sap individual strength and jeopardize fraternity. The arts, presupposing and multiplying a dangerous luxury, extirpate virtue and leave in its place a superficial urbanity that disguises ambition and jealousy. Throughout the *First Discourse*, Rousseau develops his argument as a series of rhetorical contrasts between present-day depravity and the virtuous past of ancient Sparta, republican Rome, and pre-Columbian America. Everything turns on the opposition between present and past with the result that the "now" everywhere reveals itself to be the vitiated parody of a lost "then." Rousseau's movement from comparison to comparison allows him to universalize his thesis but leaves unaddressed the question of exactly how humankind came to move from ideal past to malignant present.

The *Discourse on the Origin of Inequality* of 1754 rehearses, refines, and extends the argument of the *First Discourse*. Rather than relying on parataxis, Rousseau sets out to articulate a careful sequencing of the events and stages that led from natural freedom to social enslavement, from hypothetical past to appalling present. Rousseau's genealogy of inequality confronts its Enlightenment readers with what amounts to an historical anthropology of their depravity. For Claude Lévi-Strauss, the *Second Discourse* establishes Rousseau as the founder not only of ethnology but of *les sciences de l'homme* as a whole. Rather than espousing any civic ideal such as Sparta or republican Rome, Lévi-Strauss's Rousseau radicalized his argument by insisting that any valid evaluation of the present must begin by hypothesizing *man* as one with nature rather than *men* as distinct from nature by reason of their sociability.[9] In the state of nature, man is alone, self-sufficient, and, above all, free. Radically solitary, living only in the present, unencumbered by any reflection anticipating the future or recalling the past, Rousseau's natural man is defined by a consciousness that alternates between two psychological states: that of desire born as a response to the very object able to satisfy it; and that of fear provoking the immediate solution of flight. Living life as a concatenation of desires satisfied and dangers avoided, primitive man enacts an ethics which is a version of the Epicurean postulate that the good life consists of maximizing pleasure and minimizing pain. Untroubled by any sense of obligation extending beyond the self, Rousseau's primitive experiences a eudemony of pleasure indifferent to any notion of communal well-being.

Rousseau's challenge to both the secular optimism of the *philosophes* and the Christian understanding of history lies less in his hypothetical point of origin than in the careful sequence of stages which he describes as producing our modernity through the modification and corruption of individual consciousness. Rousseau's genealogy of inequality articulates the movement from the lone primitive to temporary groupings aimed at accomplishing limited tasks, to the more stable clan structure of what he calls *l'état des cabanes*, to the interdependencies generated by the simultaneous discoveries of agriculture and metallurgy, to the institution of private property, and finally, to the universal warfare that will provide the justification of the civil state. For Lévi-Strauss, the overwhelming achievement that establishes Rousseau's *Second Discourse* as anthropology's ur-text is a vision of history that refuses to invoke any *religious* principle which would establish man as apart from and above nature.[10]

To approach the *Second Discourse* as alien to any sense of the religious has, however, two disadvantages. On the one hand, it overlooks Rousseau's reliance on a patterning of human history derived from the properly religious tradition of pre-Socratic cosmology. On the other hand, any notion of a radically secular Rousseau compromises our appreciation of how his reshaping of history generates an ethical imperative that establishes him as the evangelist of what is nothing less than a new religion of liberty and equality. In his biography of Rousseau, Leo Damrosch makes the claim that the *Second Discourse* represents what he calls a "radical re-imagining of human experience."[11] In some sense, that is true; but that idea of radical novelty obfuscates the very real debt Rousseau's anthropology owes to the classical world's most influential representation of human history: Hesiod's seventh-century B.C.E. *Works and the Days*, that period's fundamental cosmological and ethical treatise.[12] The concept of the Ages of Man, a cycle which Rousseau and his contemporaries knew best from its frequent illustration in woodcuts and prints, is decidedly consonant with the rejection of Enlightenment optimism that structures the *Second Discourse*. The Ages of Man, amplified by Ovid's *Metamorphoses* and by the medieval compilations known as the *Aetas ovidiana*, was a favored topos for Northern European engravers throughout the sixteenth and seventeenth centuries. Its vision of history as a passage through the four successive ages of gold, silver, bronze, and iron quickly acquired a canonical iconography.

A particularly significant version of that cycle was produced by the early seventeenth-century Flemish artist, Hans (or Jan) Collaert. His engravings of the cycle, published by Johannes Gallé in 1612, begins with *The Age of Gold* (fig. 16), depicting that stage as a peaceful juxtaposition of couples in perfect harmony with nature. This image of human felicity, situated in a period clearly later than that of Rousseau's hypothetical lone primitives, corresponds most closely to the stage of human development which Rousseau describes as "the golden mean" (*le juste milieu*).[13] With no fixed social structure, with no state or city, these happy couples dwell within an eternal springtime. Milk, honey, and fruit abound. No work need be done and old age never threatens. As in the time of Rousseau's golden mean, these men and women live in a joyous present unsullied by envy, law, or any form of communal coercion. In a way that curiously anticipates Watteau's *fêtes galantes*, Collaert

Fig. 16. Hans Collaert, *The Age of Gold* (1612), engraving, 20.2 × 26.3 cm. Fine Arts Museums of San Francisco, Achenbach Foundation for the Graphic Arts.

disperses his happy couples over a broad sweep of welcoming nature. To the lower right of the print, couples enraptured by their shared pleasures gather along a watercourse in a scene not unlike what Rousseau describes as the discovery of passion's force at the communal well in his *Essay on the Origin of Languages*.[14] Collaert's *Age of Silver* (fig. 17) depicts a world remade by a Rousseauian change in climate, a shortening of spring, and the division of the year into four distinct seasons. To survive the rigors of winter, humankind, profiting from what Rousseau would describe as the simultaneous discoveries of agriculture and metallurgy, has learned to plow, to sow, and to raise livestock. Again, as during Rousseau's golden mean, small clans have formed and begun to build fixed dwellings that combine the natural terrain with fabricated appendages. *The Age of Bronze* (fig. 18) takes us to a world remade by what Rousseau will call the institution of private property. Farming and the technologies of agriculture have been supplemented by those of a warfare waged among communities claiming possession of their products. Organized societies and walled castles now exist. Humanity finds itself immersed in forms of hierarchy and inequality that subject it to constant labor

Fig. 17. Hans Collaert, *The Age of Silver* (1612), engraving, 19.7 × 25.8 cm. Fine Arts Museums of San Francisco, Achenbach Foundation for the Graphic Arts.

and strife. In the distance depicted at the print's center, opposing armies are engaged in a pitched battle for control of the castle. In the harbor adjacent to the castle, armed war-galleys and masted cargo ships share a disputed sea. From the hill overlooking the harbor, smoke billows up as a man-made darkness obstructing the sun. To the lower left, swords, maces, bows, and shields have replaced the instruments of farming as the age's epitomizing symbols. Collaert's final image, *The Age of Iron* (fig. 19), presents us with a world in which violence and carnage have become universal. Bands of soldiers rape and pillage. The large open window at this image's far left serves as a framing device through which we see a soldier pursuing a fleeing peasant. The fear that now defines life is inscribed on the face of another single man being led off by an armed soldier. The fate that awaits him can be glimpsed in the two bodies that hang from the gibbet erected on the distant knoll visible above him and to the right. This image, the final stage within the four Ages of Man, stands as an illustration of what Rousseau would call universal warfare (*la guerre générale*): a violence of each against all which will motivate the

Fig. 18. Hans Collaert, *The Age of Bronze* (1612), engraving, 19.7×25.4 cm. Fine Arts Museums of San Francisco, Achenbach Foundation for the Graphic Arts.

final consolidation of inequality in a vitiated social pact that brings only the peace of servitude.

Borrowing the shape of its history from Hesiod's cosmology, Rousseau's *Discourse on the Origin of Inequality* uses that cycle to reframe the moral complexity of the present he shares with its readers. The major thrust of Rousseau's argument is that it is humanity itself, in its desires, dependencies, and ambitions, that has determined its sad fate. Rousseau's history of inequality not only argues that we have misunderstood the past, but it deploys its vision of that past toward a radically different understanding of the present. The ethical imperative of Rousseau's argument emerges in the essay's final section, in what he describes as following from his distinctly anti-*philosophe* version of the age of iron and its generalized violence.

For the eighteenth-century French reader, the notion of all-engulfing warfare would have been associated with the sixteenth century's wars of religion. And surely, that reader would assume, the two centuries since those conflicts have brought with them a more enlightened and irenic social order.

Fig. 19. Hans Collaert, *The Age of Iron* (1612), engraving, 20.2 × 25.6 cm. Fine Arts Museums of San Francisco, Achenbach Foundation for the Graphic Arts.

Rousseau's discourse directly challenges that assumption. It not only extends his history to the present he shares with his readers, but imbues that present with a binding moral imperative. Tightening his focus to a specific moment within the history he narrates, Rousseau describes how, at the nadir of warfare's chaos, one individual—the richest and most cunning, the person best able both to recognize the precariousness of his position and to take measures to protect it—formulates a plan that will transform his adversaries into his protectors. For the first time since the "This is mine" (Ceci est à moi) (3:164) that marked the birth of private property in the opening sentence of the *Discourse*'s second part, Rousseau sets aside his third-person narrative voice and offers his readers a verbatim rendition of the consummate exercise in duplicity that stands as the cornerstone of the modern state. The rich man's ruse consists in his appeal to an alternative vision of the future that serves to motivate what must be done in the present. This speaker's argument relies for its cogency on the seductive verbal portrait he paints of a time to come when all will benefit equally from a beneficent reign of justice, law, equality, and peace. "Let us unite," the rich man appeals to all,

> to protect the weak from oppression, restrain the ambitious, and secure for everyone the possession of what belongs to him. Let us institute regulations of justice and peace to which all are obliged to conform, which make an exception of no one, and which compensate in some way for the caprices of fortune by equally subjecting the powerful and the weak to mutual duties. In a word, instead of turning our forces against ourselves, let us gather them into one supreme power which governs us according to wise laws, protects and defends all the members of the association, repulses common enemies, and maintains us in an eternal accord. (3:177)

What would the reader of 1754 have seen in this appeal? Far from evoking the rise of absolute monarchy that in fact checked the violence of France's wars of religion, this carefully crafted speech instead rehearses with biting irony—and labels as the great lie—the very program proposed by *les philosophes* as the most progressive political ideal of midcentury republican thought. Rousseau's entire history of humankind is structured in such a way that, at the point where his audience would least like to hear it, one of its principal figures steps forward and confronts the reader with a speech echoing all the optimistic promises of solidarity and equality that his most enlightened readers saw as their shared hope. Here, however, those promises are denounced as pure rhetoric, a false and manipulative vision of the future that serves only to protect the rich and enslave the poor. This foundational speech, an illusion woven of words, is a mirage that blinds its listeners to the reality it masks. "Such was, or must have been, the origin of society and laws, which gave new fetters to the weak and new forces to the rich, destroyed natural freedom for all time, established forever the law of property and inequality, changed a clever usurpation into an irrevocable right, and for the profit of a few ambitious men henceforth subjected the whole human race to work, servitude, and misery" (3:178).

Rousseau's denunciation, making no mention of the status quo of monarchy, chooses as its target not the real but the ideal: the republican ideal of consensual government which the most enlightened *philosophes* presented as the goal toward which society must advance. Forcing his readers to recognize precisely how and why they have become dupes of that rhetoric, Rousseau redefines the premises of political morality. In the same way that his vision of human history borrowed its shape from classical mythology, so also his vision of the present culminates in a new version of the Fall and of sin, of the culpability at the core of what purport to be the age's most enlightened political ideals. Rousseau's entire anthropology prepares this radically discomforting moment, this moment of denunciation, when his readers are asked to imagine differently the moral valance of all they have esteemed as most beneficent, most equitable, and most just. Rousseau leaves his readers no middle ground: either they are the guilty accomplices of an ideology serving only the rich or they must part company with all that has presented itself as most enlightened. Rousseau's readers, forced to behold themselves in the mirror of the richest and most cunning, must recognize that their most damning sin is to have become his dupes. For the Christian, sin is what blinds the soul to Christ's sacrifice and the spiritual salvation it makes possible. For Rousseau as the father of modernity, sin is a deluded acquiescence to the illusions of a false liberty and a false equality. The most grievous sin—now of mind rather than of soul, now of understanding rather than of belief, and now political rather than spiritual—is our unwitting collaboration with voluntary servitude. In terms of the anthropology proposed by the *Discourse on the Origin of Inequality*, any eudemony of liberty becomes problematic. Rousseau's enlightened readers are invited to see themselves as at worst hypocrites and at best dupes. Bringing his history to a close, Rousseau compares the hypothetical *homme sauvage* with which he began his analysis to the eighteenth century's *homme policé*. As beginning and end, they find themselves aligned in damning congruity: "Here all individuals become equal again because they are nothing" (3:191). With enslavement now so universal that it has become imperceptible, eudemony—be it as civic concord or as individual pleasure—becomes the delusion of an ignorance willfully chosen.

In the closing paragraph of the *Second Discourse*, Rousseau insists that his history of inequality is rooted in "the light of reason alone independently of the sacred dogmas" (3:193). If Rousseau can so effortlessly elide all mention of established religious dogmas, it is because liberty has assumed the status of a new religion, its inaccessible god at the center of a theology which is exclusively negative. This new religion of liberty is a faith so demanding that no one, least of all Rousseau, can assume that he has achieved justification. It is this dilemma that will generate, as the successive stages of his impossible quest for salvation within a fallen world, each of the major works that Rousseau would produce before his turn to autobiography. *The Social Contract* sets out to establish a complex dynamics of individuals absorbed within the mystical body of the general will as the premise of true liberty within an organized society. *Émile*, shifting its focus from the community to the individual, attempts to show how, guided by the hidden hand of the *précepteur*, a single child might be prepared to lead a life of true liberty. *Julie, or the New Heloise* conjures up a utopia built on passion's renunciation and sustained by the confected freedom of a symbolic order that is one with Wolmarian reason. Each of these attempts, however, fails to provide the desired salvation. The social contract is haunted by an incipient tyranny of the majority; Émile will find true freedom only as a slave in Algiers; and the idyll of Clarens falls to pieces around Julie's death.

Rousseau's religion of liberty had as its most paradoxical consequence the redefinition of eudemony as a state which must renounce all hope for any salvation that extends beyond the single individual. In his final years, as though returning to some private version of what Leo Strauss called "nature," Rousseau would find refuge from a feeling of exclusion bordering on paranoia only in the self-contained pleasure of writing and rereading his *Reveries of the Solitary Walker*. In that work, Rousseau, as a consciousness forever plumbing a past cut off from all community with his fellows, reverses the trajectory of the *Second Discourse*. Stepping outside of a society he now sees only as threat, Rousseau becomes the affective equivalent of *l'homme de la nature* with whom everything began: "I am now alone on earth, no longer having any brother, neighbor, friend, or society other than myself" (1:995). In the same way that natural man experienced pleasure within the pure present of moments lived in isolation from past and future, so also, at the end of his life, Rousseau, the now resolutely solitary walker, draws his only solace from a synthesis of memory, reverie, and imagination that generates once again the eudemony of an escape from time and from the world of other men.

One of Rousseau's most intriguing statements on pleasure and its intensification comes in his discussion of music in the *Essay on the Origin of Languages:* "Every man in the universe will take *pleasure* in listening to beautiful sounds; but unless that pleasure is animated by melodious inflections that are familiar to him, it will not be *delightful*, it will not become *voluptuous*" (5:415; italics mine). This reflection on pleasure and the dynamics of its increase is part of

Rousseau's stating of his position in relation to the *querelle des bouffons* that pitted the partisans of melodic Italian opera against the complex harmonics of Rameau and the French style. For Rousseau, what makes melody a source of pleasure that can lead to delight and even *volupté* is its direct mimesis of emotions and its ability to move the enchanted listener far more effectively than the superficial complexity of harmony's intervals and consonances.

To clarify the dynamics of this pleasure provided by music, Rousseau looks to the way a similar choice must be made in music's sister art of painting.[15] Just as the composer works with melody and harmony, the painter elaborates his image as a synthesis of *dessin* and *couleur,* of line and color. In an age that did not recognize abstract or nonrepresentational art, it seemed self-evident that a beautiful and moving painting could never consist only of a play of colors or of some purely chromatic harmony. A painting's power to move and delight its viewer is a product not of color but of line deployed in such a way that a recognizable image—a face, a countryside, an instructive vignette—emerges from the work's array of tones and colors. Just as melody makes music a pleasing rhapsody of sentiment, so also line and representation allow painting to put the spectator in contact with a dimension of meaning *beyond* the mute chromatic surface.[16]

Rousseau's statements as to the relative importance of color and line are in one sense an echo of the seventeenth-century controversies opposing Rubens and Poussin.[17] In a particularly intriguing way, this same opposition plays an important role in Rousseau's first articulation of his specifically social critique. In the opening pages of his *Discourse on the Sciences and Arts,* after extolling humankind's slow ascension to the enlightened present, Rousseau abruptly reverses the direction of his argument. With only commas punctuating the shift in his position, he unveils his true thesis: "While Government and Laws provide for the safety and well-being of assembled men, the Sciences, Letters, and Arts, less despotic and perhaps more powerful, spread garlands of flowers over the iron chains with which men are burdened, stifle in them the sentiment of that original liberty for which they seemed to have been born, make them love their slavery, and turn them into what is called civilized peoples" (3:6–7). Here, in Rousseau's first appearance as the champion of liberty, he expresses his thesis through a figure that contrasts the work of color and of line. Within his metaphor, the pleasing colors of the garlands may produce pleasure, but it is a pleasure that ultimately serves only to disguise the firm lines of our chains.

This metaphor may set the hook of Rousseau's argument, but it is, upon reflection, a surprising choice on his part. At one level, it is strange that a man who, throughout his life, would draw immense pleasure from gathering and collecting flowers into carefully assembled herbals should choose them as his emblem of evil. Here already liberty and pleasure take separate paths. The flowers may delight, but, as Rousseau's esthetic theory insisted, their truth lies finally in the firm line of the chains they obscure. It is only as line and as chain that these colors reveal the counternarrative of our enslavement. As the paraclete of liberty, Rousseau saw it as his duty to fix his readers' attention on the chains of servitude beneath the alluring colors of our illusions. Refusing the flowers' diversion of only apparent pleasures, we must look directly to line, to meaning, and to the tragic narrative of human history.[18]

This intersection of Rousseau's esthetic and political theories within a metaphor of garlands that hide our chains allows us to return to the two prints with which I began this chapter. The scene depicted in the frontispiece to the *Discourse on the Sciences and Arts* (see above, fig. 14) can in fact be read as another narrative of color's deceptions: of how the torch's captivating rubescence blinds the satyr to the dangers of its fire. This mythological vignette meant to summarize the *First Discourse* also prompted Rousseau to articulate an implication of his religion of liberty that extends well beyond the torch's danger. In his response to Claude-Nicolas Lecat's attack on the *First Discourse*, Rousseau pointed to Lecat's inability to understand this frontispiece as the crowning proof of his adversary's imbecility: "I would have believed I was insulting my readers and treating them like children by interpreting such a clear allegory for them—by telling them that Prometheus's torch is that of the sciences, created to inspire great geniuses; that the satyr who, seeing fire for the first time, runs to it and wants to embrace it, represents common men, seduced by the brilliance of letters, who surrender indiscreetly to study; that the Prometheus who cries out and warns them of the danger is the Citizen of Geneva."[19] If, then, Rousseau cast himself in the role of Prometheus, it was less as the bearer of fire than as the victim of his benefaction—as the figure whose liver would be consumed by Zeus's eagle.

When we look at the frontispiece itself, however, there are three distinct figures present. In terms of the wording of his letter to Lecat, Rousseau seems to see this image as containing two different versions of Prometheus. The first, the paternal figure to the left who holds the torch, is the traditional Prometheus of myth. The second, the angelic young man who stands between the fire bearer and the satyr, is for Rousseau a second version of Prometheus—not *Prométhée*, but *le Prométhée*—who, as the Citizen of Geneva, has as his mission to warn everyone of fire's danger. While perhaps a "great genius," that middle figure's attitude is one of neither admonition nor fascination. The soft features of his face set him apart both from the muscular power of the figure to the left as well as from the brute carnality of the satyr to the right. While the Prometheus of myth, never touching the ground, descends from above, the satyr, whose cloven hoof supports his leap toward the flame, literally springs from the rough earth. Between them, the third figure stands statue-like on the pedestal of a first step away from the animality of the satyr and toward the world-to-come of Prometheus's fire. With his arms extended away from his sides, he assumes a pleading, almost crucifixional pose. As though anticipating what lies ahead—the price to be paid for proclaiming liberty's truth—this figure accepts the immolation that will be a corollary to the fulfillment of his mission. Distinct from both Prometheus the fire bearer and the satyr, this supplicant figure incarnates the dilemma at the core of Rousseau's religion of liberty. With the torch's flame directly above his head, Rousseau's sacrificial stand-in is infused with the pentecostal knowledge of a loss of liberty so inevitable that eudemony finds itself excluded from the narrative of history. Here, in the first of his political writings, Rousseau's vision of liberty's truth serves to set him apart from the present yet costly pleasures of the satyr as prenarrative man.

If this frontispiece to his first published work already prefigures the foreclosure of pleasure that would devolve from his public vocation, the Boucher print Rousseau would so cherish during the last decades of his life stands as an emblem of what would be the phantom pleasures and postnarrative consolations of *The Reveries of the Solitary Walker*. Within an empty, surreal space, a single female figure lifts toward her face a small bird whose wings flutter in joy as it moves toward their shared embrace. The world beyond girl and bird is present only as a carefully drawn cage that sits on a high bureau whose vertical slats suggest a concatenation of prisons. Line and its work of narrative are present in this image, but only to delineate a prison. And it is outside the confines of that prison that a reconciliation of the human and the natural, of skin and feather, produces a moment of ecstatic reverie.

What is it about *Woman with Bird Cage* that made it a source of so intense a pleasure for Rousseau? This scene, so different in style from the frontispiece, works not as narrative but by association, by the way this dreamlike image reverberates with psychic remnants of Rousseau's remembered past. The prominent ribbon around the girl's neck evokes those passages in both book 2 of *The Confessions* and in the fourth promenade of *The Reveries*, where Rousseau agonizingly retells his own story of a ribbon. While a servant in the household of Mme de Vercellis, and after being caught in possession of a stolen pink and silver ribbon that belonged to the pretentious Mlle Pontale, Rousseau defended himself by claiming that he had not taken it but that it had been given to him by the innocent serving girl Marion. That lie, as Rousseau tells the story, led to Marion's immediate dismissal, condemning her to a life of poverty and prostitution. Even more important, the trauma of that lie left him with what he calls "the long remembrance of crime and the unbearable weight of remorse," which, even forty years later, "far from growing weaker, becomes inflamed as a I grow older" (1:84). That story of the ribbon establishes the Boucher print as a wish fulfilled and a past rewritten. Finally, the real goal of his theft—giving the ribbon to Marion as a gift—has been achieved. In a different register, the bird's dance of joy on the girl's finger and the trilling song that inspires her to lift it to her lips make it an icon summarizing the transformative desires born of the first gatherings at the communal well as they are described in the *Essay on the Origin of Languages*. There, young boys and girls, who before had only fled from one another, draw together. The feelings that this proximity inspires provoke an outpouring of dance and song expressing their newly discovered emotions: "There the first festivals took place; feet leaped with joy, eager gesture no longer sufficed, the voice accompanied it with passionate accents; mingled together, pleasure and desire made themselves felt at the same time" (5:406). In still another dimension, Rousseau's fascination with this print echoes the fantasy he experienced during the 1752 performance at Fontainebleau of his *Le Devin du village* (*The Village Soothsayer*). Realizing, from the sighs of pleasure uttered by the women around him, that the melodies of his opera had moved them to tears, his intense wish became that he might, like a bird, fly from woman to woman and, with each, satisfy "the desire to collect with my lips the delicious tears I was causing to flow" (1:379).

In addition to these psycho-biographical associations, Rousseau's affection for this print also relates to what he may have known of Boucher as the eighteenth century's *peintre des grâces*. While there is little evidence as to how familiar Rousseau may have been with Boucher's work, we do know that Boucher was his first choice as the illustrator for *Julie*.[20] As concerns this print's relation to Boucher, what is most apparent is that its grays and white elide entirely what we saw to be a paramount dimension of his style: the sensuous use of color. Because the Boucher painting that inspired this print has been lost, we know nothing of its actual choice of colors. To Rousseau's remembering eye, however, the ribbon might easily have taken on the pink and silver hues of the gift that finally reaches Marion. As for the lone female figure, that stand-in for Marion would surely have acquired in Rousseau's eye what he remembers as her "freshness of coloring that is found only in the mountains" (1:84). All the elements making up this scene—hair, skin, fabric, and feather—coax the eye to imagine more than the grays and whites it sees. And we do, in terms of Boucher's larger corpus, know something about what those colors may have been. Boucher's painting *The Cage* (see fig.7 in Chapter 4) relies on a delicate contrasting of the young woman's skin tones against the blues, browns, and blacks of feather and beak. Furthermore, this scene underlines how, for Boucher, the pairing of girl and bird is always a synecdoche: a part both taken from and standing in for a larger whole. The tactile delight of the wing's delicate fluttering on the cheek stands as a metaphor of the more intense pleasures still to be shared by the two figures.

Rousseau's print depicts not a couple but a young woman alone. Yet at the same time, her trancelike gaze suggests that her solitude is one peopled by memory and anticipation. Were we to ask what form this reverie might take, the beginnings of an answer can be found in Boucher's larger iconography. His work titled *The Bird Catchers* (fig. 20) is an oil on canvas done in 1748. It dates from a period when Rousseau, still one of Diderot's closest friends, may well have accompanied him to the Louvre and viewed this work when it was exhibited as part of that year's Salon. The movement within this painting leads the viewer's eye from right to left, from architectural construction to the faint beginnings of a forest. It is an image of high pastoral whose young male and female figures, rustic yet richly dressed, are concerned only with the pleasures of nature and of one another. The anchoring female figures at the right and left, seen in profile, appear almost as versions of the young woman in Rousseau's print. What is most distinctive about *The Bird Catchers* is its combination of rich color with clear narrative development. As the eye moves from right to left, this painting displays four distinct chapters within

Fig. 20. Francois Boucher, *The Bird Catchers* (1748), oil on canvas, 294.6 × 337.8 cm. The J. Paul Getty Museum, Los Angeles.

a single story. The first chapter, centered on two couples, opens as the girl to the extreme right lifts the door of the cage so that the bird inside might jump to the hand of the boy in blue. The second chapter presents a central female figure in white who entertains the child to the left with the bird's flying at the end of the string she holds in her hand. The third chapter shows a single woman in brown who, with one finger raised in admonition, trains the now nearly tamed bird to remain on her hand even with no restraint. The fourth and final chapter brings the story to a close in the most explicit anticipation of Rousseau's print, as the girl in pink and ocher lifts the now docile bird on her finger toward her kiss as her face expresses a state ambiguously between solitary reverie and involvement with the two figures beside and above her.

In the larger context of eighteenth-century French art, Boucher's *Bird Catchers* offers his own version, working through metaphor and metonymy, of Watteau's famous *Departure for Cythera* (fig. 21), in which a series of couples act out the stages of an amorous encounter placed under the sign of Venus, the goddess represented by the stele at the painting's far right. As in Watteau's image, the juxtaposed groupings of Boucher's painting emblematize the larger cycle of attraction, desire, capture, and memory of which Rousseau's beloved print is one isolated moment. The full panorama of *The Bird Catchers* clarifies, in other words, what might be the absent pleasures of the solitary female figure's extended reverie. What I have described as the final chapter of *The Bird Catchers* does not only repeat the print's trope of bringing bird to lips; that fuller version presents this image not in the gray solitude of absence but in the full chromatic pleasure of eyes lifted toward but never meeting those of the boy in the straw hat. Situating Rousseau's *Woman with Bird Cage* print within the context of Boucher's more narrative painting makes clear how much this print's eerie sense of nostalgia depends on its status as synecdoche, as the fragment of some larger whole. The pathos of Rousseau's print lies in the fact that, while it evokes that lost whole, it provides no bridge back to its moments of pleasures shared.

This visual and textual itinerary, moving from the frontispiece of Rousseau's first published work to the Boucher print so dear to him in his

Fig. 21. Antoine Watteau, *Departure for Cythera* (1717), oil on canvas, 194 × 129 cm. Charlottenburg Castle, Berlin.

final years as well as from the two *Discourses* to *The Reveries* as his final autobiographical work, helps us to see why, within Rousseau's eudemony of liberty, pleasure became accessible only in the key of loss, only as nostalgia. Rousseau's religion of liberty, like his mission as the appointed paraclete of liberty's truth, foreclosed his choosing any option of a pleasure cut off from his commitment to the greater happiness of the community. As, however, every avenue toward happiness within the community proved impassable, as a world of chains and cages refused ever more adamantly the truth he would speak, his only idiom of pleasure became the fragment of a lingering trauma, a synecdoche severed from its sustaining whole. The pleasure Rousseau drew from his print of *Woman with Bird Cage* came not *in spite of* its absence of color, story, and sensuality, but precisely *because* the pale lines of its solitary figure speak as shards of what is lost.

Rousseau's refuge within this image, like his solitary embrace in *The Reveries* of a nature where others are present only as memories, points to the paradox of his place within the larger history of enlightened pleasures. Reacting to what he saw as the choice made by his fellows to ignore his message of liberty, Rousseau became in the last decades of his life the prototype of the alienated romantic. Seeing only hostility and corruption in the society around him, he found himself, quite simply, with nothing more to say to a community that refused the truth he would speak. In the optimistic days of the two *Discourses*, he may have relished in the irony of claiming to "leave aside the sacred dogmas" while putting in their place the Ovidian Ages of Man as a cycle explicating humankind's expulsion from unmediated pleasures to the brutal chaos of universal warfare. A quarter century later, left to plumb only his own anguished consciousness, he turned away from history in all its competing versions.

History, however, would hardly turn away from Rousseau. In the decade and a half following his death, events would make of the solitary walker the preeminent theoretician of a new civic community. It would be his name and his call for a unanimous general will guaranteeing true liberty and equality that the spokespersons of the newly born Nation would invoke as they prepared a Terror that would prove as antithetical to pleasure as Christianity at its worst. To accuse Rousseau of being the father of totalitarian dysdemony is both absurd and inevitable.[21] It is absurd because, even as he composed his most virulent indictments of the status quo, Rousseau made it clear that he intended to foment no revolt and that history shows that, in our postlapsarian state, such insurrections only intensify the enslavement they purport to remedy. As though anticipating what history would so bloodily demonstrate, he wrote in his dedication to the *Second Discourse*: "Once peoples are accustomed to masters, they are no longer able to do without them. If they try to shake off the yoke, they move all the farther away from freedom because, mistaking for freedom an unbridled license which is its opposite, their revolutions almost always deliver them to seducers who only make their chains heavier" (3:113). Yet linking Rousseau to the totalitarianism of the Terror is inevitable. Independently of his intention, the Revolution chose to read the *Social Contract* and its ideal of a unanimous general will, not as the utopian alternative to the moment of the rich man's ruse of the social pact as it was described in the *Second Discourse*, but as a practical blueprint for the radical reweaving of France's complex social fabric. That choice to enforce a political program as a duty compelling all to be free or to die was a civic enterprise which would carry the executioners as well as the executed to the very antipodes of pleasure.

6. Laclos' Anthropology of Pleasure

Conceptualizing pleasure was never an uncomplicated enterprise in eighteenth-century France. As Rousseau illustrates, there emerged in the second half of the century a new set of reasons why pleasure, when compared to its other-directed cousin of happiness, came to be associated with appetites and situations seen as dubious if not immoral. Even for those who rejected Christian idealism, pleasure evoked a dimension of human experience too redolent of the sensual and the selfish. If pleasure had to blush in the polite company of happiness, things became even more complicated when one raised the question of what might be a woman's pleasure.

That subject, it would seem, was best left to the period's libertine if not pornographic novels. Could one, in other words, even ask the question of woman's pleasure without slipping toward what the period called "women of pleasure"? Thérèse may fully discover pleasure only when she becomes an Epicurean *philosophe*, but, as her friendship with Bois-Laurier made clear, the heroines of such novels are women dangerously close to the vast world of eighteenth-century prostitution.[1] It was only after Rousseau's *Julie* and the ensuing triumph of the novel of sentiment that another novelist, himself much influenced by Rousseau, dared to offer the portrait of a woman of impeccable social standing who nonetheless insisted on her pleasure. Mme de Merteuil, the central figure in Laclos' *Les Liaisons dangereuses*, stands as the singular and stunning example of a female character who, until her undoing, reconciles an appetite for pleasure with unquestionable social respectability. Her station as a marquise and her seemingly unfailing prudery assure her the protection of even the most censorious *dévotes* within Parisian society. All that, however, counted as nothing for the venerable Marie Riccoboni, herself a well known novelist and astute critic of woman's difficult place in society. In an exchange of letters with Laclos, she makes it perfectly clear that any woman ready to act so outrageously in the service of her pleasure must, no matter what her rank in society, be seen as nothing more than a woman of pleasure. Pulling out all the stops, Riccoboni labels Merteuil "a vile creature, determined from her earliest youth to become the champion of vice, to make evil her guide, and to fashion for herself a mask hiding from all her determination to embrace the morals of those unfortunate creatures forced by poverty to live in infamy."[2]

Given the intensity of Riccoboni's reaction, and she was hardly alone in so reacting, one must ask what it was that Laclos was trying to say about woman's pleasure in this novel, which presents itself as a collection of letters from, to, and shared with this central character whose chosen mission is to refuse all the limits her society would set on the pleasures available to a respectable woman. The complexity of Laclos' ambition as a novelist of manners, his interest in fashioning a female character different from a Thérèse, a Margot, or a Manon is made clear to the reader from the start. On the novel's title page, immediately below a set of initials designating the anonymous author, there is an apparently innocuous epigraph: "I have seen the morals of my century and I have published these letters." That statement becomes, however, more heavily charged when its source is identified as *Julie*, Rousseau's blockbuster epistolary novel of some twenty years earlier.[3] To suggest a similarity between Julie's epic of virtuous renunciation and Merteuil's devotion to unbridled sensuality—the idea that Merteuil might be some yet newer New Heloise—was nothing short of scandalous.

A constellation of ironies comes into view when the reader juxtaposes these two novels. Merteuil and Julie are the most unlikely of sisters; Laclos' portrait of a corrupt and corrupting aristocracy is the antithesis of Wolmar's rural Clarens as regenerative utopia; Valmont's sexual predations stand in stark contrast to Saint-Preux's chastened devotion. In sum, Laclos' chronicle of clandestine Epicureanism and Rousseau's idyll of virtuous Stoicism could not, it would seem, be more dissimilar. Limiting one's focus to these differences, however, distracts us from Laclos' very real debt to Rousseau—for example, the curiously ponderous phrase Laclos places on the title page between his title, *Les Liaisons dangereuses*, and the brief epigraph from *Julie*, cited above: "Letters collected in one society and published for the edification of certain others." This slightly different version of the epigraph that follows elides Rousseau's "I" and puts in its place the letters themselves as objects that have been collected and published by some undesignated agent. Laclos' readers, familiar with Rousseau's best seller and the controversies it generated, would surely remember that Rousseau's own insistence on the evidentiary value of letters immediately follows his lapidary claim that "great cities must have theaters; and corrupt peoples, novels" (2:5). This summary disqualification of fiction in turn lays the cornerstone for Rousseau's argument that, just as the letters his reader is about to begin must not be taken for a novel, so also he himself, as the editor of those letters, must not be confused with a novelist. Far from pandering to the depraved pleasures of a corrupt society, he is sharing with his public actual letters which, as a chronicle of regenerative virtue, could never be the product of a novelist's imagination. Rousseau's tenacious insistence in both his first and second prefaces to *Julie* that his epistolary novel is not a novel at all was his defense against the charge that only the most consummate hypocrite would dare publish a novel after having himself so vociferously denounced that genre—as well as all the other products of the arts and sciences—in the two *Discourses* that brought him to the public's attention. In choosing his epigraph, Laclos acknowledges his debt to Rousseau the anthropologist, whose *Discourse on Inequality* hypothesized polite society as an inferno of violence, hypocrisy, and enslavement. In a very real sense, *Les Liaisons dangereuses* asks to be read as a re-creation, under the veneer of Parisian high society, of the same state of universal warfare which Rousseau described toward the close of his *Discourse on Inequality*.

What I am calling Laclos' anthropology of pleasure is the result of his being an assiduous reader of the beginning as well as the end of the *Second Discourse:* Rousseau's portrait of natural man as he hypothesizes he must have existed within the self-sufficiency and solitude that preceded the beginnings of society and its multiplication of dependencies. Rousseau's vision of presocial man so fascinated Laclos that, less than a year after publishing *Les Liaisons dangereuses*, he found himself composing what could be described as his supplement to Rousseau's *Discourse on Inequality*. In a way uncannily similar to Rousseau's reaction thirty-some years earlier to an essay subject proposed by the Academy of Dijon, Laclos' foray into what we would today call anthropology was triggered by the announcement, in March 1783, of a *concours* sponsored by the Academy of Châlons-sur-Marne on the subject: "What might be the best measures for perfecting the education of women?" Laclos' immediate reaction to that question produced a five-page essay most striking for the way he writes himself into a dead end. In this short essay Rousseau's influence is again evident from Laclos' opening epigraph. The short quotation—"Evil is beyond remedy when vices have become customs"—is from Seneca, but it also stands as a succinct summary of the thesis at the core of Rousseau's two *Discourses*.[4] After a rapid summary of what passes as education for women in eighteenth-century France, Laclos arrives at the conclusion that the question posed by the academy is absurd. Is it logically possible, he asks, to perfect something which does not and cannot exist? "Wherever there is slavery, there can be no education. In every society women are slaves. Therefore women living in society are beyond education" (391). The sharpness of this dismissive syllogism unmasks the very posing of this question as an exercise in mystification. Laclos' manuscript ends with the unfinished sentence "Without liberty there can be no morality and without morality there can be no education . . ." (392).

This abandoned draft is important, not only for the radical nature of the position it takes, but also for the shift it signals in Laclos' interest away from the epistolary mode of his novel to the philosophical and speculative approach of the essay as a form.[5] After arriving at an impasse in his first attempt to respond to the academy's ill-conceived question, Laclos began a different and more ambitious essay. Very much under Rousseau's influence, he set out to explain how and why society has reached a point where any project claiming to foster the education of women must necessarily be an exercise in ideological obfuscation. The resulting eighty-page essay, although known under the title "On the Education of Women," might more fittingly be described with the Diderotian title: "A Supplement to Rousseau's Hypothesis."[6]

In the first footnote of his essay, Laclos brings up Rousseau's natural man. Quoting directly from the *Discourse on the Origin of Inequality*, he points out that he too will offer "hypothetical and conditional arguments more suited to shedding light on the nature of things than to revealing their true origin" (393). Rather, however, than focusing on Rousseau's heuristic construct of natural man "such as he was fashioned by the hands of nature," Laclos will examine what lies on the other side of the gender divide. His hypothesis will involve a careful portrait of natural woman as she *may have existed* in the state of bucolic freedom and self-sufficiency that preceded society. Laclos' subject will be, as Chantal Thomas has put it, woman as "a purely physical presence, whose development introduces us to a paradise of transparency and immediacy."[7] In other words, Laclos' supplement will complete Rousseau's hypothesis with a gender-specific history of natural woman and how her fate came to be sealed as organized societies were formed. While closely following the stages of Rousseau's progression from natural freedom to social enslavement, Laclos' essay is also a supplement in the sense that he will take his story of womankind further than did Rousseau. The *Second Discourse* ends, as we saw, in a dystopia of lies and exploitation as civil society's illusory equality of all before the law ends the state of generalized warfare by consolidating the reign of the rich and powerful. Laclos continues that story by including within his speculative history a phase that extends beyond servitude: a strategic retaking of power by women that is made possible by the new dynamics of pleasure that accompanies organized society.

Laclos' natural woman is defined by three characteristics: freedom, strength, and health. Able to satisfy all her needs for food and shelter, she tends to a solitary existence that eliminates any extended reliance on other human beings. In this, Laclos stays quite close to Rousseau. Where he departs from him is in the prominence he gives to a paradigm of individual consciousness which is sensationist and Epicurean. Because he grounds all appetites and the strategies for satisfying them in the body and its senses, Laclos is less concerned than Rousseau with preparing those dimensions of consciousness which will at some later period develop independently of the physical body. Language as the expression of consciousness is, for the more materialist Laclos, less a mystery that must have its own separate history than it is a repository of concepts that are false precisely because they ignore, mask, and contradict the data of the senses. Language as a means of communication between individuals will, for Laclos, have little to do with the beginnings of sociability or with the coming together of couples as protofamilies. For Laclos' natural woman, the first movements toward interaction with another occur as a corollary to the bodily changes that define the onset of puberty: "Already her form becomes more rounded and her bosom larger at the same time that her reproductive organs tighten and are covered with budding hair." When, during a hunt or some other short-term task undertaken by a group, her hand happens to make contact with a male's, she discovers that her response to that touch has a dimension she has not previously experienced: "A sweet tremor moves throughout her body. She pulls her hand back and blushes involuntarily, not from modesty, but from unrest. She feels desire, but is fearful of touching him again." A need for solitude and reflection—"She draws back into herself and for the first time she will be concerned with her thoughts"—may accompany this event, but it is the change of her physical body that is decisive: "She remains in this state until her first menstrual flow calms her by preparing nature's laboratory" (400–401).

Puberty transforms the world around her into occasions of pleasures which are real in themselves but which also hint at an augmented dimension of pleasure as yet only suspected: "She casts ardent and troubled glances all around her. She is transfixed and enchanted by the morning's spectacle. The sweet perfume of the flowers prepares her for voluptuousness *[la volupté]*. Birdsong is no longer a vain noise but a touching harmony that speaks directly to her heart" (401). Becoming one with a universal symphony of sensual longing, her chance perception of a figure in the distance provokes a response that is the pure expression of instinct: "Then in the distance she perceives a man. A powerful yet involuntary instinct leads her to run toward him. As she approaches him, she becomes timid and stops. Drawn forward again, she joins him and grasps him in her arms. . . . Delicious pleasure [*jouissance*], who could attempt to describe you?" (401).

Because words could never capture the sensual intensity of that first moment of sexual pleasure, Laclos ends his portrait of puberty and begins a new chapter devoted to what he calls *l'âge viril* of natural woman. Before continuing his hypothetical history, however, he interrupts his portrait to give a Rousseauian warning that his readers must resist any tendency to project back onto this state of nature concepts and behaviors which are the products of a later and much degenerated age—an age that would see the end of woman's freedom in nature. The intense pleasure of these couplings between presocial women and men must not, Laclos cautions, be imagined in terms of such concepts as what his contemporaries would call "beauty" and "love." As concerns beauty, the rugged body and weathered skin of natural woman in no way correspond to the pale, delicate, and sensitive skin which has become the hallmark of feminine beauty. For Laclos, the characteristics any given society happens to designate as constituting beauty in a woman are the results of arbitrary preferences for certain traits that are grounded far more in cultural choices than in physical reality. Rather than any confected and parochial beauty, what establishes natural woman as irresistible for her partner is the robust healthiness Laclos calls "the state most favorable to sexual pleasure *[jouissance]*" (403)—with *jouissance* understood here as the pure, unmediated pleasure of senses that have been totally satisfied. As concerns what is now called love, Laclos sees it as a purely linguistic construct, an illusory and compensatory term which draws its power not from pleasures experienced in the present but from what is absent and longed for: "Love is what society offers as a consolation. Socialized man has paid for it with everything natural man once possessed" (403).

Laclos is quick to anticipate the difficulties his readers will have with his distinction between (natural) pleasure and (socialized) love. Yes, these encounters between natural woman and natural man, who "come together without ever having seen each other before, and, in a moment, will separate never to see each other again" (403), take place entirely outside the social construct of any "sustained passion." At the same time, however, the members of such a couple do experience *at the level of sensation* what amounts to the full narrative of a beginning, middle, and end marked by "all the nuances of sentiment" (403). In choosing the word *sentiment*, Laclos consciously forces that term back to its etymological roots in the experience of the senses as opposed to that of the mind. In describing nature's love story Laclos systematically emphasizes the embodied reality of movements, gestures, and touches as more forceful versions of what his contemporaries experience essentially as adventures of language. "Their first caresses serve as a *declaration*. The woman by turns draws back and provokes. It is in this way that their desires grow. Soon those desires reach their height and give birth to inebriation. It expresses itself *not with elegant phrases*, but in the sultry looks and burning sighs which are part of every language" (403; italics mine). Laclos' prioritizing of the senses as more natural and more forceful than the language-embedded emotions that today accompany what people call love emboldens him to ask his sadly socialized female readers to compare themselves with their sisters from the lost past he describes: "Is there even one among you who has taken pleasure *[joui]* constantly, without fear, without jealousy, without remorse, and without the tiresome boredom of duty and uniformity?" (403).

This natural sexuality based entirely in pleasure precludes any continuing relation with the male. Similarly, in the midst of a bountiful nature, a child's dependence on the mother lasts only through the first four years of nursing. These facts in turn allow him to articulate the most subversive premise of his anthropology: the refusal of the family unit as a natural form of conviviality that preceded humankind's socialization. For Laclos, the family is not the natural building block with which societies will construct themselves. A continuing sexual and familial relation between female and male must not, in other words, be seen as the given of nature, as a *status quo ante* out of which more complex social structures will develop. In fact, the very possibility of any such continuing relation will be, for Laclos, the first and determining problem which any nascent social order is obliged to address and resolve. It is, in other words, not the *union* but the *conflict* between equally independent females and males which any society must resolve if it is to become stable and endure.

Once the independent sexuality of natural woman has been established as the indispensable hypothesis for evaluating woman's true status in society, and after a lengthy consideration of objections by Buffon and Voltaire to the idea of a state of nature that precedes society, Laclos begins his historical anthropology of how natural woman and man have come to be as they now are. The chapter "On the First Effects of Society" begins with the ultra-Rousseauian axiom that "nature creates only free beings; society produces only tyrants and slaves" (419). It is this coercion at the core of every social relation which will explain why, because women are less physically strong than men, they passed from a state of natural freedom to one of social vassalage: "If the oppression of the weak by the strong is not a natural law in the sense which moralists give to that term, it is nonetheless a law of nature, or rather it is the first vengeance which a forsaken nature takes against socialized man" (419). For Laclos, no matter how eloquent the lip service paid to such ideals as equality, respect, and mutual protection, "every convention established between two subjects of unequal force produces, and can only produce, a tyrant and a slave" (419).

According to this argument, the fact that women are less physically strong implies that, as they were drawn into early social formations, they found themselves enslaved. For Laclos, the first social groupings were exclusively masculine collectives of individuals who, because they were more or less equal in strength, were able to overcome natural man's innate wariness toward any sustained interaction with his fellows. Those men, however, "soon felt the need for women, and therefore set about forcing or cajoling them into joining them" (420). It was this decision made by men that decided the sad fate of womankind: "Whether by force or by persuasion, the first woman who gave in [to that proposition] forged the chains that would bind her entire sex" (420). During an initial stage women were held in common by the group—"all women belonged to all men" (420)—and the men's greater physical strength allowed them to heap upon women the duties of labor and menial tasks. As these groupings stabilized, this debasement of women's status led to their becoming, under the guise of marriage, a form of property held by men in the same way they did lands and chattel. Set on confirming his anthropological hypothesis with ethnographic data, Laclos then embarks on a review, drawn largely from the travel literature of his period, of the various forms the enslavement of women has taken among Lapps, Koreans, Lebanese, Hottentots, and other societies imagined by Europeans as the most primitive and therefore the closest to our origins.

Once he has completed his ethnographic review, Laclos shifts his focus to what he sees as a historical paradox. On the one hand, women today, like their sisters of long ago and far away, are still disadvantaged by patriarchal society's organized oppression of the weak by the strong. On the other hand, compared to the abject misery that is woman's lot in primitive societies, there are numerous modern examples of women who have set limits to male hegemony and even acquired power over men. How is it that, starting as tribal drudges, women have produced clear exceptions to a tyranny of the strong over the weak based on gender? More important, what lessons might contemporary women draw from those examples?

For Laclos, the answer to those questions lies in the dynamics of pleasure as a phenomenon able to mitigate and even reverse the hegemony of gender: "They [women] realized that if force has made them dependent on men, pleasure could make those same men dependent on them" (421). What Laclos here calls pleasure is both sensorial and sexual. Unlike the beatific *jouissance* fleetingly shared by women and men in the state of nature, pleasure is the possible but by no means certain modality of sexual congress as it is practiced in societies that have redefined sexuality as the privilege of men and the duty of women. Experienced in two such different ways, sexuality for men leads to and ends with satisfaction; sexuality for women, to the contrary, becomes a site of strategic reflection. If it was women who became the true theorists of pleasure, this was because "more unhappy than men, they were obliged to learn more quickly than men to think and to reflect" (421). Once that reflection born of servitude began, what women learned was that the complex dynamics of pleasure makes it the ideal terrain on which they might "substitute skill for force" (421).

What is it that women were able to learn from their reflections on pleasure? First and foremost, that, as an experience of the senses accompanied by imagination, pleasure is always less than and inferior to what had been anticipated: "Pleasure never measured up to the idea they had conceived of it, and imagination always surpassed nature" (421). Within the state of nature, before the formation of stable societies, an encounter between a woman and a man could have one of two outcomes: to couple or to flee, with both options quickly followed by separation and forgetting. It was only within the confined sphere and continuous contact of society that there came to exist an interval between what the excited mind might imagine and what the sensate body would experience. It is that interval, and the alchemy of imagination that presides over it, that gave birth to desire as pleasure's deprived twin and as a force which woman's superior intelligence could turn to her advantage: "From the moment they understood how to inflame men's imagination, they also knew how to foster and direct his desires" (422).

This jujitsu of turning a force back against the agent wielding it was the result of women's skill at manipulating two values generated by social consensus: what Laclos calls "preferred beauty" (*la beauté de choix*) and "possessive love" (*l'amour exclusif*). Both are social constructs that mirror yet go beyond less alienated phenomena that existed within the state of nature. Preferred beauty is an attractiveness grounded in the arbitrary norms and tastes of a given society and for that reason different from the unadorned vigor and strength that made natural woman so appealing. Possessive love is a force grounded not in any attributes of the beloved but in the competing, triangulated desire generated by the perception of a rival. Within society, it is never simply one woman and one man who come together; it is the mediated and confected desires of society as a whole that act themselves out in the scenario of every encounter.

Suffering women were the first to learn that the tensions of deferral and refusal that exacerbate imagination could be turned to their benefit. "Once they had understood these first truths, women learned to veil their charms in order to intensify curiosity. They perfected the difficult art of refusing even when they wished to consent" (420). No longer locked in servitude by reason of her lesser physical strength, socialized woman can become the adept negotiator of pleasures imagined and deferred, a formidable opponent able to turn to her own benefit the very strength that could be used against her: "Struggling always, occasionally triumphing, and often, because they were more skilled, they turned to their advantage the very forces directed against them" (420).

Laclos agrees with Rousseau that society is the realm in which the arbitrary and the idiosyncratic disguise themselves as the necessary and the universal. Nowhere is the status of society's norms and preferences as local and parochial more apparent than in the genesis of beauty. How, Laclos asks as he considers what he calls preferred beauty, can one explain why societies differ so vastly in their sense of what constitutes beauty? How, even within a single society, does it happen that individuals differ so sharply as to what they call beauty? In posing those questions Laclos has two goals: one philosophical and the other strategic; one focused on the genesis of value and the other on the exercise of power. Philosophically, Laclos' explanation of beauty's genesis takes the distinctly non-Rousseauian tack of grounding it in Epicurean materialism. The stimuli leading an individual to designate something as beauty always begins in the senses, in sensations experienced as pleasurable. Over time, multiple experiences of such pleasure will coalesce within the mind as an incipient paradigm of beauty. "Beauty is, as we see it, nothing other than the appearance most promising of pleasure, a way of being that inspires dreams of the most delicious pleasure" (423).

We saw earlier how, even as Laclos described the brevity of sexual pleasure in the state of nature, he insisted on articulating its momentary physicality into a scenario endowed with a beginning, middle, and end. As societies developed, and as natural beauty came to be inflected by the diverse criteria of preferred beauty, pleasure's temporality became even more complex. Living in close proximity with their fellows, and perceiving them as potential rivals, men entered the realm of the comparative. They continually measured themselves and their situations against those around them. Rather than living within nature's present, men came to see that present as having meaning only in relation to a past and a future: "Man set about comparing his ideas: his memory retrieved the past and his imagination portrayed the future. Memory and anticipation developed together and exerted a strong influence on him" (423). From Laclos' sensationist perspective, this more involved consciousness, while grounded in sense experience, displaces it into the more complex temporality of a past preserved in memory and a future grounded in anticipation: "As soon as his memory became adept at recalling the effect of sensations he had experienced, he compared his pleasures from the past and drew from them conclusions as to pleasures still to come" (423). As a result of this augmented temporality, pleasure acquires a new dimension. While triggered by a stimulus situated in the present, pleasure's allegiance to a remembered past and a hoped-for future valorizes the moment of perception as the promise of a pleasure that synthesizes present, past, and future. "The woman who had brought him the most intense pleasure became the most precious to him. He sought her out again. When she was absent, he chose the one who most nearly resembled her" (423).

In terms of Laclos' Epicureanism, a beautiful woman is less an integrated whole than a juxtaposition of constituent traits each of which provokes greater or lesser pleasure on the part of the beholder. Soft yet firm skin entices the sense of touch. An ample figure promises the delight of being enfolded. It is only within the mind that this data from the various senses will be synthesized into the unified ideational whole of the beautiful woman. The mind's repertoire of sensations associated with pleasure makes possible a movement between the part and the whole, a passage from data provided by a single sense to a judgment as to the whole. Synecdoche, the interplay of part and whole, becomes the defining trope of the beautiful.

Moving from the philosophical to the strategic, Laclos insists that understanding beauty and the ways men perceive it is essential for any woman living in our postlapsarian, socialized world. Yet that is no easy task. Beauty is, as we have seen, relative, and it changes from individual to individual as well as from society to society. The dynamics of beauty is further complicated by the protocols of polite civilization. While beauty as a semiology of promised pleasure may have been unambiguous in an age when all were naked and the entire body was visible to the beholder's eye, modern customs, in offering less, give even more sway to the imagination. "When women began to cloth themselves, the imagination was obliged to add its part to what the eye could no longer perceive. But imagination is easily seduced and frequently in error. Curiosity prodded desire and desire in turn embellished its object.... Men grew accustomed to desiring before they had experienced; and illusion accompanied every desire" (424–25). As clothes and corsets cloak and form the body to appear different from its reality, those parts of the body still uncovered, primarily the face, come to play a central role in the display of beauty and the quest for pleasure it provokes. For the beholder who "knows objects only by the impression he receives from them" (425), the visible face became a crucial synecdoche providing the imagination with a compelling clue to the tenor of the pleasure promised by the body as a whole. Beauty impresses itself upon its beholder through a synthesis of sense perception and imagination. The imagination volatilizes the data provided by the senses through both a memory of pleasures past and a movement between part and whole. To behold beauty is to read a limited field of signs and, on the basis of sensations recalled, to fantasize an imaginary whole from visible parts.

Given this complex chemistry, the signs of beauty are readily susceptible to simulation and adornment. In his closing chapter, "On Finery" (Sur la parure), Laclos offers a series of surprisingly practical counsels as to how women might best exploit "the art not only of profiting from the gifts of nature, but even more so of adding to them the charms of imagination [in such a way that] it become a stimulant to voluptuousness" (429). His suggestions are varied: never confuse dressing sumptuously with dressing well; follow a careful diet to preserve an appearance of freshness; avoid excesses of alcohol and sun, both of which destroy the complexion. Above all, the truly prudent woman will protect her always visible face from the ravages of emotion and excess: "If you do not rein in too frequent movements of anger, your muscles will acquire a dangerous mobility and soon your expressions will be nothing more than grimaces. . . . Be especially careful of the fatigue that follows pleasure. In that state of exhaustion, your drooping eyes, your faded lips, and your pale cheeks will never inspire a desire which it is obvious you are not ready to share" (431–32).

The subject of *parure* leads to that eminently eighteenth-century art of *maquillage:* how the refined artifices of make-up allow women to control what the visible face suggests about the hidden body.[8] Laclos warns, however, that the magic of make-up brings with it a real danger: that of refashioning the face as a sign so misleading that it prepares a humiliation to come. To indulge oneself in creating excessive gaps between signifier and signified, between sign and reality, is to opt for an illusionism that produces only disappointment. The truly wise woman never confuses the function of the part with that of the whole: "The face attracts, but it is the body which holds captive. The first is the net and the second the cage. The prudent bird catcher, before setting his traps, makes certain that he has the means to hold on to whatever prey he might snare" (433).

Laclos' essay moves from a gendered anthropology to tactical considerations of how women in modern society might use the dynamics of pleasure to resist and even reverse masculine oppression. If his argument espouses a conscious instrumentalizing of pleasure, it is as a corollary to the unjust social order with which his readers must contend. Women's subordination to men may be a perversion of nature, but it is nonetheless the necessary starting point for any effective understanding of what is possible within the present. Woman's condition within society must be approached not as a tragedy to be lamented but as a drama whose denouement is yet undecided. While Rousseau's *Second Discourse* ends within an entirely negative denunciation of the evils humankind has wrought upon itself, Laclos' anthropology of pleasure postulates society as a synthesis of reality and illusion whose scrutiny can yield strategies through which women might reverse the tyranny of the masters.

The difference between these two perspectives is clearest in their respective treatments of imagination. For Laclos, the imagination is, as we have seen, an integral component of pleasure deferred, an intensification of pleasure's force which women might learn to solicit and direct. Rooted in an inevitable surplus of desire over fulfillment, it opens up a space of manipulation in which the positions of master and slave can be reversed. For Rousseau, to the contrary, recourse to the imagination is the hallmark of monstrosity and depravation. As Julie succinctly puts it in one of her early letters to Saint-Preux: "So many people talk about love, and so few know how to love, that most of them take as its pure and gentle laws the vile maxims of an abject traffic that soon satiated by its own devices calls on monsters of the imagination and falls into depravity in order to sustain itself" (2:138).

The pure love in whose name Julie would condemn imagination is, for Laclos, a social and ideological construct. His strategic counsels to women assume as biological givens both woman's lesser physical force and a quest for pleasure that animates relations between the sexes. These givens constitute what he sees as the only natural foundations of gender distinctions. As such, they determine how women and men are both similar (in their seeking of pleasure) and different (in their physical strength). Laclos' anthropology seeks to show how the *physical* difference between woman and man has been transformed within society into the *political* difference between slave and master. Within that framework, he analyzes how woman's manipulation of pleasure and desire can counterbalance and even reverse masculine domination. For Laclos, the gendered social order is political. And, like all things political, it is subject to change, compensation, and reversal. Gender, in other words, determines strategy, not outcome.

The nineteenth-century poet Charles Baudelaire provocatively titled one section of a long-planned but never completed study of *Les Liaisons dangereuses* "How People Made Love during the Ancien Régime." In it, he notes that "it was all lies; but people made no pretense of adoring their fellows. They fooled one another, but they fooled themselves less."[9] Baudelaire's cold-eyed summary of Laclos' world—where deception is assumed and where self-deception becomes the only unforgivable sin—underlines the different mode in which what I have been calling Laclos' anthropology of pleasure was already at work in the novel that would make him an emblem of eighteenth-century France on the eve of Revolution. What so many readers denounced as the scandal of Merteuil's hypocrisy, her diabolic finesse at duping all those around her, might more calmly be read as a narrative anticipation of Laclos' anthropology. In his anthropological essay, as he moves from woman's natural freedom to her social enslavement, it becomes clear why all women of consequence must be some version of Mme de Merteuil.

What changes entirely in these two works separated by little more than a year is the moral posture they impose on their readers. Laclos' essay is a philosophical response to a theoretical question: how might one rewrite Rousseau's *Essay on the Origin of Inequality* if it founded its argument on the hypothesis not of natural man but of natural woman? Presented as a hypothesis, the essay allows its reader the distance of someone entertaining a possibility and evaluating the implications of that different way of looking at things. *Les Liaisons dangereuses* places its reader in a very different position. A collection of letters written in the first person and purporting to be real, it compels its readers, for the duration of their reading, to become one with a cast of intricately interlocking deceivers and dupes. To entertain the idea that, within an oppressive patriarchy, women are obliged to better their lot through manipulations of masculine desire is one thing. To become the intimate confidant of such hypocrisy in action is something quite different. It was this forcing of the reader to see the real motivations behind society's polite rituals that prompted Baudelaire, in another of his notes on Laclos' novel, to describe it as a "manual of sociability" (70).[10] Sociability is certainly the shared subject of Laclos' novel and his speculative essay. At the same time, reading the novel and vicariously becoming its characters replaces speculative distance with moral outrage. The genius of Laclos' novel was to use that rush to moral judgment to place his would-be castigators in the even more uncomfortable position of implicitly espousing all the prejudices of polite society. Morally indignant readers may well applaud the unmasking of the hypocrites at the novel's end, but in so doing they became doubles of Cécile's so easily duped mother, Mme de Volange, the most conventional and limited of all Laclos' characters.

Laclos' novel, like his essay, is fundamentally a work about women. Its unifying subject is a topology of the options available to women within society, and all its most carefully drawn characters are women.[11] Valmont certainly has his place in the long line of the eighteenth century's Don Juans, but Laclos' version of that figure is most profoundly defined by a pathetic failure of lucidity. Always ready to launch into the grandiose rhetoric of the sexual buccaneer, his boast and bluster finally become a form of self-deception, a way for him to hide from himself the infatuation with Mme de Tourvel that Merteuil is more than happy to manipulate toward her own ends. Writing at the time of the novel's appearance, Friedrich Melchior Grimm described perfectly the uneven relation between the novel's two main characters: "As sublime an example as he may be of his type, he nonetheless remains quite inferior to the Marquise de Merteuil, who inspires him, guides him, and surpasses him in every way.... Valmont is little more, one might say, than the secret minister charged with her pleasures, her hatreds, and her vengeance."[12] The novel's every episode has as its immediate or remote cause Merteuil's determination to occupy a position and to exercise a power her society is unwilling to grant to any woman. Its center and circumference, she is the novel's enabling premise.

Looking at Laclos' novel in terms of his anthropology of pleasure brings to the fore an important question: how did Merteuil, a character unlike any other woman in the novel, become Merteuil? In his philosophical essay, as we saw, Laclos attributed women's awakening to a long history of suffering and reflection. Their ability to turn the dynamics of pleasure to their advantage was "what the experience of many centuries had taught them" (421). Given Merteuil's singularity within the novel—the many ways in which she is different from all its other female characters—she clearly cannot be read as an example of ontogeny repeating phylogeny, of one individual's development recapitulating that of the entire species. The real answer to the mystery of Merteuil's genesis is, appropriately enough, one that she herself provides. Letter 81, Merteuil's autobiographical *Bildungsroman*, explains how she has become the person she is. This gesture of self-definition grows out of the fury she feels when she reads Valmont's condescending warning that she is over her head if she thinks she can confront the wily Prévan and undo his plan to disgrace her socially. What Merteuil finds intolerable, and what motivates every stroke of her self-portrait, is that Valmont—a man protected by all the unearned privileges society confers upon men—should presume not only that he understands her but that he can help her: "And you would like to teach me, to direct me! Oh, my poor Valmont, what a distance there is between us! No, all the vanity of your sex cannot make up for that disparity. Because you would not be able to carry out my plans, you decide that they are impossible!"[13] Far from overreaching, she insists, her joust with Prévan will bring her to the threshold of her unique mission as a woman: "Should you not therefore have concluded that I, who was born to revenge my sex and master yours, have been able to discover methods of doing so that were unknown before me?" (170).

Situating her life's purpose at the intersection of the sexual and the social, of gender and power, Merteuil is like no other woman. A Galatea who is her own Pygmalion, she describes herself as the self-fashioned creation of a strict adherence to principles that set her apart from all other women: "I say my principles, and I say it intentionally. They are not, like those of other women, found by chance, accepted without thinking, and followed out of habit. They are the fruit of profound reflection. I have created them, and I might well say that I have created myself" (170). The principles that guided this autogenesis—to distrust appearances and uncover the secrets they hide, to control absolutely every indication one gives about one's own feelings and intentions, to remain masked while unmasking all others—establish Merteuil's voice as the synthesis within a single consciousness of all the lessons that Laclos' anthropology of pleasure designates as the fruit of womankind's long centuries of suffering and reflection.[14]

As Merteuil summarizes it for Valmont, her public life began when, like Cécile in the novel's opening letter, she learned from her mother that she was to marry a man much older than she. That union may have brought her sexual initiation, but, for her, that realm of the senses and their pleasures immediately became a new terrain for cold and lucid observations, allowing her to extend her control of self and domination of others to the most private precincts of intimacy. What other women might experience as a *libido sentiendi* triggered, for Merteuil, only a *libido sapiendi:* "I had no wish to take pleasure, I wanted to know . . . and I saw my various sensations only as facts to be noted and meditated upon" (172). Her brief marriage and subsequent widowhood had as their most important premium her status within society as a woman now free from the authority of both husband and father. Thanks to an always vigilant manipulation of the perceived and the hidden, she is esteemed by the public as a woman of impeccable reputation while enjoying in the privacy of her *petite maison* all the pleasures of her choosing. Early on in the novel, in letter 10, Merteuil feeds Valmont's jealousy by offering him the detailed narration of an evening she spent with her lover of the moment, Belleroche. Her description of the six hours they spent together becomes an illustration of the strategic manipulation of pleasure Laclos would describe in his essay. Incarnating the fine art of coaxing and modulating every contour of her partner's pleasure, Merteuil exercises a power that is never more complete than when it masks itself as surrender. Even as she overwhelms Belleroche with limitless delights, her real goal is the far more exquisite pleasuring of the self that she finds in manipulating him. As she recounts that evening for Valmont, she chooses a metaphor for her situation that captures perfectly the polarities of apparent and real power. Belleroche may imagine himself a sultan in the midst of his harem, but that reiteration of his potency becomes the surest proof of the control she exercises over him through pleasure. "After supper, now childish, now reasonable, now playful, now sentimental, at times even lascivious, I amused myself imagining him a sultan in the midst of his harem while I played in turn a succession of his favorites, so that, each time he paid his respects, it was to a different mistress, although the same woman received them" (31). Woman in the long lost state of nature, unencumbered by any continuing relation with the men she encounters only momentarily, may have been able to act as an untroubled Epicurean responding to the promptings of her senses and seeking only her pleasure. Within society women must, like Merteuil, temper that natural Epicureanism with the Stoic's skills of distance, reasoned reflection, and a control of self that allows the manipulation of others.

At one point in letter 10, Merteuil explains in a single sentence why she was so pleased by her evening with Belleroche: "I think I have never taken such care to please, nor ever felt so satisfied with my success" (31). Later in the novel, in a letter which Mme de Rosemonde sends to Mme de Tourvel, we hear the voice of a very different female character. The wise and virtuous Rosemonde, Valmont's elderly aunt, is writing to Tourvel as a young women whom she counsels as she would an adopted daughter. Responding to Tourvel's admission that she has yielded to Valmont, that she loves him, and that her life will henceforth have no meaning without his love, Rosemonde struggles to express her acceptance of whatever Tourvel decides is best for her, yet she also articulates her trepidation over where she fears that choice is leading. Rosemonde speaks to her young friend not of individuals but of universals, of men and women, and of how they are different: "A man takes pleasure from the happiness he feels, a woman from the happiness she gives. This difference, so essential and so little noticed, nonetheless influences the whole of their respective conduct in the most remarkable way. The pleasure of the one is to satisfy his desires. The pleasure of the other is, above all, to arouse them. Giving pleasure for him is only a means to success; while for her it is success itself"(304).

Surprisingly, this description of the relation between the sexes, offered by a character utterly unlike Merteuil, presupposes the premises of Laclos' anthropology in the same way as did Merteuil's declaration of satisfaction. The same understanding of gender that Merteuil wields as a weapon is proposed by Rosemonde as a consolation. For both, it is assumed that men act always as rigorous Epicureans concerned only with maximizing their pleasure. Women, to the contrary, must acquire the skills of the Stoic at distancing themselves from, understanding, and manipulating the pleasures that draw men and women together. The irony of this surprising similarity between the two positions goes even further. Laurent Versini, in a note to Rosemonde's sage analysis of gender, points out that for readers of the period her counsel was a clear echo of seventeenth-century preciosity. That delicate femininity—clearly out of fashion in 1782 but hardly surprising in a character of Rosemonde's advanced age—postulated, as Versini puts it, that "women alone are capable of that 'true love' which seeks only the happiness of the beloved." For the *précieuse,* far removed from the Epicurean appetites of men, "true love" is entirely an affair of feeling and sentiment. It would divorce itself completely from the body were it not for what Versini describes as "the satisfactions demanded by the egoism of masculine desire" (1365).

If Laclos underlines the similarity between the positions of these two very different characters, it is because, in terms of his anthropology, women always find themselves obliged to assume one of two postures toward the social order. One option, and everything invites them in this direction, is to subscribe to the belief that a woman's true love brings with it the untroubled ideal of an innocent transparency of the soul far superior to the baser pleasures of the senses. The other option—the option Baudelaire underscores with his observation that in a world given over to lies there is an inverse proportion between deceiving others and deceiving oneself—is to spurn the mystifications of true love while manipulating them in one's partner. Women who, like Merteuil, choose manipulation recognize that true love's imaginary alternative to the oppression of women within society comes only at the highest of prices. To pine for true love is to become the victim not only of an arbitrary social order but also of that very imagination which allows the lucid woman to emerge as victor rather than as dupe.

Society's concatenation of masters and slaves places women and men in relations of power that cannot be elided. To the masculine prerogative of force woman must oppose, not her own deluded true love, but a strategic manipulation of masculine imagination that can check and even redress her oppression. Laclos' anthropology of pleasure allows us to understand that Merteuil's downfall comes not because loving women must triumph over lucid women, but because her commitment to lucidity is irretrievably compromised by the very need to be applauded for her accomplishments that led her to initiate her secret correspondence with Valmont. Tzvetan Todorov has pointed out that *Les Liaisons dangereuses* is a novel that tells two different stories: one about the characters who exchange the letters we read and one about how those letters come to be gathered together and offered to the reading public.[15] Those two stories finally become the same story and all the novel's characters meet the fate they do because the letters Merteuil and Valmont intended only for each other are now read by all.

Returning to Merteuil's enumeration of the principles guiding her self-creation, the reader can only be puzzled when she writes to Valmont: "From that moment on my way of thinking was my private affair, and I revealed only what I found it useful to reveal. . . . These precautions, along with those of *never writing letters* and of *never providing evidence of my defeat*, may appear excessive, but to me they never seemed enough" (171–75; italics mine). Ironically, Merteuil violates her principles even as she proclaims them, and the contradiction between what she writes and what she does prepares her social disgrace. If she does so, if she unwittingly arms Valmont for the battle in which both will be undone, it is because she too has fallen victim to the kind of mystification she denounces in the women around her. To provide Valmont with the means to unmask her reveals her own illusory hope that the lucidity they share in deceiving others can also become the recuperation of a lost Epicurean ideal of unguarded pleasures. Her fate is sealed when she forgets the lesson of Laclos' anthropology: that within the society of always Epicurean men, women can be free only through the Stoic's mastery and manipulation of pleasure.

7. Recasting the Epicurean Novel

Mirabeau's *La Morale des sens*

What was the fate of the new Epicureanism so closely associated with the giddy effervescence of France at midcentury in the very different context of the decade leading up to the Bastille and Revolution? How did the novel portray enlightened pleasures for a readership that, for almost two decades, had been fascinated with the ethos of sentiment introduced by Rousseau's *Julie* and its epic of virtuous self-denial? What relevance could stories of serial seductions by privileged males have within a society that more and more explicitly challenged the prerogatives of birth? *Les Liaisons dangereuses* of 1783 offers some answers to those questions, but also sidesteps them by situating its story within a society from the past ironically designated as inconceivable as part of the present its editor shares with his readers. A more direct answer can be glimpsed in a philosophically titled novel written by the brother of one of the Revolution's most famous orators. That author, embodying the ambiguities of his times, was an ardent defender of the monarchy yet also a frank Epicurean who produced biting critiques of the hypocrisies of both the ancien régime and the virtuous citizens of the republic to come.

In 1781, at the age of twenty-six, the least well known of the three Mirabeaus, André Boniface Riqueti, Vicomte de Mirabeau, published in London a short and strangely iconoclastic novel titled *La Morale des sens*. Five years younger than Honoré Gabriel, the famous Comte de Mirabeau, André Boniface shared little with his older brother beyond a knack for infuriating their father, Victor Riqueti, the Marquis de Mirabeau, best known as an economic theorist of physiocracy, famous for such works as *L'Ami des hommes ou traité sur la population* of 1756 and *Théorie de l'impôt* of 1760. Both sons spent considerable time in royal prisons as a result of the *lettres de cachet* which were their exasperated father's response to what he saw as their scandalous sexual escapades. Both also used that time in prison to refine their talents as writers of fiction. The older brother, Honoré Gabriel, best known as the author of the 1789 version of the *Declaration of the Rights of Man and Citizen*, became a major figure of the period before his premature death in 1791. Even while a counselor to Louis XVI, he was one of the Revolution's most eloquent orators.

André Boniface took a very different path. The younger Mirabeau began a military career at the age of seventeen when he was named *sous-lieutenant* in the Légion de Lorraine. Three years later, in 1775, he became a knight of Malta, but was expelled from the island and the order that same year for the hardly chivalrous feat of attacking and destroying the religious statues that had been prepared for a local procession. In 1778 he was named to the cavalry in the Régiment de Nivernois, where he was described by a superior as a "notorious rake" and acquired the nickname Mirabeau Tonneau (Mirabeau the Barrel) for the corpulence brought on by his love for wine and food.[1] The least dubious period of his military career began in August 1780, when he participated as a volunteer in the French military expedition sent to the aid of the insurrectionists in the American War for Independence. After participating in a number of raids on English forts in the Caribbean, Mirabeau was given command of a regiment under the Comte de Rochambeau and played an important role in the Battle of Yorktown in 1781. Promoted to the rank of colonel by Lafayette, he was decorated at Versailles as a chevalier de Saint Louis by Louis XVI in March 1782.

Back home as the Revolution approached, he was elected to the Estates General as a representative of the nobility of the Haut-Limousin. Vehemently opposed to revolutionary projects which he saw as half-baked utopias that would do far more harm than good, Mirabeau distinguished himself by the comic parodies of his adversaries' rhetoric and goals that were always part of his performances during the official sessions of the National Assembly. One of the most wittily caustic satirists on the right and a constant annoyance to the left, he never hesitated to espouse a position simply to provoke.[2] Hardly pious and, as we shall see, a sharp critic of the Church as an institution, he nonetheless argued vociferously that, in a properly Gallican form, Catholicism should be proclaimed the national religion of France. Ridiculing his opponents in an endless barrage of comic interventions in the deliberations of the Assembly as well as in printed pamphlets, his frustration at the success of the very different political choices made by his older brother led to his resignation from the Assembly and his emigration in July 1790.[3] Once in exile he raised from the ranks of the émigrés a pro-monarchist regiment known as the Légion noire. His own insurrection was cut short when, in August 1792 at the age of thirty-eight, and a month before the Battle of Valmy, he died in the Black Forest town of Frieburg from a cerebral congestion said to have been brought on by a bitter dispute with one of his own officers.[4]

The Vicomte de Mirabeau massively and unabashedly chose the wrong side in the defining political upheaval of his short lifetime. For the reader of *La Morale des sens*, a work composed in the relative calm of almost a decade before the taking of the Bastille, his choices stand as a surprising sequel to the portrait of French society he offers as a novelist. On the one hand, Mirabeau the novelist, clearly in sympathy with the subversive Epicurean materialism of La Mettrie and Diderot, writes as a caustic satirist of the ancien régime's fundamental institutions, from the Church to the tax farmers, from a social order based on birth to all forms of personal piety. On the other hand, as Jane P. Sctrick has well described it, this novel, republished in London in 1792 with a set of eight erotic engravings,[5] is nonetheless shot through with what she calls "nostalgia for an epoch swept away like no other by man's madness for virtue."[6]

For the twenty-first-century reader, *La Morale des sens* is puzzling and paradoxical. Out of joint with its time, it is distinctly unlike such carefully constructed classics of the period as Rousseau's *Julie* and Laclos' *Les Liaisons dangereuses*. Divided into fifty chapters of two to six pages each, along with an opening epistle to Babet and a brief conclusion, it opens with the arrival of its unnamed hero at the University of Nan*** and proceeds to tell the story of his amorous encounters. Early on, however, any semblance of a linear or integrated narrative structure is fractured. Chapter 16 abruptly introduces a previously unmentioned character named Méricour who tells how an equally unanticipated Damon set out to test the virtue of his new bride by feigning impotence. Seven chapters later, the narrator receives a letter from his father that sends him to the country marriage of an uncle where new adventures and an entirely different cast of characters await him. Chapter 33 brings another letter from the father that sends the narrator to the capital, where he will spend two years as a novice in a religious community. By chapter 43, after being defrocked for conduct unbecoming of a monk, the narrator embarks on a brief military career as a general's adjutant.

Always witty and blithely skimming the surface of events, the narrator describes himself and the characters he encounters in a diction unconcerned with providing any sense of a progressive or cumulative comprehension of those figures. Strikingly anomalous for its period, *La Morale des sens* challenges its readers to understand its esthetic as something other than a throwback to some primitive stage of the storyteller's art, to a time before the French novel addressed, to use Georges May's phrase, its defining "dilemma" through a reconciliation of subjectivity and realism.[7] Mirabeau's anomaly in relation to the novelistic rhetoric of his day declares itself from his very choice of a title. Somewhere between philosophy and allegory, it joins two abstract terms whose connotations appear to move in opposite directions. On the one hand, the title tells us that the novel will deal with the senses. Mirabeau's variation on the Virgilian *arma virumque canto* becomes, in his first chapter, the distinctly Epicurean "I shall speak of my pleasures" (19), which foreshadows what will become the chronicle of his sexual escapades. His first discovery of sexuality, with a compliant landlady, is described as an overload of sensory delight so intense that it sweeps away all contact with the self as a stable foyer of experience: "If only I could paint for your eyes that zest of soul, those tumultuous transports of the senses that I then experienced for the first time.... I passed from one delight to the next. Nothing could hold me back. Like a butterfly flitting from flower to flower, I gathered nectar, I took flight, and I returned again to whatever object drew my fancy" (47). On the other hand, the title's first term evokes the more sober enterprise of articulating a *morale*, an endeavor that assumes a posture of reflective and even Stoic remove from the immediacy of the senses. It is the narrator as moralist who cautions the beautiful Églé, convinced that giddy happiness will follow her departure from the restrictive world of the convent, that life never quite works out that way: "Can we ever count ourselves happy here below? Sufferings come, as they say, one upon the other; and however unfortunate we are, wisdom tells us that still worse awaits. Such is life"(22).

What were readers to make of this tension, underlined in the title, between a chaotic parade of episodic sensual delights and the enterprise of molding them to the controlled articulation of a moral treatise? Robert Darnton, speaking of the novel everyone of Mirabeau's generation knew well, has argued that Rousseau's *Julie* taught its readers a new way of reading and a new way of relating to what they read. As we saw earlier, that new way of reading was the result of Rousseau's erasure of any clear boundary between fiction and reality, as he encouraged his readers to believe that his characters must actually have existed and must have written the letters we read. Summarizing what he sees as Rousseau's achievement, Darnton claims that "Rousseau even attempted to teach his readers how to read and, through reading, tried to touch their inner lives. . . . Rousseau threw himself into his works and expected the reader to do the same. He transformed the relation between writer and reader, between reader and text."[8]

Darnton's description of Rousseau as encouraging a different way of reading novels is important to *La Morale des sens*, not because Mirabeau was attempting something similar, but because the new benchmark of Rousseau's revolution brings into focus the real stakes of the very different choices made by Mirabeau. While the intensely sentimental dilemmas of Rousseau's characters generated alluring facsimiles of subjectivity that coaxed his readers to identify with them, Mirabeau remains adamantly at the surface of his characters and their reactions to the events they experience. The narrator and the cast of characters who make up his conquests, rivals, and accomplices embark on their adventures as pure sensoria situated entirely in the present and unencumbered by any conflicted subjectivity of reflection or anticipation linking them with past or future. Beginning always anew, they may be in dialogue with the characters around them but only in ways that highlight the decisiveness of action as opposed to the uncertainties of introspection.

The strangeness of Mirabeau's novelistic diction for a work published in 1781 becomes even more apparent when we compare it with Laclos' almost contemporaneous *Les Liaisons dangereuses*. Laclos caustically adapts the strategies of the epistolary novel perfected by Rousseau to the more somber lesson that all language, even the language of sentiment, relies on mediating sign systems that lend themselves equally to the cause of duplicity as to the cause of truth. *Les Liaisons dangereuses* mimics perfectly Rousseau's semiology of sincerity, but at the same time places its readers in a house of ever-shifting mirrors. When Laclos juxtaposes the radically different voices which Merteuil and Valmont adopt when writing to each other and when writing to their dupes, he makes clear that the diction of sentiment—once the hallmark of indubitable sincerity—has become a convention, a jargon, a snare set to catch the unwary. *Julie* offered its readers the inebriating pleasure of absorption within effusions of sentiment the reader longs to be true. *Les Liaisons dangereuses* forces its readers to understand, as they pass from one letter to another, that even the most eloquent tropes of passion offer no guarantee of the feelings they purport to express. Following Rousseau, yet contradicting *Julie*, Laclos substitutes distance for absorption and irony for identification.[9] Ironizing irony, Laclos makes even of Valmont's claims to act as the quintessential libertine deceiver a mask with which he finally deludes only himself.

Both *Julie* and *Les Liaisons dangereuses* help us to understand what is so different about Mirabeau's novel of pleasure. Consciously eschewing both absorption and irony, Mirabeau refuses the primacy of subjectivity and its premise that an effective narrative must provide the reader with access to the characters' ever-shifting eddies of self-conscious reflection. With a diction that opts for the description of action rather than the analysis of sentiment, Mirabeau challenges the Cartesian privileging of subjectivity as a higher distillation of experience that we find in both Rousseau and Laclos. It is this choice that makes it so difficult to read *La Morale des sens* today without mistaking its esthetics for a narrative primitivism, a naïve luxuriance in plot and action that missed the boat to the higher realm of conflicted subjectivity. It is a testimonial to the enduring dominance of the Cartesian legacy within the French novel, pace such experiments as *le nouveau roman* and *le chosisme*, that it remains so difficult to acknowledge the very different premises of a work like *La Morale des sens*.

In a way unlike Rousseau and Laclos, Mirabeau too asks his readers to read differently and to understand differently the world his novel evokes. If the implications of Mirabeau's esthetic choices are so easily misunderstood, it is because his different way of reading and understanding derives not from a Cartesian primacy of mind but from the materialist and sensationist tradition of Locke, La Mettrie, Condillac, and Helvétius. According to that materialist paradigm, the subjectivity that soars above experience and sense perception always carries with it heavy liabilities of delusion and self-deception. Limiting his diction to event and perception, Mirabeau favors surface over depth. To read is to interpret, but what Mirabeau asks his readers to interpret is the spectacle of unanticipated events and their power to engulf his characters in a constant process of fractured identities and displaced valances. Individuality in the world of Mirabeau's novel is grounded, not in consciousness and the sovereignty of subjectivity, but in the body as a site of the ever-changing sense perceptions generated by the random encounters that bring the novel's characters into contact with one another.

As a representation of experience *La Morale des sens* is the logbook of an expedition through a world of surfaces grasped always through the senses. As a narration of experience, it is intended to provide its reader with a lesson as well as an itinerary. Mirabeau begins his novel with a prefatory epistle to Babet. In it the narrator explains that his decision to write what we are about to read represents the continuation under another form of the kisses they shared in the past—but with an added premium: "Before I gave you kisses, and now I shall give you advice. I won't tell you again how charming you are or that you have no rival in wit and grace. That you know only too well. But what you have not yet acquired is that experience which comes only from a long study of the heart" (17–18). If the narrator offers his story to Babet on the eve of her marriage to a much older husband, it is because his story will provide her with an instructive example of how she might find her way in the world. This gift replacing their kisses of the past must, however, take the form not of abstract knowledge but of a story, a sequence of events and encounters, attractions and repulsions, that reveal the true tenor of life as an experience of the unexpected and the random.

In framing his novel this way, Mirabeau subscribes to the doctrine of exemplarity. He places himself within the long tradition that posits the story to be told as a simulacrum of experience allowing its readers to achieve a more complete understanding of the world they share with the narrator. Paradoxically, the first such episode narrated for Babet's instruction calls directly into question this traditional itinerary of understanding. The narrator begins his story with his arrival at the university. He focuses on how he, along with his new friend Belcour and their fellow students, are attempting to apply the scholar's skills of analysis and definition to the subject of love. "One day, when we were at table with two of his friends and with glasses raised like true Epicureans, . . . our conversation turned to love. What is love? Is it the coming together of two souls destined to love each other? Is it what gives life to all that breathes? Is it, suggested a third of a more scientific bent, a mechanical impulse of the senses that leads persons of one sex to unite with those of the other? After a host of definitions each clumsier than the last, we reached the point where none of us could agree" (20). Encompassing definitions that range from pure Rousseauian sentiment to a materialist mechanics of the senses, this attempt to articulate some essence of love ends up illustrating instead the irreducibility of experience to abstract definition. The only conclusion the narrator can draw from these attempts at scholastic classification is its irrelevance to life and its pleasures. "Giving up on resolving that question, I left them to argue, to distinguish, to split hairs, and to offer proofs for as long as they wanted. Drawn instead by my taste for pleasure, I thought only of how I might find it" (20). This parody of the search for a Platonic ideal comes to an abrupt close, and finds itself propelled in a very different direction when, putting an end to their disquisitions, Belcour's sister, the beautiful Églé, suddenly appears in their midst. The sight of her exquisite beauty puts an end to all concern with reflection as the narrator finds himself swept up by the power of what his senses perceive: "A brilliant carriage makes a noisy entrance and stops in the courtyard. Everyone runs to the window! . . . What do I see! My God, what an incarnation of charm! . . . It is the delightful Églé, my friend's sister, who was returning from convent school. What radiance . . . how beautiful I found her! How pitiful all our definitions now seemed to me! Pensive, alone in the midst of my friends, I see only her, I sense only her, I dream only of her" (20). The first rule of this novel's exemplarity is the upending of abstraction by the surprises and power of the unanticipated moment.[10]

Privileging event over introspection, Mirabeau's narrator asks the reader to understand this novel's exemplarity differently. "I will not be telling you what I said and what I did when I arrived home. I am not like those novelists who see forgetting to report their hero's slightest thought as stealing something from their reader" (57). Early on in his courtship of Églé, in a chapter titled "Novels," the narrator directly addresses the question of the genre's power to modify the reader's understanding of the world. The subject arises when the narrator happens one day to find Églé alone and, much to his surprise, quite distraught: "Trembling as I approached her, I ventured to ask what was bothering her. *She had just finished reading a novel* whose heroine, even though quite touched by her lover's suit, resolved to show him only cold indifference. That poor young man, driven to despair by such severity, signed on as a soldier and was killed in battle only a few days later" (34; italics mine). The intensity of Églé's reaction to that novel's melodramatic courtship suggests to the narrator a way he might turn to his advantage what he sees as a particularly feminine susceptibility to the novel's ambiguous border between reading and experience, fiction and reality. Resolved to enlist in his favor the effects her reading has on Églé, he supplies her with a different kind of novel, with works populated by "more ardent and daring heroes as well as by far less prudish heroines" (35). The narrator excludes from his reading list all novels on the model of Rousseau's *Julie* and its luxuriance in the tortured subjectivity of denial. If he opts instead for works that portray the pleasures of the senses, it is because he sees the Rousseauian novel of sentiment as little more than an artificially reheated version of seventeenth-century preciosity and its pastoral tales of chaste longing. "I was careful not to give her anything like *L'Astrée, Cyrus,* or *Cassandre,* whose sentimental heroes are always ready to die kneeling before their beloved, or any of those novels that keep the reader languishing in sadness through twelve volumes" (35).

Convinced that the proper reading program will "shorten my enterprise by six months" (35), the narrator postulates reading as an access to a freer and liberating alternative to experience. For Mirabeau, the right kind of novel functions like a prose version of the Epicurean Stoicism we saw at work in Boucher's paintings. As an esthetic object, it can offer its reader portraits of powerful sensual experiences yet, consisting only of words, it holds that pleasure safely at a distance and carries with it none of the dangers that accompany actual experience. As a representation of pleasure at a distance, the novel provides a way of trying on and trying out options that, as reality, would trigger only reluctance. As Mirabeau puts it, "Timidity can stop a young woman from giving their full weight to a lover's arguments. When read alone, their power is much greater" (35). The novel's power to reshape even tenaciously held principles also derives from its having on its side the combined suasion of what appears fashionable and expected. "The force of example, it is well known, is a torrent that drags us with it. That is why even what might first repulse us slowly finds its way to our hearts. . . . Fashion and custom are our tyrants: all that comes from them is good; all else is arbitrary" (35). This vision of the novel as a school for pleasure encourages the narrator to push his argument to an almost Swiftian extreme: the state, if it wishes to combat effectively the dangers of depopulation, should offer cash prizes to the right kind of libertine novelist. In a parody of the careful fiscal proposals elaborated by his economist father, Mirabeau *fils* suggests that, should the funding of such prizes place too heavy a burden on an already depleted treasury, there is an obvious solution: "A small tax should be levied on those mothers whose daughters are innocent and on those husbands whose wives are charming but chaste. They are after all the two groups for whom such novels could do the most good by correcting the prejudices of the first and the scruples of the second. Well executed, this project would provide a sure way to increase the birth rate" (34–35).

Chapter 22, the near midpoint of the novel, is the last to follow the loose intrigue centered on the triangle of Églé, the narrator, and his rival, Florval. That chapter also brings an abrupt shift in subject and diction. After a brief opening paragraph mocking the now definitively banished Florval, the narrator abandons that story and launches into a philosophical disquisition. Echoing La Mettrie and Helvétius, he articulates an Epicurean materialism proclaiming the Ovidian primacy of love's pleasures as the force that propels the metamorphoses of our world: "Love is the force that drives all things. It reproduces all, animates all, vivifies all. Men, plants, animals, elements—everything has been created to feel and to love. Differences of form imply none in sensation and in pleasure" (89). Mirabeau combines a Pascalian sense of humankind as poised between the infinitely great and the infinitely small with the Diderotian hypothesis that all things, inanimate and animate, are but different forms of a universal matter within the circle of being.[11] "Radiant and majestic globes, unfurling above us torrents of light; innumerable and sublime stars, whose impenetrable movements separate only to move back together, why should you be bodies devoid of feeling? . . . We imagine those parts of our bodies that are hard and solid to be insensitive, and we have wrongly concluded that all things similarly hard and solid must also be incapable of feeling" (90–91). Collapsing what are imagined as distinct natures and orders into one continuous whole, Mirabeau's argument becomes an epistemological challenge to the supremacy of consciousness as well as to any distinction between sentient life and unfeeling matter.[12] "We make judgments only by comparison, and we believe our judgments to be infallible. We are incapable of understanding that there exist beings organized in wholly different ways, and we dare to assume that we alone are capable of thought" (91). Once, the argument continues, we acknowledge the unity of all within a single movement of matter orchestrated by sensation and pleasure, the illusions of separateness and distinction yield to the recognition of life's single all-encompassing law: "Nature cries out to us: all must love. Such is the sacred law she imposes on all things" (91).

At this point the narrator's argument shifts from the cosmological to the historical. Were we to pass in review all the most illustrious conquerors of antiquity, the narrator claims, it would become clear that even their most sanguinary feats derive from the same universal impetus. History's conquerors become a repertory of those whose devotion to Mars served only to prepare their homage to Venus. "They hastened from victory's brilliant war chariot into the arms of their mistresses, and it was with them that their bolts of lightening found their one true mark" (91). Having completed this vast sweep of all that is and was, the narrator's diction of universals gives way to the specificity of personal pronouns, of an *I* and a *you* which establish the narrator's until now unidentified interlocutor as the real target toward whom this entire argument was directed: "But following on the heels of all those great men, can *I* dare speak to *you* of *myself*? *I* adore *you*, beautiful Églé; yes, *I* adore *you*" (91; italics mine). As amorous pleading replaces philosophical argument, this chapter—the only one with a double title, "A Pompous Declaration" and "Chaos Resolved"—has come full circle. As it completes its trajectory, it brings together in a way that mirrors its materialist premise what would seem to be two distinct registers. What began in the narrator's glee at Florval's departure provokes a grandiloquent tour of cosmic space and historical time that itself becomes a mock-heroic inflation of the battle he is now ready to win for Églé's favor. This elaborate juxtaposing of the personal with the universal is meant to exemplify how the chaos of the particular resolves itself within the coherence of the whole. At the same time, however, the universal is destined to become real not as an abstraction but as a movement of tangible bodies mobilized by pleasure and desire: "So as to give more feeling to my words, I took her in my arms and placed her hand over my heart.... She could feel it beating.... I watched her eyes, her beautiful eyes, come slowly alive with passion. She drew me to her without realizing it, pressing me to her breast.... Our tears began to flow and merged on our cheeks.... My God, what a moment!" (91–92).

This seriocomic conflation of the philosophical and the sensual, of universal law and the couple's pleasure, underlines the shape of Mirabeau's insurgency against the Cartesian model of novelistic exemplarity. The narrator not only refuses to share his thoughts with the reader, and mocks those novelists who do so, but the interaction between characters foregrounds not their individuality but their generality, their status as interchangeable instances of pleasure's universal law. In Chapter 46, while seducing the wife of a provincial visitor to Paris, Mirabeau's narrator offers a single answer to her questions as to who exactly he is: "Why should we need to know who we are? Between us, my dear soul, there are no names. There are only feelings" (175). Later still, on the brink of the novel's denouement, the narrator, disguised as a nun, finds himself wandering a convent corridor. At his approach, the curtains of one of the women's beds are parted. There ensues a scene of mistaken identity where the force of desire melts away the distinctions of both gender and individuality: "'Is that you, my dear friend [*ma chère amie*]?' 'Yes,' I answered in a whisper, 'it's me.' 'I thought I heard the Mother Superior!' 'No need to fear that,' I answered. With that, she took my hand and placed it on her breast. I gave her a passionate kiss which she returned even more passionately. The most libertine desire flowed through our veins. I wished only to prolong her error; but that beautiful woman for whom pleasure unshared was no longer pleasure soon sought to show me her gratitude" (186).

What emerges from Mirabeau's chaotic narrative is a new version of the novel that foregrounds the way all characters, whatever their station or gender, become examples of the Epicurean law that "all must love." The individuality of his characters derives from the fragility of their pretenses at being beyond the sway of pleasure's law—be it as modest virgins, faithful spouses, or chaste religious. Rather than a drama of tortured subjectivity, this novel offers its readers a comedy of the inevitable stumbles that await all who would set themselves apart from what they really are.

For the novelists of tragic subjectivity, the genre's bedrock is the option it offers the reader of dwelling within, understanding, and identifying with the singular virtue and insidious vice of characters who stand out from the world around them. For Mirabeau as Epicurean materialist, the novel's goal is to show how the world works, how a universal quest for pleasure tugs individuality toward universality. Structural rather than romantic, social rather than personal, this narrative stands outside what had become and would remain the mainstream of novelistic practice within an age seduced by the genre's illusion of living life vicariously. Given its eccentricity, *La Morale des sens* presents its reader with a singular challenge. Published in 1781, it offers few hints of any revolution to come. Mirabeau's characters relate to the conventions and assumptions of their society as illustrations rather than as insurgents. His decision to portray rather than to protest is not, however, a passive complicity with the status quo. What he offers his readers is a shift of perspective, a recasting of society's workings as they might be perceived through the prism of Epicurean materialism. The narrator's adventures delineate the vast geography of ruses and self-deceptions that preside over sentient bodies as they struggle within the constraints of an arbitrary social order.

At the most immediate level, that social order is composed of gendered bodies. While the distinction between male and female may be grounded in nature, its implications are everywhere ambiguous. Men, especially older men, appear, through wealth and property, to control the circulation of female bodies. The opening epistle to Babet defined the novel to follow as a counsel offered by the narrator to a former mistress as she prepares for a hardly enticing marriage. If he suggests she should accept the challenge of "warming the ice-cold heart of an old man," it is only because doing so will allow her "to ride in a brilliant coach more stunning for your charms than for its luxury. A superb palace will replace your hovel" (18). Similarly, one of Églé's first suitors will be "Old Bertigni." He will be eliminated as a rival not by the narrator but by what Églé learns from her friend, the bisexual Mlle To***. Speaking as a "friend concerned only with her education" (24), Mlle To***'s lesson is that, rather than spurning Bertigni, Églé should use him to develop the feminine wiles that will be so useful for her on a far broader field of play. "After all, an old fool like Bertigni whom you can lead around by the nose would be the perfect match for your first experiments after leaving the convent. Everyone has to start somewhere, and Bertigni is exactly what you need. Look at him as a doll on which you can practice your tricks for the men to come" (25). Mlle To*** distills a century of libertine doctrine into the angry retort with which she replies to Églé's naïve insistence that a woman should listen only to the heart: "The heart! What a joke! Do you realize what you are saying? A mistake like that can ruin a woman for life. With men, the best course is always to deceive them. . . . Of all the virtues, those which most lower us in their esteem are good faith and trust" (25). Anticipating the gender resentment Merteuil will articulate in letter 81 of *Les Liaisons dangereuses*, Mlle To*** concludes that, even within a de jure patriarchy, feminine charms can provoke a de facto reversal of oppression: "Beautiful and in the flower of age, your charms will avenge us all. We must teach our tyrants to fear us, to see in us their rivals and never their slaves" (26).

The power to challenge patriarchy is not limited to charming bodies. Women, especially within polite society and its *cercles*, can turn to their advantage the same force of fashion's reshaping of conduct which the narrator pointed to as he chose Églé's reading program. In chapter 30, "The Reigning Fashion," the narrator, now in Paris, frantically composes verse and prose pieces in the hope that they will gain him entry to the receptions given by the all-powerful and hardly charming Comtesse de Saint-O***. The Comtesse, presiding as the "Grand Inquisitor" over what is nothing less than a "literary Holy Office," issues unimpeachable judgments as to who will be the winners and who the losers in a universal "frenzy for being esteemed witty and smart" (120). As recognition and prestige prod masculine ambition no less tyrannically than beauty excites their senses, the Comtesse rules as the absolute arbiter of fashion's hierarchy. "This was the tribunal where reputations were made, academic honors distributed, and books appraised. It decided how long they would be in fashion and was pitiless in burning at the stake any rebellious writers who questioned its authority" (120).

Mirabeau's portrayal of relations between the sexes reconfigures an entire set of gender stereotypes inherited from the libertine tradition. Chapter 27 and its description of the final stages of the narrator's courtship of Églé is titled "The Siege and Taking of Égléopolis." In it, the narrator may show a predilection for those military metaphors so dear to the libertine novel: "She grabbed hold of a cushion and covered herself with it as though it were a bulwark meant to delay the enemy's advance. But, mistakenly defending herself against what was only a diversionary advance, she imprudently exposed her main fortress to attack" (110). At the same time, however, Mirabeau's Epicureanism recasts the dynamic of this apparent warfare. The postures of masculine aggression and feminine resistance as Mirabeau uses them point, not to some implacable hostility between male and female, but to a reciprocal and pleasurable yin and yang. Subsumed within the Epicurean trope of an all-encompassing continuity, the apparent opposites of attack and defense as well as of advance and retreat ultimately collapse into a larger cycle of life and change, of action and reaction. Mirabeau's narrative reshapes the libertine's gender war toward a celebration of pleasures shared and life continued.

> Ce couple heureux sur un grabat
> Se faisait tendrement la guerre,
> Et livrait alors un combat
> Qui ne dépeuple pas la terre. (40)
>
> [This happy couple on a mean bed
> Tenderly made war on one another,
> And engaged in that combat
> Which never depopulates the earth.]

Within society's geography of deception and repression no institution exercises a more extensive power than the Church. With women as its target of choice, it is not surprising that *La Morale des sens* begins with Églé's return home after her convent education and closes as the narrator helps his beloved Sophie to escape from a convent which has become her prison. Mirabeau's portrayal of the Church has little to do with theology or doctrine. The Church is present within this novel not as the mediator of any relation to the deity but as a force noxiously perverting nature, sexuality, and pleasure. Églé, the perfect product of her convent education, enters the scene as a repository of futilities: "Locked up in a convent from her earliest youth, she learned to sew, embroider, and babble. As she was to have a proper education, she also acquired the skills of singing in a choir, assembling scapulars, and saying her prayers" (21). Whatever the limits of the convent's curriculum, puberty signals its term: "Églé, so innocent as a girl, became less naïve with each passing day. Her eyes burned with a new fire. She became more spirited and lively. . . . She reached that age when nature awakens our instinct for pleasure, and when convent life becomes intolerable. Églé had to get out" (21). If a young woman's initiation to sexuality so often occurs as a seduction, it is because, as we saw in *Thérèse philosophe*, the Church has systematically indoctrinated women with its repressive construct of *pudeur* (from the Latin *pudere*, to be ashamed). Usually but imperfectly translated as "modesty," *pudeur*'s catechism of feminine shame compels the male posture of aggressive seduction: "The first task is to overcome her timidity, set aside her self-effacement, and finally overcome that dreadful monster known as *pudeur*" (100).

With men, the Church has a different strategy. During his stay in Paris, the narrator joins a religious community. He quickly discovers there how Gargantuan feasts become the preferred form of the orgy, how sexuality is sublimated into a massive overloading of oral pleasures: "I arrived in a large refectory where the aroma of a hundred exquisite dishes delighted my sense of smell. In an instant all the plates that covered the tables began to disappear and the thick ranks of bottles began to thin out. A second service followed the first; and it served only to prepare for a third. Finally there was a fourth. Delicious wines flowed like water. We drank, we ate, we discussed. Everyone got drunk while praising sobriety" (135). This jocular portrait of excess prepares a more serious indictment of the Church on two related counts. Awakening one day from the nap that inevitably follows those protracted feasts, the narrator finds himself reflecting on his situation: "I thought back to everything that had happened to me in this house of grace and prayer. I marveled at how many delights its austerity bestowed on those truly committed to their salvation, and with what profusion Providence spread its blessings on the chosen. All this while millions of the less fortunate who actually do useful work are deprived of even the bare essentials" (137). As the narrator passes from the refectory to the library, its shelves evoke the Church's role as the active proponent of the divisiveness and intolerance summarized in "the dreary compilations of these holy swashbucklers who spend their whole lives fighting over a single word" (138). Alongside those monuments to the disputations of theology, he finds another more militant genre: all those pious works meant to "incite the members of one flock to cut devoutly the throats of all others" (138). Reflecting on what the Church has accomplished from its suppression of early heresies through the more recent wars of religion, the narrator is moved to ironic admiration. "Yes, I cried out, I adore the sublime truths set forth in these books. Let us take up sword and fire against our friends, slit our brothers' throats, plunge daggers into the breasts of our sisters and mothers, crush infants still nursing: heaven has ordained it, and all is well. How can anyone doubt that these are God's orders as he has revealed them to those charged with executing his will on earth!" (138).

While social mores and religion pervert the lesson of the senses, Mirabeau's countryside—echoing both the sensuous pastoral of works like Boucher's *Bird Catchers* and the presocial simplicity of Rousseau's *Second Discourse*—

emerges as a last refuge of pleasure's truth. Chapter 23, "The New Arcadia," finds the narrator traveling to his uncle's wedding. On the way there he happens upon a group of young shepherds and shepherdesses. Refreshed as much by their absence of hypocrisy and mistrust as by "the pure country air," he can say of himself: "I felt my worries evaporate as my heart opened up to joy" (93). If the young country folk tending their flocks provide a lesson for the narrator, it is because they are untouched by urban or religious *pudeur:* "These young men and women gathered together with all the friendly simplicity that is characteristic of country life. Among them there was no trace of that timid mistrust and caution that young people learn so early in our cities. Even as children they learned to look at the opposite sex as objects of love rather than of fear" (94). Inspired by their simplicity, the narrator indulges in a reverie as to what these happy peasants tell us of a lost and more natural past: "Such innocence and candor! Thus is nature! What sublime simplicity! How much these people can teach us about the goodheartedness and frankness of the earliest centuries." (96)

Later, in chapter 28, "The Hermitage," Mirabeau pokes fun at how that Rousseauian trope has become a cultural cliché. Mocking the way such imaginary country folk function as a construct of urban nostalgia, he stages an encounter between citified aristocratic women and a dubious version of the hardy peasants such women delight in imagining as embodiments of a direct and uncomplicated response to the promptings of pleasure. In this episode, rather than real peasants, it is the narrator and his friend Lainville in disguise who have decided to take full advantage of that urban stereotype. Their plan is simple. They will appear to be hard at work in a grove where they know the Marquise de Saint-Albo*** and the Présidente de Vauxcoul must pass as they travel to a country pilgrimage. The premise of their ploy is that, once in the languid countryside, "The high born set aside their airs. The duchess can act like a shepherdess with no fear of embarrassing herself. And the Vestals, busy with other things, let the sacred flame go out . . . Moss, greenery, grottos, ferns—everything we need is there for our games of love" (112). As they hoped, when the Marquise sees the narrator she is immediately beguiled by his "large blue eyes . . . his muscles—and a promising air of health" (113). Needing no pretext more complicated than the weather, the Marquise moves things along quickly: "Turning to me, she asked: 'Would you be so kind as to take me to the closest spring? This heat is quite unbearable'" (113). As she removes one garment after another at the cool spring, it is the Marquise who leads the narrator as shy rustic in a duet that reverses the stereotypes of masculine aggression and feminine resistance. "Finally she drops all pretenses and displays the full beauty of her charms. The more I feign timidity and shyness, the more adeptly she charms me with contrary forces. Soon she is looking at me with the most inviting eyes, and she does her best to inspire in me the fire that consumes her blood" (114). As this scene draws to its obvious close, the narrator emphasizes how it calls into question the social constructs not only of gender but of rank: "She looks directly into my eyes and I no longer have the force to resist the torrent of voluptuousness they provoke in me. I sigh; we fall into each others arms; and the beautiful aristocrat becomes one with her Colin" (115). Mirabeau's country scenes are comic vignettes showing how Epicurean materialism enlists a truncated version of Rousseau's natural man in support of its claim that, once freed from the hypocrisies of society and religion, women and men dance only to the music of pleasure.

Mirabeau's programmatic treatment of such broad categories as gender, religion, and countryside is a corollary to what I have described as his structural vision. Offering a broad panorama of society from the perspective of militant Epicureanism, Mirabeau opts for a novel of types rather than of characters. His focus is on identity as a performance of already written social roles far more than on the idiosyncrasies of subjectivity. Even when a character is given a specific name, individuality disappears within type. Mlle To***, Églé's libertine tutor, may surprise the narrator, but only as a startling juxtaposition of stereotypes—an amalgam within a single person of the diverse roles available within society's repertory of the feminine: "Mlle To***, on the contrary, always seemed different, and she could appear to be any type because in fact she was none of them. Lively or indolent, a prude or a coquette, libertine or sanctimonious, her single person was an abbreviated gallery of her entire sex" (24). This same primacy of type and role extends to Mirabeau's male characters. Florval, the narrator's rival, is "a man of his century" because, like a weathercock responding to every breeze of fashion, he has "mastered all the jargon, all the mannerisms, the airs, the tone—and for all that he is no more than a fool. The capital and the provinces are full of such automatons!" (43). In terms of Florval's real talents, a less calcified society would have assigned him a very different role: "In another century, and without his rank and titles, Florval would have made an excellent tailor. His talents went no further than being able to choose the right pleat or sleeve and knowing how to wear clothes with grace and elegance" (44). For Mirabeau, society amounts to a colossal mismatch of type and station. Florval's absurdity is that of an entire society: "In creating us, nature gave to each different advantages. One man might live in the humblest circumstances, but his integrity, his impartiality, and his wisdom suit him to be the perfect judge. Another, who infuriates everyone with his babble, scandalizes honest citizens with his ostentation, and trails a legion of valets behind him, deserves at most to occupy the seat of his coachman" (44). Mirabeau's incongruous juxtapositions of type and role allow him to cut to the quick of the nearly *ancien* regime. Beneath the society of orders defined by birth there is a debilitating incompatibility between station and talent.

Mirabeau, as his political choices would make clear, was in no sense a revolutionary. What his novel does express, however, is the dilemma faced by the Epicurean sensibility within a society on the brink of revolution. Chapter 50, the last in the novel, is curiously titled "The Gallery." The *Grand Robert* offers three different meanings for that word, all of which Mirabeau brings into play. A gallery can be an architectural configuration, a space allotted to spectators, or a room for the display of statues. In its architectural sense, the gallery is a covered passageway, a narrow corridor much longer than it is wide. In this closing chapter that narrowness becomes a metaphor of the narrator's dilemma. The story he has told of his life, its concatenation of encounters and adventures, becomes for him a gallery less within space than within time: a gallery of situations recalled and figures remembered. "I like to remember far back into the past and count again my conquests" (189). As sweet as those conquests may have been, their retelling has revealed them to have all the shortcomings of the gallery: a narrowness of vision that is the product of a pervasive narcissism. Focused on the self as the single shared element within that gallery, the narrator's story leaves unaddressed the broader question of how he will be judged by the larger world. It is that question that brings into play the second sense of the gallery as a space designated for spectators: "But yet, when I tally up my glory, is there that much to be proud of? Couldn't just about anyone have come out as well as I did? Was anything I did so extraordinary that it astounded my century?" (189).

How, in a novel that rejects the esthetics of tragic subjectivity, can Mirabeau's narrator make any claim to significance as an individual? How can his story have any real meaning within a world populated only by types, by performers struggling with roles beyond the scope of their talents? This concern with a doubtful glory brings into play a tension between the narrator and the third sense of the gallery as an array of statues. If the characters punctuating his story are stereotypes lacking all substance, how can they testify to anything other than his own insignificance. Of Églé, he admits that "her portrait is that of a hundred thousand others, and my role was that of any man who was not a complete fool" (190). As for the Marquise de Saint-Albo***, he can only conclude that "if, from the thousands of scatterbrains in the capital, you were to chose one by chance, you would have the exact equivalent of the Marquise" (190). From the midst of this crisis there emerges a single redeeming figure: Sophie, the cloistered nun whom the narrator meets toward the end of his story in a chapter titled "Salvation." If the novel comes to a close with Sophie, it is because she alone stands outside the world as gallery: "But you, Sophie! I would not demean you by equating you with the statues in this gallery" (191). Unlike all the other characters we have met, she combines within her person "the advantages of the richest beauty . . . a noble, delicate, generous, and sublime soul," as well as "the finest and most cultivated mind" (191). Transfixed by her uniqueness, the narrator finds the answer to the question of his own value. No longer the conqueror of insignificant others, he finds himself instead in the new identity of a connoisseur able to recognize and respond to the paramount value that Sophie incarnates: "O Sophie! My true glory lies not in conquests, but in my having been able to appreciate you, to value you, and to sacrifice everything for you" (191).

 This new glory, and its shift from conquest to appreciation, occupies less than a dozen lines in the last paragraph of "The Gallery." Following that final chapter there is a conclusion of a single page which takes the reader to the time, set in the present, that follows Sophie's escape from her convent, her marriage to the narrator, and—with a collapsing of time similar to the endings of both *Le Guerrier philosophe* and *Thérèse philosophe*—the twenty years that the two have spent together in perfect Epicurean bliss: "With her, I have passed twenty years of delicious days, never knowing satiety, and in a perpetual ecstasy of happiness" (193). At one level, this ending might be read as an example of bringing closure to the narrator's list of conquests in the kind of resigned marriage and return to traditional values that we saw in La Morlière's *Angola*. Here, however, something different takes place. Mirabeau's description of what the narrator and Sophie find together—"delicious days . . . never knowing satiety . . . perpetual ecstasy"—points far more emphatically to Epicurean delight than to connubial serenity. There is, at the same time, a focus on one specific event as the foundation of their delight to come. As the narrator explains, it occurs when Sophie declares "with a courage I could only admire that she carried in her womb the fruit of our love—which flooded my soul with a trembling joy" (192). That joyous news, the beginning of their twenty years of Epicurean bliss, allows Mirabeau to end his novel with a final and corrective echo of Rousseau's *Julie*. This annunciation of a birth to come both refers to and reverses the moment when Julie d'Étange must tell Saint-Preux that she has miscarried and that, therefore, they have lost what was their final hope of compelling Julie's parents to accept their marriage.

La Morale des sens ends as it began in Mirabeau's refusal to write his novel as another version of tragic subjectivity. Consistently mocking the diction of sentimentality, he pillories the rhetoric of effusive virtue that had become the hallmark of the novel's new ethos of pleasure refused. From his Epicurean perspective, Mirabeau saw sentimentality's tortured epics of self-denial as nothing more than a grotesquely secular version of Christianity's denigration of the body and its senses. Placed in the post-Rousseauian context of 1781, Mirabeau's novel is more than a return to the clichés of *libertinage*. If *La Morale des sens* ends as it does, it is because Rousseau's seductive masterpiece had, during the two decades since its publication, created a community of readers blind to the Epicurean vision of life as an unpredictable and all-encompassing reciprocity of pleasures grasped and lost. Refusing to accommodate those readers who clamored for the dubious delights of vicarious moral and civic virtue, Mirabeau's chaotic tale recasts the Epicurean novel by turning it toward a panoramic unmasking of a society remade by the conventions and hypocrisies of sentimentality.

Mirabeau writes for a society that would soon extend its passion for heroic tragedy from the personal to the political. Struggling against that new moralism, he recasts the Epicureanism that before had drawn force from its alliance with the Stoic esthetic of distance and remove. *La Morale des sens* turns its Epicurean vision against sentimentality and its distorted Stoicism of abnegation. That new Stoicism, severed from any allegiance to the celebration of pleasure, consecrated an ethos of denial, purification, and heroism as its guiding values. Faced with that shift, Mirabeau warns his readers of how high a price one pays for the hubris of subordinating pleasure's chaotic sway to the austere dictates of virtue—be it moral or civic.

8. Theaters of Pleasure

Eighteenth-century France was smitten with theater. With our focus on the period's well-known novelists and philosophers, it is easy to overlook the fact that, as Henri d'Alméras put it, "the French have always loved theater, but never as much as during the eighteenth century."[1] For that claim to make sense, we must think of theater, not in terms of such august institutions as the Comédie-Française, but as an astoundingly widespread cultural practice, a form of conviviality and socializing that found its place at all levels of society. From rowdy pantomimes inspired by the public *foires* to private performances in the homes of the highest aristocracy, donning a costume and playing a role was an essential part of eighteenth-century social life. Theater, in this broader sense, served as a vehicle for educating the young, bettering one's station, enlivening a social event, and enacting the most intense sexual fantasies. Able to replace the tedium of identity with the mobility of performance, theater was singularly apt at opening up new vistas of pleasure.

This development was related to two intertwined phenomena. First, putting on a performance, play acting, spread beyond the official theater to become a pleasure enjoyed at all levels of society. Gone forever was any real concern with the Church's dark vision of the theater as a foyer of spiritual corruption. The Church might still refuse to bury actors in consecrated ground, and Rousseau would raise his voice against Voltaire's dream for a theater in Geneva, but the sharp debates on theater that punctuated the second half of the seventeenth century had lost their cultural edge. Second, as part of this proliferating theatricality, there emerged a new and still little-studied erotic theater that set out to stage explicit performances of sexual pleasure. Aristocrats as well as commoners crafted the theater's synthesis of bodies and words, action and dialogue, into extravagant displays of a sexuality whose pleasures and perils redefined the borders between actors and audience. Centered on eros and erections as always fleeting occasions of pleasure, this theater—extant in only the handful of sometimes dubious scenarios that have survived—uses living, speaking, and coupling bodies to stage an Epicurean subversion of rank and privilege that suited it well to the Revolution to come.[2]

Appreciating theater's centrality to Enlightenment culture is hampered by both broad and narrow preconceptions about the period. The wigs, extravagant dress, and careful protocols of court and *cercle* make it all too tempting to declare the whole of ancien régime society a protracted exercise in theater—a generality that drains theater of any specificity beyond the clichés of life-is-but-a-stage. From a different perspective, while eighteenth-century French theater has never, like the period's poetry, been pronounced utterly devoid of interest, it is too often bracketed by three predictable but questionable assumptions: first, that with tragedy in calcified subservience to Corneille and Racine, comedy alone was innovative (but only, it would seem, in the two figures of Marivaux and Beaumarchais); second, that the Enlightenment's shifting balance of social power found its most important theatrical manifestation in Diderot's *drame bourgeois* (even though he produced no stageable example of that genre); and third, that theater stagnated in France until the regenerative energy of the Revolution multiplied its venues and politicized its content. These assumptions draw their currency from the way each consolidates even broader stereotypes of eighteenth-century France: that it was a period that wanted to laugh but never to cry; that the *philosophes* championed bourgeois virtue as part of a program to discredit an irrelevant aristocracy; that only the period's culminating explosion breathed new life into its esthetic practices.

Each of these stereotypes contains some truth, but at the same time directs attention away from a crucial aspect of eighteenth-century theatrical life: the fact that writing and staging plays extended far beyond the period's public and state-sanctioned institutions. Historians of the theater as an institution understandably focus on the components and conflicts of that official theater. At the top of that hierarchy, there was the Comédie-Française, since 1680 the only institution authorized to perform tragedies as well as comedies. There was also the Comédie-Italienne, whose roots in the *commedia dell'arte* made it, after its return from exile in 1716, the venue of choice for the century's more boisterous comedies. In addition, there were the rougher, more popular troupes of mimes and acrobats associated with the left-bank Foire Saint-Germain, which ran from February through April and the right-bank Foire Saint-Laurent, which ran during July and August. Finally, there was musical theater: the Opéra as part of the Académie royale de musique and, until its merger in 1762 with the Comédie-Italienne, the Opéra-Comique.

To understand why the term *theatromania* was so often used to describe the passion for composing, staging, and acting in plays that manifested itself across all sectors of French society—bourgeois as well as aristocratic, provincial as well as Parisian—we must look beyond the institutions that set theater apart from everyday life and limited it to the exclusive domain of professional actors. Writing almost a century ago, Léo Claretie used the term *théâtre de société* to describe performances in which the roles were acted by amateurs before an audience made up of a fashionable public of invited guests. For Claretie, this society theater synthesized the salient traits of Enlightenment sociability: "The multiplication of receptions, the growing number of salons, circles, and coteries, the craze for mixing the sexes, for gallantry, for events where people could meet to exchange compliments, promises, smiles, and triumphs—all this contributed to the success of these private performances, which became a fashion, a fury, and a madness."[3] Closer to us, Martine de Rougemont, writing in 1988, describes the eighteenth century as possessed by what she calls *la folie abdéritaine*, a term derived from the Greek colony of Abdera whose inhabitants, as legend has it, were afflicted with a fever that led them to run frenetically through the streets reciting verses from Euripides. Preferring the term *théâtre d'amateurs* to *théâtre de société*, Rougemont nonetheless agrees that, for the eighteenth century, "it served as a fundamental underpinning of fashionable life and social exchange."[4]

Be it society theater or amateur theater, it was everywhere. In 1746 Mme de Pompadour, Louis XV's official mistress, transformed the gallery at Versailles leading to the Cabinet des Médailles into a performance space that came to be known as the Théâtre des Petits Cabinets. The first play presented there, to an audience of fourteen that included the king, was a performance of Molière's *Tartuffe*, with the décor by Boucher and with Mme de Pompadour herself in the role of Dorine. Five years later, the much larger theater she constructed at Belleville would provide the venue for Rousseau's *The Village Soothsayer* and for what he describes in his *Confessions* as his triumph of bringing tears to the eyes of all the ladies of the court seated around him.[5] Later in the century, Marie-Antoinette held regularly scheduled performances in the theater at Choisy. These carefully structured events consisted of a play from the classical repertoire at four in the afternoon, and, at eleven in the evening, the racier fare of popular farces in the *poissard* style (a term derived from the legend that the queen had fishmongers from Les Halles brought to Choisy to serve as voice coaches for the aristocratic guests to whom she assigned their roles). From 1780 to 1785 she herself, along with other members of the royal family, took roles in the plays she staged at the Trianon. Her most memorable performance, in August 1785, was as Rosine in Beaumarchais' *The Barber of Seville*. The king's brother, the Comte d'Artois, had two private theaters and the Prince de Conti insisted that, during his Monday receptions, the guests entertain themselves by performing comic sketches in which even the princes of the blood pulled out all the stops—the young Duc de Chartres being particularly well known for his clownish hamming.

With Versailles setting the tone for Paris, the century's theatromania took on even architectural implications. As Claretie perhaps overstates it, "In Paris, from the time of Louis XIV on, comedies were staged everywhere, at all levels of society—in chateaux, in private homes, be they of *grandes dames*, of magistrates, or of society figures. The plays were sometimes presented on improvised stages, but most often in a permanent performance space, since every stately home now had to have its own theater, a feature as indispensable as a salon" (18). Writing in 1770, Louis Petit de Bachaumont describes in his *Mémoires secrets* how the fashion of having one's own performance space had spread throughout French society: "The unbelievable rage for staging comedies grows more intense each day. In spite of the mockery heaped on our hamming bourgeois by the immortal author of *Métromania* [Alexis Piron's biting satire of a new bourgeois gentleman who suddenly discovers poetry and theater], there isn't a single magistrate who doesn't insist on having his own stage and his own troupe in his house."[6] As early as 1707 the lawyer and playwright Thomas-Simon Gueullette made a specialty of composing and staging *parades* for his aristocratic clients. These short pieces, modeled on the bawdy previews of the *théâtres de la foire* that coaxed the public into buying tickets, became delicious pretexts for hosts and guests, who had made up their faces and memorized a few lines, to launch into free-flowing improvisations on both comic and erotic scenarios. Putting on a play or staging a sketch became an enterprise that accommodated itself to every purse. In modest circumstances, rearranging the chairs, deploying a few screens, and rudimentary scenery could transform even a tight living room into a performance space. In rural settings, barns were transformed into temporary theaters. There are records of workmen's associations in Lyon and Strasbourg—and even of a Société des domestiques in Le Hâvre—which regularly staged plays.[7]

If anything, the period's theatromania only intensified as the century progressed. Describing French theater in 1732, the *Mercure de France* made the claim that "in Paris and the surrounding country estates, one can now count more than fifty well constructed and correctly decorated theaters where private groups offer themselves the pleasure of putting on plays."[8] Speaking of the same subject less than two decades later, Melchior Grimm claims in his *Correspondance littéraire* that by midcentury the number of theaters had more than tripled: "The taste for comedy and opera has become contagious. People put them on everywhere, and Paris can now boast as many as a hundred and sixty theater groups."[9] The effervescent atmosphere that followed the peace treaty of Aix-la-Chapelle in 1748 brought a proliferation of private theaters that drew such large numbers to the performances staged at private residences that the Comédie-Française took the step of officially protesting to court authorities what it saw as illegal infringements on its privileges.[10] Beginning in the 1780s, political polarization sparked an even more frenzied multiplication of theatrical spaces. As the Revolution approached and as the regime found itself unable to exercise any real control over theatrical presentations, each political faction set about staging its own parables of the world as it saw it.[11]

Dates and numbers may give some sense of the quantitative changes that marked the life of the theater, but they say little about why this polymorphous theatromania became so central to Enlightenment culture, about why some theater historians go so far as to speak of an "interpenetration of the theatrical and the social."[12] There is, as mentioned earlier, a simple but ultimately unsatisfying answer to that question. A succinct formulation of it can be found in a passage from Louis-François Métra's *Correspondance littéraire secrète* of 1787. The son of a wealthy Parisian merchant who acted as the court of Prussia's commercial agent in France, Métra the younger chose exile in Cologne after the Maupeou coup of the late 1770s. It was there that he began publishing his subscription-supported newsletter that offered regular reports on social trends and political gossip in France. Musing as to why the French so adore private theaters and amateur performances, Métra invokes the national stereotype according to which "all fashionable people are passable actors without their realizing it." As to why that is so, he suggests that "it may well be that, when they play a role in a comedy, they don't realize that they are simply doing what they always do. In their amateur theatrical groups and on the stages now to be found in every country house, they are repeating phrases committed to memory but never really felt."[13]

The problem with such facile irony is not only that it too hastily equates theatricality with hypocrisy, but that its Rousseauian moralism misrepresents the lucidity with which the period acknowledged theatricality as a component of the self-mastery essential to modern civility.[14] Preparing and performing a role, some actual experience of acting and stagecraft, were recognized as important components of the proper education of both young men and young women. Families of standing frequently hired professional actors and actresses to serve as tutors for their sons and daughters. These professionals carefully coached young women as they prepared the role whose performance at a private gathering, not unlike the modern-day debutant ball, was meant to give maximum *éclat* to their entry into adult society: "At the moment, professional actors and actresses earn huge sums for the lessons they give in private families. Acting is taken extremely seriously, and young girls begin their training quite young. . . . Their mothers, well aware of the importance this pleasure will have in their daughters' lives, would never neglect the preparation and study it demands, seeing some skill at acting as far more useful than any vain study of language or pointless knowledge of geography."[15] As for the education of young men, the Jesuits, the tutors to the elite, had long included student performances as an essential part of their curriculum. All across the constellation of their *lycées*, from its summit at Paris's Louis le Grand to the more modest institutions in the provinces, professional-level performances by the students of plays drawn from the Latin classics as well as from the repertory of seventeenth-century French classicism served as a capstone experience. An example of how demanding these performances could be can be found in the program for the end-of-the-year student presentation at the Jesuit *lycée* in Caen for 1724: "They presented, one after the other, the first acts from a French verse tragedy, from a ballet, from a Latin play, and from two comedies. They then did the second and third acts of each, ending with the fourth act of the ballet and finally a full-cast dance piece."[16]

For women and men, the role one happened to play during those events from adolescence often provided a nickname that remained with them for life. In his *Mémoires*, Jacques Fleury pokes fun at how this practice became a badge of social standing: "This fashion, now entrenched throughout high society, has made stage acting an essential part of the education given all our dandies and coquettes. There is not a single well-born girl or any woman of court or of high finance, who can't pick out in the street the Lisette or the Célimène from a rival theater group. The most distinguished men can be heard greeting one another by the name of the character they most enjoyed playing. Monsieur le duc is Crispin; Monsieur le marquis, Dorante; this austere magistrate Damis; this musketeer Purgon or Sganarelle."[17]

Learning to take the stage in a theatrical role was an ideal preparation for the culture of display that was so important to aristocratic conviviality. In *La Femme au dix-huitième siècle*, Edmond de Goncourt takes obvious delight in developing his argument that, for well-born women of the period, the preparation and execution of a role in such private performances provided all the inebriating pleasures of a seduction aimed not at a single target but at an entire audience.

> This was the great seduction that society theater had for a woman: it allowed her to become an actress. It put her on stage. It provided her the fun of rehearsals, the elation of being applauded. It put on her cheeks the garish make-up she wore so proudly, and then touched up for the supper that followed the performance even though she pretended she had removed it. It added to her life the illusion of comedy, the lie of the stage, the pleasures of the wings, all the giddiness that came with intoxicating the hearts and heads of her public.

Goncourt ends his description of how seriously these private performances were taken with a comment by the Prince de Ligne as to how surprisingly talented these amateurs could become: "As the Prince de Ligne insisted, 'Nearly a dozen of our high-society women act and sing far better than any actress I have ever seen in our best theaters.'"[18]

Amateur theatrics were also part of the rituals of the *cercle* or salon. While noted for the premium they placed on witty conversation, even those salons most famous for the spirited improvisation of their conviviality needed less-demanding activities as a ballast to their heady moments of brilliance and repartee. In some cases, that alternative took the form of gambling, the other great passion of the eighteenth century. But gambling had the disadvantage of breaking the group up into the smaller worlds of each separate table. Later, after the Revolution, that ballast would be provided by the multiplication of balls and their interludes of dancing as an ideal accompaniment to the conversational arts of the salon. During the eighteenth century, however, the most frequent practice was the staging of amateur theatrical performances. The presentation of scenes and even whole plays prepared by and for the group merged perfectly with the guiding ethos of the salon as an institution. Playing an already written role may have relaxed the demands of improvisation, but it opened up new dimensions of nuance, bodily display, and choreographed interaction that allowed each individual to shine before the group.[19]

As part of a discrete celebration or as an option within the protocols of the salon, this multifaceted society theater provided a coming together of reality and performance in such a way that each inflected the status of the other. For a theater historian like David Trott, the ease with which a drawing room or salon could be transformed into a performance space amounted to what he calls an "auto-reflexivity" between theater and society. From that perspective, Marivaux's choice in a play like *Le Jeu de l'amour et du hazard* (*The Game of Love and Chance*) to stage the action, not in Spain or on some exotic island, but in the home of the very contemporary Monsieur Orgon stands as an example of how life and theater had come together.[20] No matter how closely the professional stage might mimic actual social space, however, the appeal of these amateur theatrics derived from their power—whether a few short scenes or a full-fledged play—to conjure up a new dimension within the event of which they were a part. The homogeneous space of the salon gave way to a distinction between the stage as a miniworld of make-believe for the players and the still quotidian world of their audience. The performance might well be staged in a space which only moments before all had shared, but, once it began, it created a second world serving as an esthetic metaphor of its environs. Amateur theatrics introduced into the salon the new temporality of a staged world regulated by the clock of a performance distinct from its venue. This other world of the performance also brought with it a coherence—a satisfying progression from beginning, to middle, to end—whose power depended on its being distinct from the larger social interaction of which it was a part. The pleasure and magic of society theater were a function of what became possible within its synthesis of difference and similarity.

What kinds of plays made up the repertoire of these theaters of pleasure? The options were many, some predictable and others far less so. In terms of tone and structure, they ranged from short, fluid, and often highly improvisational sketches, *parades,* vaudevilles, and masquerades to the more demanding classics of the seventeenth century. The more ambitious society theaters also provided an alternative staging possibility for plays whose public performance had been delayed or forbidden by the often strict censorship exercised over professional theaters. Works such as Charles Collé's *La Partie de chasse de Henri IV* (The Hunting Party of Henri IV) and, far more famously, Beaumarchais' *The Marriage of Figaro* were performed in private theaters well before they were staged at public venues. Private theaters were also used for test runs of less controversial works before their official debut. Voltaire, for instance, frequently used both his own theater and the Duchesse de Maine's to stage working previews of his plays.[21] There was also the genre known as *proverbes:* more morally serious versions of the *parades* that were easy to learn and recite, often accompanied by songs, and brimming with bonhomie. Louis de Carmontelle and Mme de Genlis, both specialists in the genre, published collections of these short works composed for private performances.[22] If the lighter fare of *parades* and *proverbes* was an important part of the repertoire, it was because their brevity and wit made them a perfect match for the spirit of the salon. Unlike a classical tragedy or even a three-act comedy, their premium on improvisation also lent itself well to the period's predilection for surprises and humor that turned on the moment. In the introduction to his translation of some of these short pieces, Daniel Gerould underlines how "they avoid the architectonically predictable in favor of spontaneity and surprise. The microdramatist cuts through the circuitous unfoldings of full-scale playwriting into the bright, epigrammatic world of dreams, jokes, and aphorisms."[23]

Among the private theaters that developed over the course of the eighteenth century, there is one variant that stands out for the premium it placed on the staging of pleasure in a tangibly sexual form.[24] With titles like *Le Bordel, ou le Jeanfoutre puni* (The Brothel, or The Dickhead Punished), *Le Luxurieux* (The Rake), and *Les Putains cloîtrées* (The Cloistered Whores), the surviving examples of this erotic theater give ample evidence that their staging of sexuality included the body as well as language, physical actions as well as spoken exchanges. Its characters—women as well as men, amateurs as well as professionals—not only talked about sex, but performed sex. Opening even broader vistas, it frequently happened that, when these plays were performed, the actors appeared cross-dressed, men taking female roles and women male roles.

Understanding this erotic theater has suffered from the sometimes misleading titles of the few studies devoted to it. Writing in 1905, Gaston Capon and Robert Yve-Plessis referred to it as a "clandestine theater," a tradition continued by the title of "secret theater" (*Geheimtheater*) chosen by Arthur Rabenalt for his much broader study of 1963.[25] Yet, for the wealthy patrons and high society courtesans most often associated with these productions, they were far from clandestine. Sponsored, and often acted in, by aristocrats and the mistresses they lavishly kept, these erotic performances were staged as gifts, as displays of wealth and daring intended to impress not only the recipient but the wider circle of peers and rivals who composed audience and cast.

Given their tone and content, it is not surprising that, in spite of their importance, these theaters of pleasure have received scant attention even from those who argue most forcefully for the inseparability of the eighteenth century's amateur theatrics and the larger culture. Martine de Rougemont declares amateur theater to be a "connective tissue" for the period: "Theatrical life in eighteenth-century France was built on the tight connective tissue of private performances. They were available to savants and illiterates, to rich and poor, in a way that no commercial enterprise or artistic production could hope to match." Yet, she dismisses this erotic theater as a representative only of an embarrassingly universal proclivity for which some excuse must be found: "Purely pornographic events can be found in almost all periods . . . but during the eighteenth century they were never as frequent and notorious as they are today."[26]

Her approach to the genre continues a tradition, going back to the beginnings of modern literary criticism, of dismissive discomfort with the unbridled sexuality of these works. In his 1887 study of the eighteenth century's hypersentimental genre known as *la comédie larmoyante,* Gustave Lanson alludes in passing to high society's taste for erotic theater as an anomalous example of an infatuation with vulgarity gone haywire:

> Filth overflows . . . and provides the only comic element. Such a profusion of coarseness is distressing, and one cannot help but wonder how so polite and refined a society could be amused by jokes and double entendres which today would not amuse even the most jaded of our music-hall regulars. Perhaps the attraction was that they offered the players and spectators some momentary relief from the weighty burden of manners and good taste. Fed up with elegance, propriety, and wit, from time to time they needed to slum. Acting like common people wasn't enough; they became rabble drunk on stupidity and obscenity.[27]

Closer to our time, Jacques Truchet, in his introduction to the Pléiade's 1974 anthology of eighteenth-century French theater, replaces Lanson's indignation with a more debonair condescension. In his description of what he classifies as a minor form at the antipodes of "high comedy," Truchet underlines its use of "sustained bawdiness, ribald stories, and an affected immorality" to justify his conclusion that "the essential was that these little plays be amusing. And they are that, *but in very small doses* [italics mine]."[28]

It would be misleading to claim that Victorian prudery and academic pomposity alone explain the paucity of attention accorded this theater. As a cultural phenomenon, these sexual farces left only ambiguous traces. Some scenarios did find their way into print, but always as clandestine publications produced by shadowy publishers more interested in brisk sales than in preserving any authentic trace of the works' earlier status as staged performances.[29] One of the most intriguing examples of the genre, a three-act comedy with the paradoxical yet portentous title of *L'Esprit des mœurs au XVIIIe siècle, ou la petite maison* (The Spirit of Manners in the Eighteenth Century, or The Little House), and usually attributed to Simon-Pierre Mérard de Saint Just, begins with an *avertissement* that insists on the dual status, and considerable differences, between the work as a script to be read and as a scenario to be performed. Large portions of the dialogues, the author-posing-as-editor maintains, should be eliminated in any actual performance of the play and replaced by sexual pirouettes accompanied only by appropriate sound effects. In addition to these ambiguous published scripts, there are also, in memoirs and correspondences of the period by Collé, Bachaumont, and others, occasional references to specific performances: where they took place, the architecture of the theater, and who was in attendance. Often, however, these reports have the ring of dubious confections concocted in the service of some larger polemic. With slightly more objectivity, there are also references in police reports of the period to instances when the authorities intervened to shut down a performance and make arrests.[30] Rarely, however, do we have for these performances information allowing the cross-corroboration of facts with which the historian would be comfortable.

We do know more about where these performances were staged. On the one hand, they were often part of the rituals associated with that eminently eighteenth-century space known as *la petite maison:* a private house like Merteuil's located away from one's official residence and devoted to the enjoyment of private pleasures. Often, in spite of the *petite,* they were large, richly appointed premises used for late-night suppers, sexual dalliances, gambling, and other forms of amusement. For a period when social standing and prestige were a function of lavishness and ostentation, it is not surprising that *la petite maison,* which may have begun as a secret and strictly private space, often became a locus of display—at least for those of a certain standing. In a society infatuated with theatrical performances, it was only logical that the most prestigious *petites maisons* would include their own performance space. The Comte de Clermont used the theater that was part of his *petite maison* to stage a wide variety of erotic farces. Men from the highest ranks of society, as well as women wearing discreet masks, arrived there in carriages temporarily stripped of their family crests and accompanied by servants who wore only anonymous gray *livrées.* When Clermont staged Pierre Laujon's *La Gageure des trois commères* (The Three Gossips' Bet) in November 1754, not only did his guests make up the cast, but all the players were assigned roles that were the opposite of their sex: the comte's mistress, Mlle Le Duc, played the male role of Cassandre while Laujon himself played Mme Jean-Broche, and Monsieur de Bressay took the role of Mme Cassandre.[31]

The historical figure most frequently associated with the *petite maison* and its signature genre of erotic comedy was Philippe, Duc d'Orléans (1725–81). The grandson of the regent and the father of the ill-fated Philippe-Égalité, who would be guillotined in 1793, his family tree was itself a résumé of the century's turbulent transformations. As a young man, Philippe, then Duc de Chartres, made his first foray into erotic theater when his guests were invited to join hired courtesans in performances that followed late-night suppers at the property he had purchased on the rue Cadet in the faubourg Montmartre. After his father's death in 1752, when he inherited both the Orléans title and the family's vast properties, his theatrical enterprises began in earnest. He commissioned the construction of a large state-of-the-art theater at Bagnolet and hired Charles Collé as his private playwright, who was expected to turn out scripts and musical scores specially tailored for the actors who would make up the cast of any given production. A few years later, in addition to his theater spaces in the rue Cadet and at Bagnolet, the duke purchased another *petite maison* in the faubourg Saint-Martin, where he constructed yet a third theater.[32] This constellation of private performance spaces formed a kind of circuit where his mistress, Mlle Gaussin, herself an actress at the Comédie-Française, revealed the full extent of her talents in such Collé farces as *Isabelle précepteur* (Isabelle the Tutor) and *Léandre étalon* (Leander the Stallion), works distinctly different from the tragedies in which she starred at the Comédie-Française.[33]

The other venue associated with erotic theater was, unsurprisingly, the up-market brothel. At her establishment in the rue de Clichy, a certain Mme Lacroix (or Delacroix) made the genre her specialty. Well attuned to the theatrical tastes of her wealthy clientele, she announced with much fanfare that, for New Year's day of 1741, her theater would present a one-act verse ballet baldly titled *L'Art de foutre, ou Paris foutant* (The Art of Fucking, or Paris Fucking). The scenario was written by Baculard d'Arnaud and the music done to the score of André Campra's *L'Europe galante*. The production's commercial success was assured by the promise that each of the female roles would be played by one of Paris's most renowned prostitutes—Mlles Petite jeune, Lesueur, Rosette, Mouton, and Lempereur—with each performing the specialty for which she was most renowned. *The Art of Fucking* even included as its penultimate scene a police raid which is happily aborted when a group of musketeers, themselves faithful customers, arrive with swords drawn and send the police packing. Unfortunately for Mme Lacroix, actual events took a different turn. The sensation provoked by the performance as well as the clandestine publication of Arnaud's scenario led to the author's arrest and to Mme Lacroix's consignment to Bicêtre, the Paris penal hospital for prostitutes who had become too notorious.[34]

Lacroix's twist of using Paris's best-known courtesans as her leading ladies underlines the complex relations between eighteenth-century theater and prostitution.[35] On the one hand, as had long been the case, actresses (and actors) were automatically excommunicated from the Church. Excluded from the sacraments, actresses could not marry, nor have their children baptized, nor be buried in consecrated ground. On the other hand, a woman's official admission to the company of the Comédie-Française or to the Opéra royale provided her with a juridical autonomy that was otherwise unavailable to women. In terms of civil law, a woman remained under the tutelage and control of her parents until, upon her marriage, their authority passed to her husband. When, however, an unmarried woman was formally admitted to a recognized theater or opera company she was, as it were, emancipated: even though unmarried, her parents no longer had a claim to her income and could not exercise over her personal and sexual life the control afforded by the ancien régime's institution of the *lettre de cachet*, so easily available to the parents of wayward children. Given the independence available to women officially recognized as performing artists, that status became a safe haven. For a woman who made her living through some form of prostitution, the good offices of a well-connected protector could be used to obtain the lucrative independence of formal admission to such companies. Margot, the central character of Fougeret de Monbron's *Margot la ravaudeuse* (Margot the Mender), reaches the apex of her social ascension from street urchin to independent woman of means when the combined efforts of her wily pimp and a generous protector result in her appointment as a dancer at the Paris Opéra.

Erotic theater was a bridge between the theatrical world and that of prostitution. For the plays he staged in his first *petite maison* in the rue Cadet, the Duc d'Orléans regularly recruited, as we saw, bevies of prostitutes. The immensely wealthy tax farmer Le Riche de la Pouplinière had no scruple about building in the rue de Clichy a private theater where his wife, the well-known actress Mlle Deshayes, starred in erotic farces written by Crébillon but which her husband liked to claim he himself had composed. Established actors and actresses did not hesitate to take advantage of the lucrative opportunities afforded by the fashion of erotic theater. In 1752, Mlle Duménil, a member of the Comédie-Française, had a *petite maison* built in the rue Blanche. A short time later, her colleague, the actor and playwright Grandval, also of the Comédie-Française, purchased a separate property on the adjacent rue Royale. After connecting the two, they constructed there a small private theater where, for more than a quarter of a century, they staged all of Grandval's most successful farces—works with titles like *L'Eunuque, ou la*

Fidèle infidélité (The Eunuch, or The Faithful Infidelity), *La Médicine de Cythère* (Cythera's Medicine), and *Sirop-au-cul, ou l'heureuse deliverance* (Syrup-up-the-Ass, or The Happy Deliverance), the last a work Grandval categorized as a *tragédie héroï-merdifique*. Similarly, but on an even grander scale, Mlle Guimard, a star dancer in the Académie royale de musique, tapped the resources of her lovers, the tax farmer Benjamin de la Borde and the Prince de Soubise, to finance the construction of a private theater on the Chaussée-d'Antin. Designed by the architect Claude-Nicolas Ledoux, with wall panels by Fragonard (who also painted a well-known portrait of Guimard), it could accommodate up to five hundred guests. Splendidly appointed, its loges, with red taffeta wall coverings, included elaborate grillwork that insured the spectators' privacy. Adjacent to the theater there was a winter garden carefully laid out so as to provide discreet nooks for the intimate conversations expected to occur there during intermissions.

Even in its rich architectural detail, Mlle Guimard's theater is an eloquent illustration of how the eighteenth century redefined the pleasures—and dangers—of the theater. Only a century earlier, during the bitter quarrel of the 1660s over *Tartuffe* and theater as an institution, the Jansenist moralist Pierre Nicole argued that plays and actors should have no place whatsoever in a truly Christian society. He asked his readers to think carefully about just what it meant to produce on stage before an audience, as do actors and actresses in their theaters, convincing representations of individuals caught up in the strongest passions: "It is a craft whose goal is to entertain others. In it, men and women act out the passions of hatred, anger, ambition, vengeance, and, above all, love. They must be able to express them as naturally and as forcefully as possible; and they cannot do so unless they provoke them in themselves, unless they impress them on their souls so they can then express them in gestures and words. . . . In this sense, comedy is by its very nature a school for vice."[36] A century later, Paris's new theaters of pleasure stood Nicole's warning on its head. What for the dour Jansenist made acting an occasion of sin so obvious that all forms of theater should be banned had became the drawing card that attracted sophisticated audiences to performances that prided themselves on their promise to excite the very contagion of desire that Nicole denounced. Profoundly Epicurean in spirit, this new erotic theater dissolved the distinctions between actor and prostitute, and often between actor and audience, within the universal solvent of pleasure. It is in this sense that Raoul de Vèze is right to insist that "one cannot really understand the eighteenth century and its love for pleasure without a knowledge of this literature which, although minor, is a joy to discover."³⁷

But what were these plays I am referring to as erotic theater? Given its diversity of venues and ambitions, there is no simple answer to that question. At the most general level, all surviving examples of the genre, both comic and serious, highlight the force of sexuality and the hypocrisy of its repression in the name of social norms. Rather, however, than trying to define this theater of pleasure in the abstract, it is more helpful and more enjoyable to look briefly at specific plays that, taken together, give a sense of the genre's capacious parameters.³⁸

One of its tamest forms is the comic parody of classical seventeenth-century tragedy where the central dilemma is a question of honor raised not by a conflict of princely duties but by sexual impotence. Charles Collé's *Alphonse l'Impuissant* (Alphonse the Impotent) of 1737 is a one-act play in which the central character, King Alphonse of Portugal, must either produce an heir within a year or lose his throne to the rebellious prince Alvarès.³⁹ Impotent since birth, Alphonse's solution is to order his prime minister, Alcimadure, to father a child with Queen Léonore. Two unfortunate facts, however, compromise that plan. Unbeknownst to the King, Alcimadure was kidnapped as a child and taken to Byzantium, where, before his rescue, he was castrated in preparation for service in the Sultan's harem. The even greater problem, and the motor of the play's comedy, is Queen Léonore's unfaltering commitment to marital fidelity. Just as Chimène in Corneille's *Le Cid* could never consent to marry the man who has killed her father, Queen Léonore will never agree to conceive a child by someone who is not her husband. It is her Corneillian severity as to who might share her bed that provokes Alphonse's singular lament of his tragic destiny:

Mais admire avec moi la rigueur du destin,
Jusqu'où va la fureur de son aveugle rage:
Dans mon royaume entier ma femme est seule sage,
C'est pour moi seul qu'est fait un semblable Malheur,
Et les autres époux sont comblés de bonheur. (116)

[But marvel with me at destiny's rigor,
How far it pushes the fury of its blind rage.

In the whole of my kingdom my wife alone is faithful,
It is to me alone that such a calamity has fallen,
And all other husbands are crowned with good fortune.]

In a similar vein, Alcimadure's attempt to cajole the Queen into a more accommodating posture toward the stand-in he plans to substitute for himself if he is to fulfill the King's order produces a comic parody of royal agency and its recourse to appropriate surrogates:

> Les rois ne peuvent pas tout faire par eux-mêmes,
> Tout se rapporte au roi sans qu'il en soit l'auteur:
> Il traite de la paix par un ambassadeur,
> C'est par ses généraux qu'il gagne des batailles;
> . . . .
> Tout se fait en son nom, et tout tourne à sa gloire;
> L'histoire de son temps devient sa propre histoire;
> Ainsi les héritiers que vous aurez sans lui,
> Sont à lui comme à vous, quoiqu'ils viennent d'autrui. (119–20)

> [Kings cannot do all by themselves,
> All flows from the king even when he is not its author.
> He negotiates peace through an ambassador,
> It is through his generals that he wins battles;
> . . . .
> All is done in his name, and all redounds to his glory.
> The history of his times is the history of him.
> Thus the heirs you will provide him without him,
> Are as much his as yours, even though they come from someone else.]

Involving only elevated personages who struggle with an impotence that burlesques their tragic diction, *Alphonse the Impotent* is a relatively restrained example of the genre. Distinctly different in setting and tone, there is also the erotic comedy set not in a royal palace but in a brothel. One of the best constructed examples of that category is Grandval *père*'s *L'Appareilleuse* (The Lady Brothel Keeper) of 1740.[40] Set not only in a *maison de passe* but in a distinctly down-market fifth-floor-rear-apartment brothel, the play's characters—Mme Amboisel as *l'appareilleuse* who runs the establishment, Manon as her recently arrived fourteen-year-old niece, Mme Merlet as the *revendeuse à la toilette* or used-clothing seller who expects a healthy commission for recruiting Marianne—provided delicious challenges for the aristocratic guests who performed these roles before an audience of their peers. The brothel's customers—Monsieur Gripigni, a low-level tax collector, and Monsieur Friponneau, a minor court officer—open the gates wide for the parody of bourgeois pretensions. A one-act plan consisting of ten rapidly moving scenes, it reads like a comic documentary on the protocols of low-level prostitution in eighteenth-century Paris. The play opens with the dissatisfied Gripigni complaining that the last partner Mme Amboisel provided him may have had a pretty face, but she was "devilishly spacious." As luck would have it, the recent arrival of Amboisel's niece Manon will provide the perfect remedy—but her as yet untested charms will be costly. After Amboisel and her customer negotiate a final price of thirty louis, the audience is treated to the aunt's very precise counsels as to how her niece must conduct herself with the clients she will meet in her new profession. In scene 4, Mme Merlet, the *revendeuse*, steers to Amboisel's establishment the young Marianne, who has recently arrived in Paris with hopes of finding work with a proper family as a servant girl. When Amboisel warns her that "servants have a miserable life, and earn nothing" (143), Marianne replies that she has no other alternative because, as she puts it, "My father and mother never made me learn to do anything." That lament sets up Amboisel's untranslatable play on the different senses of the verb *faire* in French: "Est-ce que vous ne savez pas faire ce qu'ils ont fait quand ils vous ont faite?" (Don't you know how to do what they did when they made you?) (144). The answer to that question, it turns out, has to be yes—as Amboisel's careful inspection of Marianne's breasts, teeth, and sex reveals that she has already been the mother of twins.

Mme Amboisel makes it clear to Manon and Marianne that the real payoff in their new profession is not so much the easy money they will make, but Amboisel's promise that "when you've saved up a good sum, I'll arrange your marriage to a big man like them, and he'll make a big woman of you" (*une grosse madame*, ambiguously meaning rich, fat, and pregnant) (138). Moving from the recruitment of new talent to the mechanics of the brothel's everyday operation, scene 7 introduces the muscular La Jeunesse. A pimp whose job is to keep order, he efficiently intimidates Friponneau, a customer who threatens to sue Amboisel because Goton, a supposedly virginal member of her staff, has given him such a bad case of the pox that he will have to undergo a fifty-day mercury treatment. The play closes when Manon's cries of alarm at the demands of her new profession attract the attention of the *commissaire*, Monsieur Coquinon, who threatens to arrest everyone. That danger is quickly eluded when Amboisel offers him two louis (which represent half his monthly emolument) and her promise that tomorrow he will sample the charms of Manon. In little more than twenty pages of witty and fast-moving dialogue, this play deploys its handful of stereotypes in a way that lays bare and makes light of the personnel, rituals, and dangers of the capital's vast network of prostitution.

The brothel, though hardly the fifth-floor-rear variety, also serves as a setting that comically brings together characters of very different social standings. *The Brothel, or the Dickhead Punished* of 1732, usually attributed to the Comte de Caylus, is a three-act comedy set in the exclusive brothel run by Mme Dru. Its plot centers on how the well-born Valère, with the help of his ever resourceful valet Valentin, sets out to debauch both his good friend, the virtuous Clitandre, and Clitandre's beloved, the innocent Isabelle, by luring them to the brothel. Valère's plan is to distract Clitandre with the ladies he has hired for his friend's entertainment while he takes advantage of the situation to seduce Isabelle. Like *The Lady Brothel Keeper*, *The Brothel* opens with the arrival at Mme Dru's of a young woman, Desprez, who is looking for work. Her colorful story of how she managed her trip from Lyon, thanks to a paid indiscretion on the coach and then letting herself be picked up on the street the night before, is interrupted when Valentin arrives to arrange the details of the gala evening Valère wants to prepare for Clitandre and Isabelle.

What distinguishes *The Brothel* from *The Lady Brothel Keeper* is its on-stage sexual activity. Scene 9 of act 1 stages the encounter between the three ladies of the house, Tonton, La Poirier, and Fanchon—to each of whom Valère promises an extra louis if they seduce Clitandre—as they manage to get Clitandre to the point where he sports a full and impressive erection. When his loyalty to Isabelle stops him from going any further, the scene shifts to the kitchen where each of the three women, frustrated by their recalcitrant customer whom they qualify as nothing more than a *bande-à-l'aise* (limp dick), finds impressive relief with the ever-accommodating Valentin. The valet's most ardent exploits, however, are reserved for Desprez as the only character who corresponds to his *idéal féminin:* a woman his master has not yet had.

The arrival of Isabelle, tricked into coming to the brothel by a letter Valère has forged over Clitandre's signature, initiates the comedy of her slowly dawning realization as to where she actually is. Looking her over, Tonton greets Isabelle with, "But what have we got here? A nicely decked out young lady, and as proper as can be. She looks like a bit of a novice, but they're the ones who have the clap up to the gills!" (52). Offended as much by Isabelle's polite diction as by her obvious ignorance as to where she is, Tonton corrects both: "If you were chatting up a customer, I could excuse your talking the way you do. But with me, it's as though you were mocking me. . . . Mme Dru is Paris's number one madame, so get it into your head that you are in a whorehouse" (53–54). All ends happily when the police, led by an unbribeable *commissaire*, enter the premises. After first making sure that Clitandre and Isabelle are discreetly evacuated from the scene, he states his mission: "Virtue is safe. Let us now root out vice" (67). According to that agenda, Mme Dru and Tonton (who, it turns out, is already well known to the police under the name "Grosse Margot") are sent to Bicêtre. The villainous Valère is dispatched to the prison of For-l'Évêque, but the other women and the always-lucky Valentin are let go with a warning.

When performed in a *petite maison*, brothel plays were a favorite for the way they insured the immediately comic element of watching one's well-born friends stretching their talents as they acted the parts of a wily madame, a sashaying whore, or a duped customer. But there was also a darker side to the brothel as setting: its close association with gonorrhea and syphilis. While the passing references to mercury treatments and "clap attics" in *The Lady Brothel Keeper* and *The Brothel* hardly compromise their comic lightness, *The Rake* of 1735 by Marc-Antoine Legrand (also published under the titles *Le Libertin puni* [The Libertine Punished] and *Étrennes libertines* [Libertine Gifts]) lends a very different tone to the brothel. A dark and misogynistic work, Legrand's play does not use the brothel as its setting—the entire play takes place in the *hôtel particulier* shared by the licentious Valère and his prudish sister Isabelle—but as the place where Valère spends all his time away from home and to which he constantly dispatches his servant for news of the latest arrivals. The plot turns on two marriages: the faked ceremony with which Valère hopes to seduce the apparently virginal Agnès and the long-postponed marriage between Isabelle and her chaste suitor, the upright lawyer Branlard. These two marriages collide when, with an almost Schnitzlerian turn, we discover, just as Valère quickly consummates his charade marriage, that Branlard has postponed his marriage to Isabelle because he is still recovering from the severe case of syphilis he contracted from none other than Agnès. In the play's closing scene Valère declares his horrifying vision of the sickness he can already feel in his veins:

> Je vois déjà, je vois cette déesse immonde
> Que l'enfer enfanta pour tourmenter le monde.
> La pâleur l'accompagne, et ses avant-coureurs
> Viennent me préparer à toutes ses fureurs. (96)

> [I see it already, I see that vile goddess
> Spawned by hell to torment the world.
> Enfeeblement accompanies her, and her symptoms
> Are already preparing me for the full brunt of her furies.]

Furious with self-pity, his misogyny and bad faith prompt him to invite Branlard to join him in the war of vengeance he would wage against all women:

> Vengeons-nous, cher Branlard, au milieu de nos maux;
> Allons nous signaler par des exploits nouveaux;
> Ne perdons point de temps, courons, de belle en belle,
> Promener le présent d'une beauté cruelle.
> Nous pouvons desormais, sans courir de hasard,
> De ce fatal présent en tous lieux faire part. (96)

> [Let us avenge ourselves, my dear Jack Off, in the midst of our woes.
> Let us blaze a trail of new exploits.
> Without wasting a moment, let us hurry from belle to belle,
> Sharing the gift that one cruel beauty has given us.
> From now on, without running any risk, we shall
> Bestow this fatal gift on every house we enter.]

One of the most ambitious examples of erotic theater, in some ways the masterpiece of the genre, is Mérard de Saint-Just's *The Spirit of Manners in the Eighteenth Century, or The Little House; Proverb in Two Acts*.[41] With a title that evokes Montesquieu's *De l'esprit des lois* of 1748, the term *esprit* has the sense of a concentrate, the very essence of the thing; while *mœurs* (manners) refers to the social customs or lifestyle of the period. The play's title, bringing together a subject of philosophical reflection with a generic place name, is provocatively ambiguous. Is *la petite maison* simply an alternative, less abstract title? Or is that second title meant to establish the *petite maison* as a larger symbol suggesting that the current century has transformed the entire nation into a locus of predatory delectation for a certain class? First published in 1789, this play is part of Mérard's fictitious *Mémoires de la marquise de Palmarèze*. The play's setting is the luxuriously appointed *petite maison* of the judge, the Président de Guibraville, and its action is precisely situated during the afternoon and evening of June 25, 1789. The play opens with a scene not of cavorting masters but of tired servants. Discreto, the Président's major domo, explains to Justine, the Marquise's chambermaid, that times have changed and that people like the Président no longer even pretend to keep their private hideaways out of public view: "Nowadays a *petite maison* is just one more indiscretion. Everybody knows who owns it, what goes on there, and which ladies are invited—just like any other house" (295).

The Spirit of Manners is preceded by an *avertissement* which Mérard uses to place his work in the best of company: "The real title we should have given to this little comedy, as will be clear from reading it, is *The Day of Madness* [*La Folle Journée* was the subtitle of Beaumarchais's *The Marriage of Figaro*], but we thought it best to put something else on the first page so as to avoid any confusion with the entertaining comedy which was such a huge theatrical success" (289). Mérard goes on to insist that, when staging this play, the director should feel free to choose names for the characters that reflect the latest scandals. He then offers, as did Beaumarchais in the prefatory material to *The Marriage of Figaro*, an analytic précis of each character that blends description with mordant satire. The host, the Président de Guibraville, has a courtroom style all his own: "the best shady dealer in Paris and the sharpest at getting you out of a jam. He may never have read a law book, but he has all the haughtiness and pedantic conceit of a man of the courts who knows nothing, but is convinced he will prevail by pure show" (290). Representing the more venerable nobility of the sword, the Chevalier de Verville is described as someone who "when a knight of Malta pushed moral depravity to its limits" and who benefits from privileges he has in no way earned: "He got his start at court with all the advantages of a charming face, which today is a bit worn. His name opens every door, but there is no substance to him" (290). Rounding out this social typography of the powerful, the clergy is represented in two distinct variations: the abbé de Guerindal as the older and slyer Paris priest—"one of those chameleons the capital is crawling with . . .

a schemer, ready to get mixed up with anything, but incapable of doing anything honest or useful" (291); and the younger abbé de Vezac who, using his theology studies at the Sorbonne as a cover for his debauchery, "shows every sign of being a perfect good-for-nothing, the very model of the court cleric" (291). Mérard, carried away by his delight in these satirical portraits, even includes in his list characters who never appear in the play. The clandestine book seller, Brochure, for instance, is "a book peddler and snitch not without wit. If he weren't on the police payroll, he could get himself a place in the French Academy by combining a little intrigue and plotting with publishing a newspaper praising mistresses and ministers" (292).

The Spirit of Manners foregrounds a question which, as we have seen, hangs over many of these plays: to what extent were they intended for performance and to what extend were they printed scripts intended for private reading? Mérard, in the voice of the editor preparing the collected memoirs of the Marquise de Palmarèze, offers specific instructions as to how what here appears as a section of that memoir should be modified for stage presentation. Complaining that the manuscript copy from which he is working shows every sign that it has been grossly overwritten for an audience of readers, Mérard insists that one all-important rule must govern the changes to be made when the play is staged rather than read: "One must freely cut the conversations and multiply the events. It is action that makes comedy come alive. But one must never cut the events and multiply the conversations" (289). Following that rule, he includes in the text footnotes that designate passages of dialogue running from a single page to three full pages which the prudent director will cut for an actual performance. "Is it even imaginable in terms of these principles," he asks in a tone that satirizes the verbosity of a Marivaux or a Crébillon, "that some have made the mistake of dragging this play out with sheer prattling, with an endless chattering that kills comedy and action?" (289). As to what he means by the all-important *action* that must everywhere be favored over words, Mérard offers a model of mythic proportions: "In this kind of a situation, Hercules does not launch into dissertations. He gets right down to brass tacks; he acts. In a single night he transforms fifty virgins. He must be our constant model when it is a question of eroticism" (289).[42] This ideal of Herculean stamina does, of course, present a real challenge to any actor aspiring to the starring role. Mérard cautions the would-be stage director that "anyone wishing to stage this erotic drama, more difficult to perform than any other, should be reminded that it demands excellent actors, of a kind now rarely to be found" (289). This wink as to the limits of male potency echoes a similar lament by Caylus in his preface to *The Brothel*. If, Caylus explains, there is little chance his play will be performed, it is not because of censorship: "It is not the case, as one might imagine, that the police will create a problem. . . . The real difficulty comes from how difficult it is to find actors who can rise to the challenge of such roles and honor the work by giving its expressive terms the full brilliance of action" (503–4). And there is little doubt that, of all the plays examined here, the question of sexual stamina—female as well as male—lies firmly at the center of the two acts that make up *The Spirit of Manners*.

After its opening scene of servants setting out a light lunch, the Marquise de Palmarèze storms onto the stage accompanied by the aptly named Baron Illacaré (He's got it sturdy). Young, insecure, and with far more reason to be jealous than he suspects, his impetuous encounter with the Marquise combines the allusiveness of libertine jargon with italicized stage directions that substantially clarify what is happening on stage:

> THE BARON, *getting up*. My divinity! With what grace you distribute your bounty. (*He begins to allow himself a certain license.*)
>
> THE MARQUISE, *in good-humor*. My roguish sir, I must, as you can see, have quite a weakness for you; and I hope you appreciate the full value of the moment when we make our peace.
>
> THE BARON, *as persistent as ever, already in command of her bosom and continuing toward other charms*. Ah! How could we ever have known a moment's disaccord! (*Touching and uncovering certain attractions.*) Good Heavens! What beauties! (*He hastily showers them with kisses, displaying at the same time proof of his own merit.*)
>
> THE MARQUISE, *eyeing an object of uncommon proportions*. Is this what you would offer me, Baron? Have mercy on me! Certainly, such a ram could never be thrust against me, my dear . . .
>
> THE BARON, *tickling her clitoris as he tries to enter*. Ah, Marquise! Did you ever doubt that I would succeed? (300–301)

During a brief pause in the action after the Baron's departure and as the Marquise retires to write a letter, a monologue by the servant Justine updates the audience as to what has happened before the curtain rose. How much longer, Justine wonders aloud, can she be expected to put up with the demands of her service? Since arriving last evening with the Marquise at the Président's *petite maison*, she has already had to prepare no fewer than four separate baths as her mistress insisted on repeating a complete *toilette* for each of the five lovers she has so far entertained. Hardly ready to slow down, the Marquise returns to the stage and continues her exploits in a series of scenes that organize themselves like selected postures from Aretino. The *badinage enchanteur* of her lesbian interlude with Mlle Lesbosie sparks for her young acolyte the delights of a gender mobility allowing the protégée to imagine herself as a ferocious grenadier: "Wouldn't you say, Madame, that as I do this to you, I look like a ferocious grenadier with his black mustache? After all, with my mouth clamped down on you, those thick curly hairs could just as well be mine as yours" (311). After the young lady retires, she is replaced by the decidedly Florentine Comte de Catso di Coulo, who entertains the Marquise with anal delights before delicately ejaculating into his handkerchief. The first act ends with the Marquise's humiliating dismissal of the abbé de Guerindal because, on only the third iteration of his attentions, "the blade," as she puts it, "has broken" (321).

Act 2 introduces an extended cast of characters who bring with them something resembling a plot and a denouement. The Chevalier de Verville unexpectedly arrives to announce that the Président de Guibraville himself, apparently having forgotten that he has lent his house to the Marquise, is on his way, accompanied by the Vicomte de Sarsanne, the abbé de Vezac, and three *filles* from the Opéra-Comique: Nécelle, Églante, and Adeline. Over the seven scenes that follow, this cast of eight engages in a crescendo of sexual activity that takes the four couples through an ever-changing succession of on-stage and off-stage pairings. The Vicomte and Nécelle, for example, are interrupted when Églante, frustrated by the flagging efforts of the Chevalier, arrives from the wings to demand that the Vicomte provide her with a much-needed supplement. The maneuvers necessary to inspire the already flagging Vicomte culminate in side-by-side columns of dialogue comically representing the couple's hard-won expressions of their shared satisfaction. Églante's "Stop! . . . You've got me so excited! . . . You're so far in! . . . Ah! Can you feel it! . . . How I love you! . . . Courage! . . . Quickly! . . . I'm losing control . . . My soul is about to leave me!" is balanced by the perfect antiphony of the Vicomte's "Squeeze me tightly! . . . Caress me faster! . . . What supple and mobile loins! . . . No! . . . Again! . . . Hold on. Don't hurry! . . . My angel! . . . I expire! . . . Receive the proof . . . What unspeakable pleasure!" (345). As scene 9 brings all the characters together on stage, the recovered Chevalier proposes that they perform what he calls *la girandole*—a term borrowed from the technical language of fireworks displays designating the closing salvo of multiple explosions.

As in the brothel plays, this concatenation of sexual permutations is brought to a close by the arrival of the police. Here, however, as this is the *petite maison* of the Président de Guibraville, it is hardly question of a raid. Instead, we learn, the humiliated abbé de Guerindal from act 1 has informed the Marquise's husband as to her whereabouts and activities and he in turn has obtained a *lettre de cachet* ordering his wife's imprisonment. The police accompanying the furious Marquis are there to arrest only the Marquise without disturbing the others. Hardly intimidated, the Marquise first throws in her husband's face the real motive for the abbé's denunciation and then dismisses her own escapades as what any reasonable person should expect from an arranged marriage like her own: "A husband who marries a woman against her will can only expect his wife to do a few things against his will" (359). Stepping out of her role, the Marquise brings the play to a close with a verse coda addressed directly to the audience:

> Avec quelque art, messieurs, et d'un pinceau souvent
>> Gracieux, large, énergique, savant,
> Un auteur inconnu, copiant la nature,
> De ce siècle pervers vous a fait la peinture.
> Montrez-vous indulgents. Vous aimez la gaîté:
> Sur les mœurs, quand on l'aime, on est moins difficile . . .
>> La Pudeur et la Volupté
> Sont rarement d'accord ensemble. (360–61)

> [With a certain art, dear sirs, and using a brush often
>> Gracious, large, agile, and wise,
> An unknown author, copying nature,
> Offers you the portrait of this perverse century.
> Be indulgent. You love gaiety:
> And when one loves it, one makes no fuss about morals . . .
>> Modesty and Voluptuousness
> Are rarely in agreement with each other.]

Mirroring the vaudeville of reconciliation that ends Beaumarchais' *Figaro*, Mérard's closing appeal to a universal spirit of *gaîté* qualifies any rush to equate these upper-class high jinks with a protorevolutionary denunciation of corruption. A less ambiguous illustration of how erotic theater adapted to the context of the Revolution can be found in an anonymous play, *The Cloistered Whores* of 1793. What makes this work valuable as an indicator of its ideological context is the fact that it was composed as the direct parody of a very different kind of work that had enjoyed tremendous popular success only a few months earlier: Louis-Benoit Picard's light opera *Les Visitandines* (The Sisters of the Visitation) of 1792.[43] While *The Cloistered Whores* relies on the standard clichés of voracious sexuality, its real significance emerges from its contrasts to the model it burlesques. Both *The Sisters of the Visitation* and *The Cloistered Whores* are two-act works that combine dialogue and song. In both, the first act takes place during a stormy night as two lost male travelers find themselves outside a locked building occupied by sequestered women: the convent of the Sisters of the Visitation in the first and the Bicêtre penal hospital for prostitutes in *The Cloistered Whores*. Likewise, the second act of both takes place inside the building which the travelers have penetrated thanks to clever disguises.

The Sisters of the Visitation tells the happy story of two young lovers, Belfort and Euphémie, who, as the play opens, have been separated for two years. After escaping from the prison where he had been held for a crime he did not commit, Belfort fled abroad, where he has had no news of his beloved. Euphémie, now the ward of Belfort's physician father, and refusing to love anyone other than Belfort, has entered the convent of the Visitation where she is resolved to take her final vows the following week. One can easily imagine Belfort's joy when, as the storm abates, he hears coming from the convent a song sung by a woman whose beautiful voice he immediately recognizes as Euphémie's. Disguising himself as a nun and his valet as a priest, Belfort manages to enter the convent, temporarily fools the abbess, and rejoins his beloved. All ends happily when—just as the ruse is about to fall apart because the abbess notices a striking resemblance between Euphémie's portrait of her lover and the new nun—Belfort's father arrives and gives his permission for the marriage that will unite his son with his ward.

The Sisters of the Visitation, a kind of *La Religieuse* (The Nun) ultralite, contains nothing even approaching Diderot's denunciation of the convent as a locus of systematic repression. It contents itself with portraying its nuns as women unlucky in love who choose the monastic life as a not uncomfortable refuge where they spend their days recalling the happier times before their less celestial loves turned bad. Well suited to the political ambiguities of

1792, *The Sisters of the Visitation* presents the convent neither as neurotic symptom nor as religious ideal, but as a locus of sisterly consolation for women who would have been far happier in marriage.

The Cloistered Whores, element by element and sometimes line by line, parodies *The Sisters of the Visitation* by transforming it into a heavy-handed sexual farce. Euphémie is rechristened Conculie (Cuntassie); the abbess becomes Sœur Souple-Fesse (Sister Smooth Ass); the physician Belfort becomes an apothecary named Vise-Cul (Aim-for-the-Ass) specializing in enemas; and the young Belfort a serial Don Juan whose father assumes he has long since died of syphilis. The community of women, now prostitutes at Bicêtre, sings together of how they compensate for their confinement:

> Vous m'avez fait, en m'éveillant,
> Ma sœur, un bien cruel dommage,
> Je faisais un rêve charmant,
> Car je rêvais de pucelage.
> Un vit, d'une énorme grosseur,
> Dans mon con faisait son entrée.
> Est-ce un péché, ma chère sœur,
> De rêver qu'on est dépucelée?
>
> . . . .
>
> En m'éveillant, au lieu d'une pine,
> Je n'ai plus trouvé que mon doigt. (365–66)

> [In awakening me, you did me,
> My sister, a very cruel injury.
> I was having a charming dream,
> For I was dreaming of virginity.
> A cock, of enormous thickness,
> Into my cunt was making its way.
> Can it be a sin, my dear sister,
> To dream of losing one's virginity?
>
> . . . .
>
> By awakening me, instead of a prick,
> I found only my finger.]

Toward the end of the play, when the presence of Vise-Cul junior, even though disguised as a nun, begins to have its effect, all the women equip themselves with dildos, and the author gives the following stage directions: "All of the women sit down, raise their skirts and spread their thighs so as to show their cunts. At stage right, Vise-Cul and Conculie also lift their skirts, and unnoticed by the others, Conculie takes Vise-Cul's cock in her hand and strokes it" (389). These examples of the play's systematic parody of its model show how the hypersexualized bodies of erotic theater found new life in the context of the Revolution. Neither the light comedy of aristocrats entertaining themselves with the rituals of the brothel, nor the extravagant imagining of excesses associated with the *petite maison*, erotic theater here assumes a different role. Like the pornographic prose satires of Marie-Antoinette as a queen of France become Messalina, *The Cloistered Whores* stages a subversive yet comic desecration of the Church as the sustaining institution of the ancien régime.[44]

As these examples demonstrate, the eighteenth century's erotic theater staged, in words and actions, performances of pleasure based on the power of adjacent bodies to inspire and excite one another. At one point in his stage directions for the final orgy scene in *The Spirit of Manners* Mérard states: "All the couples should be arranged in such a way that no one misses a single movement. As though carried away by the sight of such divine objects, *all the men and all the women find themselves, involuntarily and without realizing it, compelled to imitate with the person next to them* what is being done by the actors and actresses they are watching" (353; italics mine). Centered on the performance of sexuality, the tension driving these plays derives less from an opposition between accepted social norms and the private regimes of brothel and *petite maison*—the final-scene arrivals of the police serve as little more than a convention to bring the action to a close—than from an eminently gendered and bodily incompatibility between men who disappoint and women who remain unsatisfied.

The woman's point of view in these plays, what she expects from men, is clearly enunciated by the Marquise de Palmarèze when she presents the less than satisfying abbé de Guerindal with an enumeration of his duties: "Mark it well, you lout, that an amphibian like you . . . has to get it up fast, fuck with abandon, refuck, fuck again, start all over, and still be ready to go—until I say, 'Enough!'" (325). Faced with that stern duty, yet so frequently incapable of fulfilling it, the male characters resort to equally gendered and misogynist insults. In Alexis Piron's three-act ballet of 1773 *Vasta*, *reine de Bordélie* (Vasta, Queen of Bordelloland), Prince Vit-Molet (Prince Soft Cock) offers the following accusatory reply to Queen Vasta's question as to what might be wrong with him:

> Car si par un hasard vous vous vîtes ratée,
> Prenez-vous-en aux dieux, qui vous firent un con
> Plus d'une fois trop large et deux fois trop profound:
> Le vent, qui s'engouffrait dans ce vaste edifice,
> Me faisait débander au bord de la matrice. (203)

> [And if it happens that you find yourself frustrated,
> Blame it on the gods, who gave you a cunt
> More than twice too wide and twice too deep.
> The wind, as it whistled through that vast edifice,
> Made me fall limp at the lip of the womb.]

The human comedy that emerges from these plays carries with it the irony of a liberation that brings only vituperation. These performances of pleasure may begin as a suspension of the laws and limits of polite decorum, but they lead ultimately to the bitter acknowledgment of a disappointing disproportion between the sexes, a disproportion whose frenzy is captured in the curse hurled at Argénie by the jealous ghost of her first lover in Grandval's 1738 *La Comtesse d'Olonne:*

> Les dieux, pour t'accabler de malheurs infinis,
> Vont t'élargir le con, et raccourcir les vits;
> Les plus jeunes fouteurs auront mille faiblesses;
> Toujours à contre-temps tu lèveras les fesses,
> Et tes amants, constraints par une dure loi,
> Au milieu du coït s'endormiront sur toi.
> Pour un gueux impuissant l'amour te rendra folle,
> Tes moindres maux seront chaude-pisse ou vérole. (102)

> [The gods, condemning you to misfortunes without end,
> Will enlarge your cunt and shorten all pricks.
> Even the youngest cocksmen will swoon with weakness.
> Always at the wrong moment you will thrust your ass,
> And your lovers, obeying a stern law,
> Will fall asleep on top of you in the midst of coition.

Your love for an impotent beggar will drive you crazy.
The least of your troubles will be the clap or the pox.]

As these verse passages make clear, this erotic theater, as embodied as it is, is also, pace Mérard's counsel as to ruthless cuts, a performance of language. Its intersecting bodies express themselves in verbal exchanges informed by a style specific to the genre. The esthetics of erotic theater depends not only on a choice of acts over words but on harmonizing diction with action.[45] At the most obvious level, this verbal transgression dictates a language of directness and vulgarity. Explaining why he wants to rent a room at Mme Dru's, Caylus's villainous Valère of *The Brothel* answers, "To fuck a cunt" (31). The names given to the characters are equally explicit. In *The Rake* we meet Gobbe-Dru (Big Swallow) and Mme Grippe-Pines (Mme Cock Grabber). The women in *The Cloistered Whores* are named Encule (Up-the-Ass), Patine (Tongue Kiss), and Foutaine (Fuckette). At the same time, these plays also rely for their comic effect on an obverse linguistic practice of studied indirection. In the impotence plays, usually set in a far-away palace where a still virginal queen must contend with a singularly disappointing king, the wife's frustration becomes comic by reason of its expression in a halting, inarticulate language of innocence and ignorance. The lament of sad Queen Bellendrap (Queen Pretty-between-the-Sheets) in Grandval's *Le Tempérament* (Temperament) of 1756 becomes hilarious precisely because its careful alexandrines contrast so sharply with her almost childlike words as she struggles to explain to her new husband why his caressing hands are simply not enough:

> N'est-ce donc que pour ça que l'amour nous rassemble?
> N'est-ce donc que pour ça que l'on se couche ensemble?
> Je suis fort ignorante en amour, en hymen.
> Mais de tout votre corps quand j'ai fait l'examen,
> J'ai vu, quand vous dormiez, la forme singulière,
> Dont un homme partout d'une femme diffère,
> Et j'ai dit, en voyant votre sexe et le mien:
> La nature n'a pas mis tout ça là pour rien. (159)

[Is it only for this that love has brought us together?
Is it only for this that we now lie down together?
I may be little versed in love, and in marriage,

But of your entire body, when I examined it,
I saw, while you slept, the singular form
Of what distinguishes a man from a woman.
And I said, as I compared your sex and mine,
Nature has not put all that there for nothing.]

Combining these two registers, it is a practice of metaphor that collapses the distinction between directness and indirection that emerges as the signature trope of erotic theater. The opening scene of Legrand's *The Rake* includes an exchange between Valère and his prudish sister Isabelle which comically underlines the dynamic of metaphor as it functions in these plays. Concerned that her brother is squandering their inheritance on his paid companions, Isabelle insists to him that it is only his money those women want. When Isabelle arrives at the example of the local *charcutière* Valère resorts to the power of metaphor:

VALÈRE. Ah! ne le croyez pas. Elles trouvent en moi, ma sœur, d'autres appas.

ISABELLE. Quoi! Vous me soutiendrez que cette charcutière
N'est pas intéressée?

VALÈRE. Ah! ma sœur, au contraire; elle a le cœur si bon, qu'en mille occasions, pour avoir une andouille, elle offre deux jambons. (76)

[VALÈRE. Ah! Don't think that for a moment. They find in me, my sister, quite different charms.

ISABELLE. What! You would claim to me that the lady pork butcher is not greedy?

VALÈRE. Ah! My sister, to the contrary; her heart is so kind that on a thousand occasions for a single sausage she has offered me two sweet thighs.]

Reacting more to the figure of speech than to her brother's defense, Isabelle's verse response summarizes the function of metaphor in erotic theater: "Je devine à peu près ce que vous voulez dire, / Et la similitude a de quoi faire rire" (I can almost guess what you are getting at, / And the similarity does have its humor) (77). Later in the same scene, metaphor's power to hijack an exchange as involuntary pun asserts itself when Isabelle explains how upset she is that her own suitor, the Captain, passed by her window with only a salute and then had his men let loose their salvo in front of her rival's house: "Comment donc! devant moi venir branler la pique / Pour aller décharger ailleurs!" (Can you believe it! He waves his lance in front of me / Then shoots off somewhere else!) (79).

These plays are rife with metaphors and similes that are not so much alternatives to directness as they are unexpectedly comic collapses into similarity of things thought to be different. When, in the opening scene of *The Lady Brothel Keeper,* Mme Amboisel waxes poetic in her explanation of why there are so few virgins in Paris—"Don't you know the proverb that says that maidenheads are like partridges that fly away as soon as they have feathers?"—her customer Gripigni extends the play of difference and similarity by replying, "Oh! By all the devils! In these parts they usually take wing even before they have a bit of fuzz" (134). In act 2 of *The Spirit of Manners,* when the Vicomte translates the Abbé's brief snatch of ribald song into an Epicurean recipe—"He is wisely suggesting that we have had enough talking and it is now time to sing. One pleasure must be replaced by another for only variety holds us safe from boredom"—Nécelle's saucy reply extends the interplay of different registers: "And that must surely be why, Vicomte, I so like to change needles while I am doing my work. That way I don't notice that I am always doing the same job" (348).

Grounded in Epicureanism, this theater stages its performances of pleasure as embodied illustrations of the Lucretian clinamen. At the scale of gendered bodies, women and men, like matter's all-encompassing atoms, engage in incessant permutations and collisions choreographed by the chaotic force of sexual energy, desire, and pleasure.[46] In the opening paragraph of his preface to *The Cloistered Whores,* the anonymous author makes his point baldly: "Fucking is the very essence of nature. Every being, whether strongly or weakly, is driven by the generative power for which we are born. The pleasure of its tight embraces and charming commerce is the goal each sex creates for the other.... There is no other remedy for this fire that goads our existence, giving life and movement to all that breathes" (363). It is as illustrations of Epicurean materialism that these plays reveal the militancy of their comedy. The message they proclaim, and the unsettling directness of their diction, place their deployment of sexuality in the same register as Gustave Courbet's gesture of giving to his hyperrealistic painting of a naked female torso, reclining with legs apart and the sex exposed, the title *L'Origine du monde*. In his introduction to *The Brothel*, Caylus makes the same point in words: "Don't you understand that all those words and objects which are labeled dirty and obscene, and which so repulse you, are the very instruments and organs of human nature? (504).

This postulate of matter's universal oneness—a oneness of man, of woman, and of nature—pulses through erotic theater's esthetics of action and word conjoined, of pleasure spoken and performed. In scene 6 of Legrand's *The Rake* Agnès awakens in a panic and describes for her cousin Bibi the nightmare she has just had. In that nightmare, perhaps anticipating Valère's pretend marriage, she finds herself pulled to the ground by a naked man who begins to stabs her. When she calls out to her father for help, he appears before her, but refuses to come to her aid because he is himself stabbing her mother. Bibi, as though she had already studied Freud, shows no hesitation in identifying the subconscious resonances of her cousin's dream: "Well, let's see . . . as for the dagger I can easily guess: / It is victory, one would think; the naked man is desire; / And the stabbed woman one could take for pleasure" (84). Agnès then asks her confident cousin if she herself ever has such disquieting dreams. Bibi's answer takes the form of a poetic phantasmagoria in which the description of her dream flows out from herself, absorbing and being absorbed by the world around her:

> Je me trouve serpent, arbre, poisson, oiseau.
> Si je me vois jument, un maquignon me dompte,
> Un palefrenier me sangle, un cavalier me monte.
> Je deviens quelquefois matelas et coutil,
> Pierre où le rémouleur affile son outil,
> Barre que l'on rougit et martèle à l'enclume,
> Lampe que l'on remplit, chandelle qu'on allume.
> . . . .
> Je suis aussi souvent en chose inanimée,
> Par exemple en maison, en porte, en cheminée;
> L'on me couvre, l'on m'ouvre, on me ramone enfin;
> . . . .
> Tantôt je suis fagot, tantôt je suis bourrée;
> Tantôt je suis marteau, tantôt je suis cognée;
> On me charge, décharge, on m'emmanche, on me vend,

Avec moi l'on se chauffe, on cloue, on tape, on fend;
Je sers à tous métiers: si je deviens aiguille
Il survient un tailleur qui sur-le-champ m'enfile;
Tantôt en accolade, ainsi qu'un lapereau,
Et tantôt embrochée, ainsi qu'un dindonneau. (85)

[I become a serpent, a tree, a fish, a bird.
If I imagine myself a mare, a trader breaks me,
A groom bridles me, a rider mounts me.
Sometimes I become a mattress and its ticking,
A stone for the grinder to sharpen his tool,
Red-hot metal hammered on the anvil,
A lamp to be refilled, a candle to be lighted.
. . . .
I am just as often an inanimate thing,
For example, a house, a door, a chimney;
I am roofed, I am opened, I am swept;
. . . .
Sometimes I am kindling, other times I am firewood;
Sometimes I am a hammer, other times I am an axe;
I am picked up, tossed down, fitted with a handle, and sold,
With me, one heats, one nails, one beats, one splits;
I can be used for any job: if I become a needle
There appears a tailor who immediately threads me;
Sometimes grabbing me by the neck like a rabbit,
And sometimes skewering me like a turkey.]

This kaleidoscopic portrait of a self that is one with animals, tools, materials, and the actions of daily life speaks of how Bibi both loses herself and finds herself within an endless succession of figures and forms. A tour de force of poetic evocation, wordplay, and double entendre, her dream and its copulations of metaphor act out in language the shared premise of Epicurean materialism and erotic theater. Grounded in the materialist vision of a world where all boundaries dissolve within a continuum of atoms in motion, her words enunciate the Epicurean vision of pleasure's quest as an all-encompassing vector of energy and force. As a response to Agnes's nightmare, Bibi's dream explains why it was that she would equate stabbing with pleasure. Far from excusing masculine violence, her dream and its amplification seek to contextualize and correct Agnes's panicked choice of stabbing as a metaphor of men and women coming together. The dissolved boundaries of the self at the core of Bibi's dream point to her cousin's imagining she is being stabbed as a reaction grounded in the unreal inviolability of those who would see themselves as separate from and threatened by the rhythms of the larger world of which they are a part. Bibi's surrender of herself to a sexuality that reverberates through an ever-shifting array of objects, persons, and actions stands as a poetic summary of the Epicurean vision motivating the eighteenth century's erotic theater and its extravagant choreographies of gendered bodies. Swooning in ecstasy or trembling with frustration, their staged performances of word and action illustrate the follies and foibles of enlightened pleasure.

Conclusion
From Pleasure to Happiness

My argument in the preceding chapters has been that it was as pleasure emerged over the course of the eighteenth century as a value to be sought after, luxuriated in, scrutinized, shared, and regretted that a new philosophy of Epicurean materialism reconfigured literature, the arts, and theater. That contention inevitably suggests a question: how and for what reasons did this fascination with the lessons of pleasure come to an end? We have seen flashes of an answer in Rousseau's political writings, in Mirabeau's rejection of *Julie*'s new ethos of sentiment, and in erotic theater's sometimes trenchant satire. While it is beyond the scope of this study to describe in detail the forces that ended pleasure's reign, I would like, as the beginnings of an answer, to briefly bring together three very different individuals: the philosopher-physician Julien Offray de La Mettrie, the revolutionary orator Louis Antoine de Saint-Just, and the novelist Donatien Alphonse François de Sade. Taken together—La Mettrie as an emblem of pleasure's heyday, Saint-Just and Sade as important voices from within the Revolution—these three figures delineate a suggestion as to how it happened that pleasure yielded the scene to a new and ambiguous ideal of happiness.

Within the enterprise of thinking seriously about pleasure La Mettrie occupies an important place. Born in 1709, the son of a merchant in the Atlantic port city of Saint-Malo, he abandoned the family business to study medicine, first in Paris and then in Rheims. It was while at Rheims that he made the important decision to complete his studies, not at France's most renowned faculty of medicine in Montpellier, but in the Dutch university of Leiden. For La Mettrie, his choice of the Protestant north instead of the Catholic south had everything to do with the presence there of the eminent clinical professor and medical theoretician Herman Boerhaave. As the leading proponent of what was known as iatromechanics, Boerhaave's defining ambition was to explain the workings of the human body entirely in terms of the mechanical laws of matter.[1] La Mettrie, an assiduous student who translated a number of Boerhaave's writings into French, would not, however, choose the sheltered life of an academic. After a brief appointment as the house physician to the Duc de Grammont, he served as a military doctor and was quickly introduced to the horrors of battlefield wounds as well as to the period's severely limited means for dealing with them. The most harrowing period of his medical career came, however, not on the battlefield but during the time he struggled to contain the cholera epidemic of 1742 in his native Brittany, a scourge which took more than eighty thousand lives.

His career in France came to an abrupt end when, in 1745, the Paris authorities roundly condemned his very Boerhaavian *Histoire naturelle de l'âme*, which rejected, even in its title, any acknowledgment of the soul as a force or principle independent of the physical body. Two years later, living in Holland, he published what remains his best-known work, *L'Homme machine*, in which he set himself the task of explaining man and all his experiences as mechanical processes subject to the purely physical laws that govern the body's various organs. Vociferously antispiritualist, antidualist, and anti-Cartesian, La Mettrie—mocked by the more conventional as "Monsieur Machine"—argued for a determinism at the level of the body's organs so all-encompassing that what the theologian would call free will and the political theorist freedom were dismissed as illusions grounded only in ignorance. This doctrine, strangely anticipating some of the more extreme hypotheses of twenty-first-century genetics, proved too radical even for tolerant Holland. La Mettrie's second experience of exile ended only when he was invited by Frederick the Great to take up residence at his court as a distinguished member of the Royal Academy of Prussia.[2]

While under Frederick's protection, a year before his death in 1751, La Mettrie published his valedictory *Système d'Épicure*, a short, aphoristic work that is less a summation of his radical materialism than a final articulation of his ethics of pleasure: "We should take the events of life as they happen to us, remembering to turn our eyes in all directions and to take pleasure from the enchanting spectacle that surrounds us. Admiration should frame our reactions, and we must refuse the vain itch to explain everything."³ Even in failing health, La Mettrie's final lesson is that our highest duty is to the pleasure that we can derive from our physical existence. Refusing a philosophical hubris that can only jeopardize sensual delight, the truly wise man must recognize that mastering the distant whys and wherefores of the world is a vain endeavor. La Mettrie is most a man of his century not when he is the polemicist of radical materialism but when, as in his final work, he declares his allegiance to an Epicureanism always attentive to the ever-changing eddies of sensation provided by the world around us. Knowing he had little time to live, he drew up a surprising balance sheet of his life: "I would ask to live my life again only as I have already lived it: with good cheer and good food, in good company, and amid the joys of study and companionship." Positing the good life as a regimen of pleasures, he identifies its real enemies as excess and monotony: "My days would alternate between women and their constant lessons of grace, Hippocrates, and the muses. As much the enemy of debauchery as the friend of pleasure, I am devoted above all to that charming mixture of wisdom and folly that sharpens each against the other while rendering our lives more agreeable and more savory" (185). The questions of philosophy may draw us back to a distant beginning and forward to a fast-approaching end, but our final choice should always be in favor of the present as the only temporality of pleasure: "Let pleasure be our present, for we only are what the present is. Dead as many years as we have lived, the future yet to come is no more in our power than that past which is no longer" (186).

Written at midcentury, La Mettrie's paean to pleasure is cast as doubly personal. It is a lesson each must learn individually and it is a state that comes only by achieving an always idiosyncratic equilibrium between the aspirations of the mind and the delights of the senses. Less than a half century later, a new value and a new concept would make La Mettrie's regimen of pleasure appear not only as the relic from another age, but as a program almost childlike in its innocence. The dynamic that ended the age of pleasure and set the stage for its successor state of happiness can be glimpsed clearly in a famous phrase spoken by Saint-Just, in his address to the Convention on March 3, 1794: "Happiness is a new idea for Europe."⁴ Many would see that sentence as a deft summary of everything the Revolution was meant to be. Sweeping from the scene both the spiritual "salvation" with which the Church had so long gulled the credulous as well as the sybaritic "pleasure" which had been the franchise of a corrupt aristocracy, Saint-Just's new happiness was meant to be material, civic, and exemplary. Happiness captured in a single word everything the practice of the Revolution's liberty, equality, and fraternity promised to provide not for a privileged few but for each and all. The emphatically inaugural tone of Saint-Just's claim has assured it a long afterlife. In the years immediately following World War I, it leaped often to the lips of the signatories to the Treaty of Versailles as a way of emphasizing how different Europe would become under the aegis of the League of Nations. More recently, and with a shift in emphasis to the sentence's last word, the continent's statesmen point frequently to a postnationalist Europe that must be accepted as the precondition for its true happiness.

The circumstances surrounding Saint-Just's statement reveal, however, a less irenic genesis for this new happiness. His sentence was part of a speech to the Convention intended to encourage it to speed the implementation of the recently adopted Ventôse decrees. That legislation had as its goal to extend the confiscations of property that had already been applied to the Church and the *émigrés* to the far larger and more amorphous category of all who entertained doubts about the Revolution and who might therefore be expected to conspire against it. As a political act, the application of the Ventôse decrees was seen as particularly important on the international scene. They were meant to demonstrate to the whole of Europe leagued against it, and in a way that less audacious legislation never could, the steadfastness of the Republic's unshakeable resolve. As Saint-Just put it, "The great blow that you strike will be felt on the throne and in the heart of every king. Laws and lesser measures are but pin pricks to their hardened blindness" (673).

In practical terms the Ventôse decrees meant that every commune in France would be instructed to draw up two carefully prepared lists: one of those whose skepticism toward the Revolution rendered them unworthy of whatever property they might possess and the other of those true patriots who suffered an unjust poverty. In terms of France's domestic politics, these confiscations were meant to satisfy the radical demands of the *sans culottes* and to forestall any objection they might raise as Saint-Just and his Committee on Public Safety proceeded to liquidate the rival faction of the Hébertists. The crucial passage of Saint-Just's speech that day reads, "Let Europe learn that you will no longer accept that there be a single unhappy person [*malheureux*] or a single oppressor [*oppresseur*] on French territory. Let our example fructify the earth and propagate the love of virtue and happiness. Happiness is a new idea for Europe" (673). The true magic of this resolutely performative discourse—"Let Europe learn . . . Let this example fructify . . ."—lies in the way Saint-Just's argument hypothesizes a juxtaposition of terms which stand as opposites only as a corollary to the Revolution's new order of cause and effect. In terms of this new semantics, the "unhappy" and the "oppressors" are not only contraries, but they are assumed to relate to one another as effect to cause. We are no longer in a world characterized by the *descriptive* opposition of the "unhappy" to the "happy," but by the *prescriptive* (and proscriptive) opposition of the "unhappy" to "oppressors" who are directly and criminally responsible for that unhappiness. What the Convention is being asked to do here is to extend the scope of its powers, of the duties incumbent upon it, beyond any political limit. The French word *malheureux* derives from *heur*, a term rooted in the Latin *augurium*, designating that which occurs by chance. Etymologically, both *bonheur* and *malheur*, by acknowledging chance's inevitable agency in human affairs, recognize a dimension of life that, because it lies beyond human control, carries with it no immediate or obvious moral valence. If some are happy and others unhappy, it is because, in the world as it is, it happens that some are lucky and others are unlucky. When, however, Saint-Just declares that the operative opposition is now between the *unhappy* and their *oppressors*, it becomes not chance but the rapacious tyranny of oppressors that is responsible for the sufferings of the unhappy. Within the new world of 1794, unhappiness has become moralized and it is the duty of the state to impose its own agency in punishing those whose pleasure and property now mark them as oppressors. When Saint-Just proclaims happiness to be a "new idea" for Europe, he looks less to how France's revolutionary example will spread some new felicity over the entire continent than he does to a purge of oppressors declared to be the precondition of that happiness. His happiness, rather than a hope for things to come, is a threat leveled against all who would oppose him.

Setting La Mettrie and Saint-Just side by side brings into focus how a new understanding of civic happiness served to dismantle what had been the new Epicureans' ethics of pleasure.[5] The Declaration of the Rights of Man and the Citizen of 1789 consists of seventeen articles articulating the foundations of the Revolution's new society. Before enumerating its specific articles, however, it offers a preamble which culminates in the proclamation that the guiding purpose of all that follows is to ensure what it calls "the happiness of all" *(le bonheur de tous)*.⁶ The opposition between the pleasure of old and this new happiness is clear. Pleasure was private and personal; happiness will be public and collective. Pleasure involved an esthetics of the senses; happiness will impose an ethics refashioning the individual as citizen. Pleasure prompted a narrowing of consciousness to the delights of the senses; happiness will expand the consciousness of each to the welfare of all by enlisting the citizen within the morality of the common good.

One event, often cited as initiating the Revolution, generated a set of documents designated by a term that stands as the perfect epitaph to the age of enlightened pleasures. In 1789 the minister Jacques Necker, as he prepared to convoke an Estates General that had last been convened in 1614, issued a call from the king to his people asking that, in every parish in France, all come together to draw up what were called *cahiers de doléances*, lists of grievances (from the Latin *dolere*, to suffer). Suddenly, by ministerial decree, the whole of France was asked to reflect on and enumerate not its pleasures but its sufferings. This gesture also provides the beginnings of an answer to an important question raised by the historian Lynn Hunt in her study of the history of human rights in France. Hunt's question is intended to remind her readers how utterly unlikely it was that the notion of equality should have emerged as a guiding principle within a society so vastly different from the France we know today: "How did these men, living in societies built on slavery, subordination, and seemingly natural subservience, ever come to imagine men not at all like them and, in some cases, women too, as equals? How did equality of rights become a 'self-evident' truth in such unlikely places?"⁷ Necker's decree that, in every corner of the kingdom, people should gather together to articulate their tribulations had the effect of focusing the social conversation on a subject singularly propitious to the emergence of a new way of understanding equality and its implications. Each gathering to draw up those *cahiers* became a collective recitation of suffering's tragedy as it impinged on all members of the community. Within that tragedy, all present had an equal right to speak their parts in the communion of a shared catharsis. With suffering as the single item on the agenda, all were enjoined to situate themselves within an explosive dimension of experience at the antipodes of pleasure's untroubled acceptance of the fact of difference. Within the demarcations of ancien régime society, pleasure was private and personal. It would occur neither to *seigneur*, peasant, nor bourgeois that what gave them pleasure should somehow be the same for all. However exalted or humble one's rank, the pleasures one took were seen as the accouterments of a finally incommensurable individuality. The fact that pleasures differed greatly across the wide span of the social hierarchy prompted no compulsion to denounce as nefarious the pleasures of others simply because they were different from one's own. Those who, like Mme C... and Abbé T... of *Thérèse philosophe*, took their pleasures in unorthodox ways understood full well that they were obliged to practice a discretion that precluded their becoming occasions of scandal and disquiet. Necker's injunction that all look to their sufferings recast society's variegated textures of pleasures, imagined as well as real, in a very different light. Approached from the perspective of suffering, any pleasure enjoyed by one but unavailable to another took on the coloration of a depravation, a source of grievance and resentment equal for all.

Triggering an epidemic of envy was not, of course, Necker's intention. His decree assumed that each estate—clergy, nobility, and the faithful of every parish—as well as France's myriad corporate and professional associations would respond within the structure of the complex system of long-standing distinctions, privileges, and duties that defined the ranks and orders of ancien régime society. When, under the same impetus that produced the Declaration of the Rights of Man and the Citizen, the three Estates of France became the single nation of France, the pleasures of some but not all—now indistinguishable from hated *privilèges*—took on the very different coloration of suspect instances of inequality and injustice.[8] It was within this unanticipated context that what the Declaration called the "happiness of all" would, as events radicalized the Revolution, take the form of an ever-expanding program of confiscations meant to right the wrong of pleasures enjoyed by those who could only be oppressors. The happiness that Saint-Just saw as so new to Europe became possible only as the antithesis and punishment of pleasure.

The Revolution's reconfiguration of suffering, pleasure, and a new happiness found one of its most revealing spokespersons in the Marquis de Sade. A noble from one of France's oldest families, yet also an active member of the Commune de Paris' Section des Piques, Sade played an active role in the politics of the Revolution. Even while writing from prison, he proved himself a master of the Revolution's rhetoric, with a particular gift for capturing the heart of an idea in a single electrifying formula. Rousseau may have anticipated the Revolution's agenda when he observed in his *Confessions*, "I had seen that everything depends radically on politics, and that, from whatever aspect one considers it, no people ever would be anything other than what it was made into by the nature of its Government," but it was Sade who compressed that insight to the crowd-moving slogan: "The government makes the man."[9] In a very real sense, Sade's writings both grew out of and ended the eighteenth century's celebration of pleasure. Militantly materialist, Sade places the pleasure-seeking body at the center of his chronicles of cruelty. What sets him apart from the Epicurean tradition is his insistence on portraying his characters' discoveries of sexuality and pleasure, not as the truth of a physical body freeing itself from the lies of religion and conventional morality, but as scenarios of omnivorous aggression that express themselves through a seamless continuum of sexual violence and philosophical argument. For the Sadian hero, inflaming the body and devastating the mind are the mutually reinforcing vectors of an enlightenment that becomes indistinguishable from rape.

The relation between Sade's participation in the political maelstrom of the Revolution and his own writing is singularly apparent in the famous paratext titled "Frenchmen, yet one more effort if you wish to be Republicans," which he incorporated in his *Philosophy in the Bedroom*. That novel, first published in 1795, was begun shortly after his most intense involvement in the day-to-day events of the Revolution. At a literal level that novel's seven dialogues tell the story of how the arch libertine Dolmancé oversees the sexual and philosophical debauching of the young and innocent Eugénie. To do this, he engages the bisexual Mme de Saint-Ange, her brother Mirval, and their servant Augustin to lead Eugénie on an itinerary that establishes her as a kind of Eve in reverse. Enlightened rather than corrupted by the twinned serpents of her deflowerers' prodigious members and philosophizing tongues, she will be brought to the point where she renounces all belief in God and replaces the shame she was taught to feel toward her body with the most brazen lubricity. Her story ends when she avenges herself on the person responsible for her benighted innocence, her pious mother, Mme de Mistival, by infecting her with venereal disease and having her vagina sewn closed. "Frenchman, yet one more effort . . ." enters this tale as a political pamphlet hot off the press which Dolmancé has just purchased at the Palais de l'Égalité (the former Palais Royal). His decision to read it aloud to the assembled characters occupies almost a quarter of the novel. Outside the novel yet part of it, this pamphlet plunges Sade's story of Eugénie's enlightenment into the heated reality of the Revolution's struggle to survive the onslaught of the monarchies leagued against it. Echoing Saint-Just's grandiose rhetoric, the pamphlet points to the greatness of all that has been achieved in the few short years since the Bastille as the proof that the citizens of the Republic's new society can surely rise to the task of taking the few additional but crucial steps still necessary to complete their work. "Fellow citizens, the road we have already traveled since 1789 was far more arduous than what still lies ahead of us. We will need to change public opinion much less for what I now propose to you than we did following the storming of the Bastille when everything had to be made anew" (3:117).

In terms of its philosophical premises, this pamphlet relies on the familiar Epicurean materialism that posits a world of atoms in constant motion and all matter as the continuum of their transformations—but with a distinctive twist. For La Mettrie and the mainstream of the Epicurean tradition the lesson to be drawn from matter's constant mutation was a calming resignation to the limits of the possible as well as to the inevitable dissolution of death. For Sade, those same premises become the foundation of an obligation to participate actively in a transformation that becomes one with destruction. "If the immortality of beings is impossible, then their destruction becomes one of her laws. If this destruction is so useful to her that she cannot possibly dispense with it, and if she cannot create without drawing upon the masses of decay prepared for her by death, then from that moment the idea of annihilation that we attach to killing ceases to be real" (144). Earlier in the pamphlet, underlining how individual conduct must be rethought as a function of the exigencies imposed by the Republic's peril, Sade addresses the question of whether actions such as prostitution, adultery, incest, rape, and sodomy should be condemned because they deviate from moral standards. "Since therefore it [the republican state] is always opposed by the despots who surround it, one cannot reasonably imagine its means of preserving itself to be *moral means*, for it can only preserve itself by war, and nothing is less moral than war." In light of that necessity to move beyond conventional morality, the implications for the individual and his conduct toward others becomes clear. "Now, I ask how one can ever claim that in a State obliged to be *immoral* it is essential for individuals to be *moral*? I will say it clearly: it is good that they are not. . . . It would therefore be as absurd as it would be dangerous to demand that those charged with maintaining the perpetually *immoral* ferment of the machine should themselves be *moral* beings" (129; italics in the original). For page after page, "Français, yet one more effort . . ." extends the scope of what public opinion must learn to embrace to an ever-widening array of what the traditional moralist would label as crimes. Savoring the moral texture of each of the "crimes" it considers, "Frenchmen, yet one more effort . . ." makes it clear that the measures the Republic must take to ensure its survival and the novel's scenes of sexual mayhem come together as mutually reflecting metaphors. Dolmancé's reading the pamphlet aloud as part of the novel establishes History itself as a twin to the violence enacted within the philosopher's bedroom.

What was Sade's intention in this work? We know that he composed it during the Terror—a period when he himself was imprisoned on the surprising charge that he had shown excessive moderation in his work as a judge. When he was transferred in 1794 to the Picpus sanitarium, he found himself in a room that directly overlooked the ever-falling blade of the guillotine and reeked of death. It is perhaps for these reasons that the novel's intercalated meditation on the moral necessities of the times so often appears to parody the Revolution's rhetoric. Speaking of theft, the pamphlet makes the point that "it is certain that it fosters courage, strength, dexterity—in a word all the virtues useful to a republican constitution, and consequently to our own. I would even ask, in all impartiality, whether theft, whose effect is to equalize wealth, could ever be an evil in a state whose aim is equality" (127). On the subject of incest, it proclaims that there can be no doubt that "incest should be the law of every government founded on the principle of fraternity" (138). Extolling the uncertain paternity that would result from the pamphlet's enforced sexual availability of all to all, Sade gives a new resonance to one of *La Marseillaise*'s key refrains: "Children will not have fathers? Of what importance can that be in a Republic where all must have no other mother than the country, where all who are born become children of the country [*enfants de la patrie*]" (135).

Saint-Just and Sade provide different yet complementary perspectives on the new force that would end the age of enlightened pleasures. Saint-Just's call for a happiness new to Europe establishes each citizen's public enthusiasm for the Revolution's agenda as a value so crucial that it must be consolidated by confiscating the property and pleasures of any who would question it. Sade insists that the public's understanding of what it calls crime must be refashioned in light of the necessities of the Republic at war. As different as their programs may be, Saint-Just and Sade share a faith in the performative power of public opinion as the ultimate arbiter of political and moral values. If public opinion found itself invested with so vast a power, it was because it was now cloaked with the mantle of what was called the general will. A term born in the complex alchemy of political unanimity that Rousseau traced out in his *Social Contract* of 1762, the general will as described in that work promised a refashioning of individual wills and particular pleasures within a consensus both emanating from and imposing itself on all members of the community. In the real world of the Revolution and its struggles, that concept became the shibboleth justifying whatever happened to be the prevailing power's vision of its goals and the program necessary to achieve them—what we would today call ideology.[10] The posthumous role Rousseau would play in the sacralization of the Revolution's general will should not, however, be seen as limited to the political theories of his *Social Contract*. The redemptive absorption of the individual within the general will stands as a political equivalent of the beneficent effect Rousseau insisted his collection of letters titled *Julie* would have on its readers. Those readers, moved by the force of their sentimental identification with his characters, would undergo a personal regeneration so virtuous in itself that the distinction between fact and fiction as well as between truth and faith became irrelevant. Julie, Saint-Preux, and Wolmar had, Rousseau argued, to be real people because the feelings and sentiments their tribulations inspired for readers were so patently real and true. Transposed to the domain of the political, *Julie*'s ethos of tragic abnegation through sentimental identification—what Mirabeau so vociferously rejected in his *Morale des sens*—became a metaphor of the individual citizen's mystical movement toward congruence with the dictates of the general will. What the rhetoric of sentiment was able to achieve within the novel it fell to the oratory of ideology to perform and enforce within the debates of the Revolution.

Having overthrown the old order, the Revolution fashioned a new foundation for its political authority. Rejecting all continuity with the institutions of the past, it looked instead to the inaugural present of a general will in the making for a unanimity that consigned all who would oppose it to the status of traitors. No longer a society of orders, estates, and corporations defining the individual's place and prerogatives within them, France's revolutionary republic became a society based solely on the sway of ideology—what the historian Augustin Cochin has called a *société de pensée* in which the theoretically unanimous opinion of the collective citizenry became the unique criterion of what was real and of what was true.[11] The irony within that transformation, an irony still with us, is that the inevitable gap between the ideal of the general will as an identification of each in concert with all and the practical reality of the state's articulation of its dominant ideology inevitably compelled the state to assume the status of the very institution it had disqualified—that of a civic religion. In his *Elementary Forms of the Religious Life* of 1912, the sociologist Émile Durkheim, pointing to Robespierre's Republic of Virtue and its Cults of Reason and the Supreme Being, states that fact baldly: "Nowhere has society's ability to make itself a god or to create gods been more in evidence than during the first years of the Revolution."[12]

The eighteenth century's interlude of enlightened pleasures was born as writers, philosophers, and artists articulated together a new Epicureanism whose paramount task was the silencing of Christianity's condemnation of pleasure as antithetical to the soul's salvation. Taken together, Saint-Just and Sade show how that interlude came to an end as a new and more virulent religion of civic happiness, sanctioned by the general will and enforced by the state, made pleasure a value that no longer dared speak its name. The Enlightenment's fragile alliance between an Epicureanism that celebrated pleasure in all its forms and a Stoicism whose ethos of esthetic distance served to temper and consolidate those pleasures gave way to a new and hypertrophied Stoicism of civic duty and accountability to the state. Abhorring all that was Epicurean, the sacralized state would henceforth speak to its citizens in the name of ideology's ever-evolving versions of what it called happiness.

Notes

INTRODUCTION

1. Roland Barthes, *The Pleasure of the Text*, trans. Richard Howard (New York: Hill and Wang, 1975), 57.
2. For a variety of approaches to the question of what *libertinage* did and might mean, see *Du genre libertin au XVIIIe siècle*, ed. Jean-François Perrin and Philip Stewart (Paris: Éditions Desjonquères, 2004); and *Libertine Enlightenment: Sex, Liberty, and Licence in the Eighteenth Century*, ed. Peter Cryle and Lisa O'Connell (Houndmills, England: Palgrave Macmillan, 2004), 2–13 and passim.
3. Denis Diderot and Jean d'Alembert, *Encyclopédie, ou Dictionnaire raisonné des sciences, des arts et des métiers* (1751–57; reprint [17 vols., plus plates and supplement in 5 vols.], New York: Readex Microprint, 1969), 1:1195. The *Encyclopédie* entry on Epicureanism is in volume 1 (1:1195–97), and the entry on Stoicism in volume 3 (3:618–20). Subsequent quotations from these two entries will be followed by parentheses enclosing the page references according to this edition. All translations are my own unless stated otherwise.
4. Diderot makes this claim concerning Gassendi's importance and how the two doctrines came together in a common struggle toward the end of his entry on Epicureanism (1:1195–96). Gassendi's major work, *Syntagma philosophiae Epicuri* (The Hague: A. Vlacq, 1659), was published after his death in 1655. For a detailed study of the rebirth of classical Epicureanism in the context of seventeenth-century French literature, see Jean-Charles Darmon, *Philosophie épicurienne et la littérature au XVIIe siècle en France* (Paris: Presses Universitaires de France, 1998).
5. Cassirer's synthesis of the Enlightenment as a European phenomenon first appeared in 1932 as *Die Philosophie der Aufklärung*. Its English translation,

The Philosophy of the Enlightenment, trans. Fritz C. A. Koelln and James P. Pettegrove, first appeared in 1952 from Princeton University Press. The most influential continuation of Cassirer's approach to the Enlightenment can be found in Peter Gay, *The Enlightenment: An Interpretation,* 2 vols. (New York: Vintage Books, 1968). For a provocative and stimulating discussion of what the term Enlightenment might mean, see the Postscript to Jonathan Israel's *Enlightenment Contested: Philosophy, Modernity, and the Emancipation of Man 1670–1752* (Oxford: Oxford University Press, 2006), 863–71.

6. Max Horkheimer and Theodor W. Adorno, *Dialectic of Enlightenment,* trans. Edmund Japhcott (Stanford, CA: Stanford University Press, 2002), 1. Subsequent page references to this translation will be given in parentheses following the quotation.

7. For a more specifically French but ultimately congruent reading of the Enlightenment's nefarious ambitions, see Michel Foucault, *The Order of Things* (New York: Vintage Books, 1970), and *Discipline and Punish* (New York: Vintage Books, 1977).

8. Lynn Hunt has described how studies of the Revolution frequently shift their focus from its status as an event to the more nebulous dimension of the teleologies that event is seen as either culminating or preparing: "Recent scholarly debates around the Revolution always seem to take the event for granted. At issue in the controversies is not the character of the experience itself, but rather its long-term origins and outcomes. The Revolution merely serves as the vehicle of transportation between long-term causes and effects." See Lynn Hunt, *Politics, Culture, and Class in the French Revolution* (Berkeley: University of California Press, 1984), 3.

CHAPTER 1. THE PLEASURES OF FAILURE

1. Jean-Baptiste Jourdan, *Le Guerrier philosophe* (The Hague: Chez Pierre de Hondt, 1744), 118. Subsequent quotations from this work will be followed by parentheses enclosing the page reference to this edition. While there is no modern edition of this novel, it is available digitally both through the University of Chicago's ARTFL project and the Web site of the Bibliothèque Nationale.

2. Louis-Gabriel Michaud, *Biographie universelle, ancienne et moderne,* 85 vols. (Paris: Michaud Frères, 1811–62), 22:56–57.

3. The one existing article on this work is a study of how Jourdan's use of the term *philosophe* relates to the evolution of that word across the eighteenth

century. See Jin Lu, "Jourdan et son *Guerrier philosophe*," in *L'Armée au XVIIIième siècle, 1715–1789*, ed. Geneviève Goubier-Robert (Aix-en-Provence: Publications de l'Université de Provence, 1999), 221–27.

4. The Chevalier's intense pleasure upon discovering that it is his own letter that so delights Geltrude restages the well-known scene of voyeurism from book 4 of Lafayette's *La Princesse de Clèves*, when Nemours, spying on Mme de Clèves at Colomiers, learns that it is his own portrait that provokes his beloved's quite visible pleasure: "She sat down and began to look at this portrait with an attention and a reverie that only passion could inspire. It is impossible to express what M. de Nemours felt at this moment. To see . . . a person whom he adored, to see her without her knowing that he was looking at her, to see her occupied entirely with things to do with him and with the passion she hid from him, that was something never before experienced or imagined by any other lover." See *La Princesse de Clèves*, ed. Émile Magne (Paris: Droz, 1946), 167.

5. On the importance of the institution which we now anachronistically refer to as the "salon" and the central place within it of women not unlike Jourdan's Mlle Du ***, see Jacqueline Hellegouarc'h, *L'Esprit de société: Cercles et "salons" parisiens au XVIIIe siècle* (Paris: Garnier, 2000). See also on this subject Carolyn Lougee, *Le Paradis des Femmes: Women, Salons, and Social Stratification in Seventeenth-Century France* (Princeton, NJ: Princeton University Press, 1976); Dena Goodman, *The Republic of Letters: A Cultural History of the French Enlightenment* (Ithaca, NY: Cornell University Press, 1994); and Joan DeJean, *Tender Geographies: Women and the Origins of the Novel in France* (New York: Columbia University Press, 1991).

CHAPTER 2. MIRRORING PLEASURE

This chapter is an expanded version of my essay "Coupling the Novel: Reading Bodies in La Morlière's *Angola*," which appeared in *Eighteenth-Century Fiction* 13, nos. 2–3 (January–April 2001): 389–413.

1. The most extensive sources for La Morlière's biography are Charles Monselet, "Le Chevalier de La Morlière," in *Oubliés et dédaignés* (Paris: Charpentier, 1876), 215–67; and Adolphe Rochas, *Biographie du Dauphiné*, 2 vols. (Paris: Charavay, 1856–60), 2:24–28. See also the biographical notice on La Morlière in *Romanciers libertins du dix-huitième siècle*, ed. Patrick Wald Lasowski, 2 vols. (Paris: Éditions Gallimard, Bibliothèque de la Pléiade, 2000–2005) 1:1216–25.

2. This undoubtedly exaggerated figure comes from Charles Simon Favart, *Mémoires et correspondances littéraires, dramatiques et anecdotiques,* August 15, 1762 (Paris: Collin, 1808; repr., Geneva: Slatkine Reprints, 1970), 21.
3. It would be difficult to find an author whose critical fortunes, even more than two centuries after his death, continue to suffer as much as La Morlière's from what we know about his life and predatory expediencies. With a single sentence in his *Le Roman jusqu'à la Révolution* (Paris: Armand Colin, 1967), 387, Henri Coulet dismisses La Morlière as nothing more than an unworthy imitator of Crébillon. Robert Mauzi finds only one scene from *Angola* worthy of comment in his *L'Idée du bonheur dans la littérature et la pensée française au dix-huitième siècle* (Paris: Armand Colin, 1965), 442. Philippe Laroch castigates La Morlière as the cad incarnate in his *Petits-Maîtres et roués: évolution de la notion de libertinage dans le roman français du XVIIIe siècle* (Quebec: Presses de l'Université Laval, 1979), 157. Given this long tradition, it is not surprising that Raymonde Robert, in *Le Conte de fées littéraire en France de la fin du XVIIe à la fin du XVIIIe siècle* (Nancy: Presses Universitaires de Nancy, 1981), 241, took the step of suggesting that we accept as fact the period's highly dubious rumor that La Morlière was not the author of *Angola,* but stole the manuscript from the far more savory Duc de La Trémouille. Even La Morlière's best contemporary critics—Raymond Trousson in "Le Chevalier de La Morlière: Un Aventurier des lettres au XVIIIe siècle," *Bulletin de l'Académie royale de langue et de littérature française* 68, nos. 3–4 (1990), and Patrick Wald Lasowski in his edition of the novel for *Romanciers libertins du dix-huitième siècle,* 1:1216–36—do not entirely avoid a tone of moral discomfort when discussing the author. To a large extent, these reactions are grounded in the devastating portrait of La Morlière drawn by Diderot in his *Le Neveu de Rameau:* "This Chevalier de La Morlière, with his hat pushed down over his ear, with his head cocked, who looks at you over his shoulder when you pass, who jostles his long sword against his leg, with an insult ready for anyone not wearing one, and who seems to challenge everyone, what is he doing? Everything he can to persuade himself that he is a man of courage. But he is a coward. . . . His long and concerted mimicry of bravery has made him his own dupe. He has pretended for so long that he has ended up believing it." In Denis Diderot, *Œuvres,* ed. Laurent Versini, 5 vols. (Paris: Robert Laffont, 1994–97), 2:651.
4. The classic study of this aversion is Georges May, *Le Dilemme du roman au XVIIIe siècle* (Paris: Presses Universitaires de France, 1963).

5. Pierre Carlet de Chamblain de Marivaux, *La Vie de Marianne*, ed. Michel Gilot (Paris: Garnier-Flammarion, 1978), 47. Subsequent quotations from this work will be followed by the page number in parentheses.
6. Jacques Rochette de La Morlière, *Angola*, in *Romanciers libertins du dix-huitième siècle*, ed. Wald Lasowski, 1:730. Subsequent quotations from this work will be followed by parentheses enclosing the page number according to this edition. The use of italics in this and all other quotations from *Angola* follows this edition except when noted.
7. On La Morlière's use of italics as a satiric device, see Laurent Versini, "Néologie et tours à la mode dans *Angola*," *Travaux de linguistique et de littérature* 13, no. 2 (1975): 505–25.
8. I am following here the order of the two prefaces in La Morlière's 1746 edition of the novel. The same order is used in *Angola*, ed. Jean-Paul Sermain (Paris: Éditions Desjonquères, 1991), which follows the 1749 edition. For reasons he does not explain, Raymond Trousson, in his edition of *Romans libertins du dix-huitième siècle* (Paris: Robert Laffont, 1993), inverts the order of the two prefaces, beginning with the "Epistle to Coquettes" and following it with "We will soon get to the Preface."
9. For a broader look at the eighteenth century's assumption that erotic novels excited and corrupted those who read them, see Henri Coulet, "Le *Topos* du roman corrupteur dans le roman français du XVIIIe siècle," in *L'Épreuve du lecteur: Livres et lectures dans le roman d'ancien régime*, ed. Jan Herman and Paul Pelckmans (Louvain: Éditions Peeters, 1995), 175–90. Surprisingly, Coulet makes no mention of *Angola* in his study of this question.
10. *Mémoire du duc de Luynes*, quoted by François Bluche, in *La Noblesse française au dix-huitième siècle* (Paris: Hachette, 1995), 80.
11. Almaïr's counsel anticipates what, in letter 81 of Laclos' *Les Liaisons dangereuses* of almost forty years later, would become Mme de Merteuil's lapidary formulation of this weakness as a propensity to "confuse love with one's lover."
12. Jean-Marie Goulemot, *Ces Livres qu'on ne lit que d'une main: Lecture et lecteurs de livres pornographiques au XVIIIe siècle* (Aix-en-Provence: Alinea, 1991), 127. This work has appeared in English under the somewhat edulcorated title *Forbidden Texts: Erotic Literature and Its Readers in Eighteenth-Century France*, trans. James Simpson (Philadelphia: University of Pennsylvania Press, 1995).
13. In Chapter 1 we saw how, in Jourdan's *Le Guerrier philosophe*, the desperate Sophie gives a portrait of herself to the departing Chevalier and begs him to

have one done of himself for her. Later, Geltrude's discovery of Sophie's portrait will convince her that her lover is unfaithful.

14. René Démoris, "Esthétique et libertinage: Amour de l'art et art d'aimer," in *Éros philosophique*, ed. François Moureau and Alain-Marc Rieu (Paris: Éditions Honoré Champion, 1984), 151.
15. Mauzi, *L'Idée du bonheur*, 30–31.
16. Marie-Hélène Huet, "Roman libertin et réaction aristocratique," *Dix-Huitième Siècle* 6 (1974): 138–42.
17. Nancy K. Miller, "Libertinage and Feminism," *Yale French Studies* 94 (1998): 17–28.
18. Jean-Jacques Rousseau, *Julie, ou la nouvelle Héloïse*, in *Œuvres complètes*, ed. Bernard Gagnebin and Marcel Raymond, 5 vols. (Paris: Éditions Gallimard, Bibliothèque de la Pléiade, 1959–95), 2:23. Subsequent quotations will be followed by parentheses enclosing the page numbers according to this edition. My English translations of Rousseau's works follow those of *The Collected Writings of Rousseau*, ed. Roger D. Masters and Christopher Kelly (Hanover, NH: University Press of New England, 1990–2006).
19. Denis Diderot, *Éloge de Richardson*, in *Œuvres*, 4:155–56.
20. Robert Darnton, *The Great Cat Massacre and Other Episodes in French Cultural History* (New York: Basic Books, 1984), 246.
21. This first letter to Mme Tourvel, letter 24, all but winks at Merteuil with its perfect mimicry of all the pleading masochism of Saint-Preux's diction: "Ah, for pity's sake, Madame, deign to calm my troubled heart, to tell me what cause I have for hope or fear . . ." Pierre-Ambroise François Choderlos de Laclos, *Les Liaisons dangereuses*, in *Œuvres complètes*, ed. Laurent Versini (Paris: Éditions Gallimard, Bibliothèque de la Pléiade, 1979), 53. Subsequent quotations from Laclos will be followed by parentheses enclosing the page number according to this edition.

CHAPTER 3. LIFE-WRITING AS EPICUREAN ALLEGORY

1. The most helpful overviews of this novel in terms of its structure, significance, and attribution accompany the following modern editions: *L'Enfer de la Bibliothèque Nationale: Œuvres anonymes du XVIIIe siècle*, ed. Philippe Roger, 7 vols. (Paris: Éditions Fayard, 1984–87), 3:17–29; *Romans libertins du XVIIIe siècle*, ed. Trousson, 559–73; *Thérèse philosophe*, ed. Jacques Duprilot (Geneva: Slatkine Reprints, 1980), i–xxxiv; and Pierre Saint-Amand's notices and notes in *Romanciers libertins du XVIIIe siècle*, ed. Wald Lasowski, 1:1279–99.

2. Jean-Baptiste Boyer d'Argens, *Thérèse philosophe*, in *Romanciers libertins du XVIIIe siècle*, ed. Wald Lasowski, 1:874–76. All subsequent quotations from this novel will be followed by parentheses enclosing the page reference according to this edition. While the English translations are my own, I have benefited from the translated excerpts from this novel included as an appendix in Robert Darnton, *The Forbidden Best-Sellers of Pre-Revolutionary France* (New York: W. W. Norton), 249–99.
3. For an analysis of voyeurism and its centrality to the libertine novel as a genre as well as to Thérèse's evolution, see Darnton, *Forbidden Best-Sellers*, 104–6. For a discussion of how Thérèse as female voyeur dismantles the sexism underlying the usually male identity of the voyeur, see Catherine Cusset, *No Tomorrow: The Ethics of Pleasure in the French Enlightenment* (Charlottesville: University Press of Virginia, 1999), 92.
4. For readers of the period these two names were transparent anagrams of the principal figures in a notorious sexual abuse trial of 1731: Père Girard and Mlle Cadière. The public's fascination with this trial was grounded in the fact that Girard's status as a Jesuit made his trial a flashpoint in the much larger conflict between Jansenists and Jesuits that continued throughout the eighteenth century. See on this subject Meta Choudhury, "Carnal Quietism: Embodying Anti-Jesuit Polemics in the Catherine Cadière Affair, 1736," *Eighteenth-Century Studies* 39, no. 2 (Winter 2006): 173–86.
5. For a reading of the Dirrag-Eradice episode as a "desacralisation of the discourse of edification" and a "destabilizing of classical values," see Nicolas Miteran, "La Fureur poétique des abbés ou les illusions dangereuses: Les Discours édifiants dans *Thérèse philosophe*," in *Roman et religion en France, 1713–1866*, ed. Jacques Wagner (Paris: Éditions Honoré Champion, 2002), 86–95.
6. Michel Delon, "De *Thérèse philosophe* à *La Philosophie dans le boudoir:* La Place de la philosophie," in *Romanistische Zeitschrift für Literaturgeschichte* 8, nos. 1–2 (1983): 76–88.
7. This recognition of sexuality's legitimacy, combined with a use of extended philosophical dialogues to force the agreement of one's interlocutor, explain why, in his *Histoire de Juliette* of almost a half century later, Sade's heroine would qualify *Thérèse philosophe* as "the only work that showed what our goal should be, but without fully achieving it." Marquis de Sade, *Œuvres*, ed. Michel Delon, 3 vols. (Paris: Éditions Gallimard, Bibliothèque de la Pléiade, 1990–98) 3:591. Subsequent quotations from Sade will be followed by parentheses enclosing the page number according to this edition.

8. Natania Meeker, *Voluptuous Philosophy: Literary Materialism in the French Enlightenment* (Fordham, NY: Fordham University Press, 2006), 126–54, offers a very different reading of the Abbé's recollections. For her, this chamber pot comparison establishes the Abbé's briefly mentioned "petite fille *ad hoc*" as an emblem of what all men would make of all women. Expanding that intuition, Meeker sees Thérèse's quest for a supposedly liberated sexuality as a somber illustration of how philosophy, always and inevitably sexist, "finds its intellectual and social origins in the contingent management of constrained bodies" (134).

9. For an analysis of Bois-Laurier's deformity as a key image in this novel, see Anne Richardot, "*Thérèse philosophe:* Les Charmes de l'impénétrable," in *Eighteenth-Century Life* 21, no. 2 (1997): 89–99. On how this figure of "la femme barrée" will reappear in Sade's novels, see Chantal Thomas, *Sade, l'œil de la lettre* (Paris: Payot, 1978), 51; Georges Festa, "D'Argens/Sade: Convergences d'une esthétique," *Studies on Voltaire and the Eighteenth Century* 284 (1991): 363–69; and Jeanne-Hélène Roy, "S(t)imulating Pleasure: The Female Body in Sade's *Les Infortunes de la vertu* and *Thérèse philosophe*," *Cincinnati Romance Review* 18 (1999): 122–31.

10. The Count's acute concern for Thérèse's full consent as well as his noncoercive sexuality make him, like the Abbé, an anomalous male figure within the tradition of the libertine novel. This insistence on a perfect reciprocity of pleasure also raises the question of whether a novel like *Thérèse philosophe* might be described as feminist. For Robert Darnton in *Forbidden Best-Sellers*, 107–13, the answer is clearly yes. Lynn Hunt, *The Invention of Pornography: Obscenity and the Origins of Modernity, 1500–1800* (New York: Zone Books, 1993), 44, argues to the contrary that because such novels were written by men and for men, the answer must be no. For an excellent discussion of this entire question and especially for her analysis of how feminine laughter deflates male potency, see Catherine Cusset, *No Tomorrow*, 104–9.

11. On the basis of the list of the novels Thérèse reads before she discovers the two paintings, Jean Mainil, in "Jamais fille chaste n'a lu de romans: Lecture en cachette, lecture en abyme dans *Thérèse philosophe*," in *L'Épreuve du lecteur*, ed. Herman and Pelckmans, 308–16, argues that characters in libertine novel are always constructed as functions of the novels they read. Surprisingly, his analysis of the novel's ending elides entirely any mention of the two paintings and their decisive role in the evolution of Thérèse's pleasure.

CHAPTER 4. THE ESTHETICS OF PLEASURE

This chapter is an expanded version of my essay "Painting for the Senses: Boucher and Epicurean Stoicism," which appeared in *Rethinking Boucher,* edited by Melissa Hyde and Mark Ledbury (Los Angeles: Getty Research Foundation, 2006), 253–68, © the Getty Research Institute. I thank the Institute for its permission to use this material here.

1. On Du Bos' biography, see Alfred Lombard, *L'Abbé Du Bos, un initiateur de la pensée moderne* (Paris: Hachette, 1913).
2. Jean-Baptiste Du Bos, *Réflexions critiques sur la poésie et sur la peinture,* ed. Dominique Désirat (Paris: École Nationale Supérieure des Beaux-Arts, 1993), xxiii. Subsequent quotations from this work will be followed by parentheses enclosing the page reference according to his edition.
3. Baldine Saint Girons underlines the importance of the English influence both on Du Bos and on early eighteenth-century esthetic thought in France: "It is a fact that, at the beginning of the century, the impetus [for esthetic reflection] came from England, where empirical and experimental philosophy found a new way of posing the question of the relation between the beautiful, sense impressions, and sentiment." See Baldine Saint Girons, *Esthétiques du XVIIIe siècle: Le Modèle français* (Paris: Philippe Sers, 1990), 9.
4. For a more complete description of this controversy, see Thomas M. Kavanagh, *Esthetics of the Moment: Literature and Art in the French Enlightenment* (Philadelphia: University of Pennsylvania Press, 1996), 129–63.
5. For the complex history of taste and its role in the larger culture of eighteenth-century France, see Elena Russo, *Styles of Enlightenment: Taste, Politics, and Authorship in Eighteenth-Century France* (Baltimore: Johns Hopkins University Press, 2007).
6. On this subject, see Thomas Crow, *Painters and Public Life in Eighteenth-Century Paris* (New Haven: Yale University Press, 1985).
7. For Boucher's relation to the Dutch tradition, see Jo Hedley, *François Boucher: Seductive Visions* (London: Wallace Collection, 2004), 59–62, as well as her *Jan Steen at the Wallace Collection* (London: Wallace Collection, 1996). For a broader consideration of iconography within the northern style, see Eddy de Jongh, *Questions of Meaning: Theme and Motif in Dutch Seventeenth-Century Painting,* trans. Michael Hoyles (Leiden: Primavera, 2000); Jan Baptist Bedaux, *The Reality of Symbols: Studies of the Iconography of Netherlandish Art, 1400–1800* (The Hague: G. Schwartz, 1990); and Eric

Jan Sluijter, *Seductress of Sight: Studies in Dutch Art of the Golden Age* (Zwolle, Netherlands: Wanders, 2000).

8. For an analysis of the iconography of cabbage, see Colin B. Bailey, "'Details that surreptitiously explain': Boucher as a Genre Painter," in *Rethinking Boucher*, ed. Hyde and Ledbury, 46–54; as well as Bailey, *The Age of Watteau, Chardin, and Fragonard: Masterpieces of French Genre Painting* (New Haven: Yale University Press, 2003).

9. Jennifer Milam was the first scholar to discover and explain how the French game of *pied-de-bœuf* motivates this title. See her "A Triumph of Lucidity: Games and Play in the Art of Jean-Honoré Fragonard" (Ph.D. diss., Princeton University, 1996), 1:75, as well as her book *Fragonard's Playful Paintings* (Manchester, England: Manchester University Press, 2006).

10. This interpretation of Lancret's painting is offered in Richard Rand, ed., *Intimate Encounters: Love and Domesticity in Eighteenth-Century France* (Princeton, NJ: Princeton University Press, 1997), 96–97. Historically, the rabat was worn not only by ecclesiastics, but also by magistrates, lawyers, and even professors.

11. I refer here to Diderot's often quoted dismissal of Boucher as a painter endowed with all the talents expected of an artist except one: "This man has everything, except truth." See Diderot, *Œuvres*, 4:205. Subsequent quotations from the *Salons* will be followed by parentheses enclosing the page reference according to this edition.

12. Louis-Charles Soyer, s.v. "François Boucher," in *Encyclopédie des gens du monde: Répertoire universel des sciences, des lettres et des arts*, 22 vols. (Paris: Treuttel et Würtz, 1833–44), 3:72. Quoted in *François Boucher, 1703–1770*, ed. Pierre Rosenberg, exhibition catalog (New York: Metropolitan Museum of Art, 1986), 63.

13. Daniel Wildenstein, preface to *François Boucher*, 2 vols. ed. Alexandre Ananoff (Lausanne: Bibliothèque des arts, 1976), 1:v.

14. Georges Brunel, *Boucher*, trans. Simon Rees (New York: Vendome, 1986), 14–16. Subsequent quotations from this work will be followed by parentheses enclosing the page reference.

15. Haldane Macfall, *Boucher: The Man, His Times, His Art, and His Signification* (London: The Connoisseur, 1908), 79.

16. Examples of this approach to Boucher would include, in chronological order: Wend Graf von Kalnein and Michael Levey, *Art and Architecture of the Eighteenth Century in France* (London: Penguin Books, 1972); Norman Bryson, *Word and Image: French Paintings of the Ancien Régime*

(Cambridge: Cambridge University Press, 1981); Mary Sheriff, *Fragonard, Art and Eroticism* (Chicago: University of Chicago Press, 1990); Eunice Lipton, "Women, Pleasure, and Painting (e.g., Boucher)," in *Genders* 7 (1990): 69–86; Erica Rand, "Depoliticizing Women: Female Agency, the French Revolution, and the Art of Boucher and David," in *Genders* 7 (1990): 47–68, as well as her "Lesbian Sightings: Scoping for Dykes in Boucher and *Cosmo*," *Journal of Homosexuality* 27 (1994): 123–39; Madelyn Gutwirth, *Twilight of the Goddesses* (New Brunswick, NJ: Rutgers University Press, 1992); and Melissa Hyde, *Making Up the Rococo: François Boucher and His Critics* (Los Angeles: Getty Research Institute, 2006).

17. For the circumstances of this work, see *François Boucher*, ed. Ananoff, 1:337; and Alastair Laing, "Catalogue of Paintings," in *François Boucher, 1703–1770*, ed. Rosenberg, 208–12.

18. Jean de La Fontaine, "L'Hermite," in *Contes et nouvelles en vers*, ed. Georges Couton (Paris: Garnier, 1961), 139.

19. On the evolution of this tradition, see Michel Faré, *La Nature morte en France: Son Histoire et son évolution du XVIIième au XXième siècle*, 2 vols. (Geneva: Pierre Cailler, 1962).

20. Antoine-François Prévost, *Manon Lescaut*, ed. Frédéric Deloffre and Raymond Picard (Paris: Garnier, 1965), 19.

21. Claude Prosper Jolyot de Crébillon, *Les Égarements du cœur et de l'esprit*, ed. René Étiemble (Paris: Éditions Gallimard, 1977), 75.

22. Pierre-Ambroise François Choderlos de Laclos, *Les Liaisons dangereuses*, in *Œuvres complètes*, 108.

23. Jean-Bernard Leblanc, *Lettre sur l'exposition des ouvrages de peinture, sculpture de l'année, et sur l'utilité générale de ces sortes d'expositions* (1747; repr., Geneva: Slatkine Reprints, 1970), 55. Subsequent quotations from this letter are followed by parentheses enclosing the page number.

24. Quoted in *François Boucher*, ed. Ananoff, 1:227.

25. This choice of "speaking only to the eyes" (as opposed to the way a narrative work was seen as speaking to the mind) was one of the central charges that the critic Étienne de La Font de Saint-Yenne leveled against Boucher and *le goût moderne* in 1747. For a modern reprint of La Font de Saint-Yenne's essay, *Réflexions sur quelques causes de l'état présent de la peinture en France*, see *La Peinture en procès: L'Invention de la critique d'art au siècle des Lumières*, ed. René Démoris and Florence Ferran (Paris: Presses de la Sorbonne Nouvelle, 2001), 91.

26. Charles-Nicolas Cochin, *Lettre à un amateur en réponse aux critiques qui ont paru sur l'exposition des tableaux*, in *Collection Deloynes: Collection sur les pièces et les beaux arts, 1673–1808* (Paris: Bibliothèque Nationale de France, 1980), microfiche, vol. 5, no. 61, 4–5.
27. Eunice Lipton explicitly makes the point, in discussing Boucher's *Aurora and Cephalus*, that "the male body [is no] less beautiful or tantalizing than the female." See her "Women, Pleasure, and Painting (e.g. Boucher)," 72.
28. For an interpretation of Apollo's feminized body and the other sexually ambiguous male and female bodies in *The Rising of the Sun* and *The Setting of the Sun*, see Ewa Lajer-Burcharth, "Pompadour's Dream: Boucher, Diderot, and Modernity," in *Rethinking Boucher*, ed. Hyde and Ledbury, 229–51.
29. In her chapter titled "Rococo Quid Pro Quo," Melissa Hyde makes the point that, in Boucher's pastoral scenes, a single epicene facial type often circulates indiscriminately between male and female characters. See Hyde, *Making Up The Rococo*, 83–105.
30. Edmond de Goncourt and Jules de Goncourt, *L'Art du dix-huitième siècle*, 2 vols. (Paris: Rapilly, 1873), 1:200.
31. Daniel Wildenstein, preface to *François Boucher*, ed. Ananoff, 1:vi.
32. Thomas Crow, "The Critique of Enlightenment in Eighteenth-Century Art," *Art Criticism* 3 (1986): 56.
33. Quoted in *François Boucher*, ed. Ananoff, 1:395.

CHAPTER 5. ROUSSEAU'S EUDEMONY OF LIBERTY

1. It was in fact Diderot who acted as Rousseau's agent in commissioning the drawing for the frontispiece from Jean-Baptiste Pierre. Early in the second part of the *Discourse on the Sciences and Arts*, Rousseau mentions Pierre as one of a number of artists whose talent risks being corrupted by what he sees as the degeneracy of the period.
2. Jean-Jacques Rousseau, *Discours sur les sciences et les arts*, in *Œuvres complètes*, 3:16.
3. The lost Boucher painting on which Blondel d'Azaincourt's print is based was titled *L'Oiseau privé*. Similar prints inspired by the Boucher original were engraved by Flipart le Jeune, Daullé, and de Billy. They can be found in *François Boucher*, ed. Ananoff, 2:184–85.
4. Jean-Jacques Rousseau, *Correspondance complète*, ed. R. A. Leigh, 52 vols. (Geneva: Institut et Musée Voltaire; Oxford: Voltaire Foundation, 1965–98), 22:329 (letter 3806). On Rousseau's predilection for this image, see Frédé-

dric S. Eigeldinger, "Instructions de Rousseau pour l'illustration de quelques-unes de ses œuvres," *Bulletin de l'Association Jean-Jacques Rousseau* 52 (1999): 17–27; as well as René Démoris, "Boucher, Diderot, Rousseau," in *Rethinking Boucher*, ed. Hyde and Ledbury, 201–28.

5. Borrowed from the vocabulary of Greek moral philosophy, the term *eudemony* had a brief afterlife in Jeremy Bentham's nineteenth-century Utilitarian movement. Bentham used the word to designate what he called "the art of applying life to the maximization of well-being" (*The Works of Jeremy Bentham*, ed. John Bowring, 11 vols. [Edinburgh: W. Tait, 1843], 8:289). More recently, the term provided the title for Thomas Bass, *Eudemonic Pie* (New York: Vintage Books, 1986), a study of the attempts by the first wave of computer aficionados to fashion minicomputers that could predict the winning numbers of casino roulette wheels.

6. Étienne de La Boétie first composed his *Discourse of Voluntary Servitude* in 1552 when he was studying law. His close friend, Michel de Montaigne, devastated by La Boétie's death at the age of thirty-three in 1563, intended to include the *Discourse* within his *Essays* which first appeared in 1580. He decided against doing that when the work was published in 1576 by Protestants as an attack on the monarchy during France's wars of religion. For an excellent contextualization of this work, see *The Politics of Obedience: The Discourse of Voluntary Servitude*, trans. Harry Kurz (Montreal: Black Rose Books, 2006).

7. Leo Strauss, *Natural Right and History* (Chicago: University of Chicago Press, 1970), 253. Subsequent quotations from the work will be followed by parentheses enclosing the page number.

8. Jean-Jacques Rousseau, Lettres à Malesherbes, in *Œuvres complètes*, 1:1134–38.

9. Claude Lévi-Strauss, "Jean-Jacques Rousseau: Fondateur des sciences de l'homme," in *Anthropologie Structurale Deux* (Paris: Plon, 1973), 45–56. On Rousseau's anthropology and its relation to the implicit anthropologies of such figures as Buffon, Voltaire, Helvétius, and Diderot, see Michèle Duchet, *Anthropologie et histoire au siècle des Lumières* (1971; repr., Paris: Albin Michel, 1995), 322–76.

10. As Lévi-Strauss puts it: "Until Rousseau, the starting point had been to separate man from nature, and to assume his sovereign reign" ("Jean-Jacques Rousseau," 53).

11. Leo Damrosch, *Jean-Jacques Rousseau: Restless Genius* (New York: Houghton Mifflin, 2005), 242.

12. For an excellent discussion of the cosmological and ethical dimensions of Hesiod's text as well as of how his premise of an original golden age parallels Rousseau's "necessary hypothesis" of a presocietal state of nature, see Laura M. Slatkin, "Measuring Authority, Authoritative Measures: Hesiod's *Works and Days*," in *The Moral Authority of Nature*, ed. Lorraine Daston and Fernando Vidal (Chicago: University of Chicago Press, 2004), 25–49.
13. Jean-Jacques Rousseau, *Discourse on the Origin of Inequality*, in *Œuvres complètes*, 3:170–71.
14. Jean-Jacques Rousseau, *Essay on the Origin of Languages*, in *Œuvres complètes*, 5: 405–6.
15. Comparing the workings of music and painting as mimetic forms was a commonplace of eighteenth-century esthetic theory. In addition to Du Bos' *Réflexions critiques*, the most important statements of this syncretism can be found in Charles Batteux, *Les Beaux-arts réduits à un même principe* (Paris: Durand, 1746); and Louis-Bertrand Castel, *L'Optique des couleurs* (Paris: Briasson, 1740).
16. On Rousseau's attachment to a mimetic theory of art, see Marian Hobson, *The Object of Art* (Cambridge: Cambridge University Press, 1982); as well as my own *Writing the Truth: Authority and Desire in Rousseau* (Berkeley: University of California Press, 1987).
17. On Rousseau's familiarity with this late seventeenth-century debate between the disciples of Charles Le Brun and those of Roger de Piles, see Jean Starobinski, "De la gravure et de la peinture: L'Atelier de l'iconoclaste," *Annales de la société Jean-Jacques Rousseau* 45 (2005): 213–18.
18. Philip Robinson, discussing the primacy of narrative over sensation at the core of Rousseau's esthetic theories, describes his politicizing of the esthetic in terms of what he calls "the quasi-linguistic function of the arts in relation to their public." See Philip Robinson, "Rousseau et l'estampe: Mieux qu'un art visual," *Annales de la société Jean-Jacques Rousseau* 45 (2005): 311.
19. Jean-Jacques Rousseau, Lettre à Lecat, in *Œuvres complètes*, 3:102.
20. Rousseau expressed his preference for Boucher, in spite of his seeing his style as *bien maniéré*, in a letter of December 5, 1757, to Elisabeth-Sophie-Françoise Lalive de Bellegarde, asking her help in making arrangements for the illustrations to accompany *Julie*. See *Correspondance complète*, 4:384 (letter 587).
21. The classical formulation of this charge can be found in J. L. Talmon, *The Origins of Totalitarian Democracy* (London: Secker and Warburg, 1952).

CHAPTER 6. LACLOS' ANTHROPOLOGY OF PLEASURE

1. On the extent and variety of prostitution in eighteenth-century France, see Erica-Marie Benabou, *La Prostitution et la police des mœurs au XVIIIe siècle* (Paris: Perrin, 1987). See also the introductory essay in Patrick Wald Lasowski, *L'Espion libertin, ou le calendrier du plaisir* (Arles: Picquier, 2000), 7–25.
2. The correspondence between Riccoboni and Laclos can be found in Laclos, *Œuvres complètes*, ed. Versini, 763.
3. The phrasing of Laclos' epigraph—"of my century"—differs slightly from Rousseau's "of my times."
4. Laclos, "De l'éducation des femmes," in *Œuvres complètes*, 389. Laclos' epigraph is from letter 39 of Seneca's *Letters to Lucilius*. All subsequent quotations from the three essays by Laclos which Versini groups together under the rubric "The Education of Women" will be followed by parentheses enclosing the page reference according to that edition.
5. This first draft of Laclos' essay can also be linked to his novel by reading it as a retrospective diagnosis of Merteuil's threatening singularity. In that draft Laclos writes: "In society as it is today, a woman who has received a proper education would not be particularly unhappy so long as she keeps her place and *very dangerous if she tried to go beyond it*" (390; italics mine).
6. My reference here is to Diderot's *Supplément au voyage de Bougainville*. The three essays by Laclos now grouped together under the title "On the Education of Women" never appeared during his lifetime. The short Châlons response and the longer anthropology of woman were first published by Edouard Champion as *De l'éducation des femmes par Choderlos de Laclos* (Paris: A. Messein, 1903). The third essay, composed substantially later, was first published by Jean Dagnan-Bouveret in the *Revue Bleue* of May 1908. That third essay of approximately twelve pages amounts to a reading program intended to guide the education of a young woman of gentle birth. Laclos never gave that third essay a title and it has none of the philosophical or anthropological ambitions of the first two pieces. It is unfortunate that both Pléiade editions of Laclos (Maurice Allem's of 1944 and Laurent Versini's of 1979) have canonized the relegation of Laclos' portrait of natural woman to a title, "On the Education of Women," that is at best misleading.
7. Chantal Thomas, introduction to *De l'éducation des femmes* (Grenoble: Éditions Jerome Millon, 1991), 36. Thomas nicely titles her introduction "A Portrait of Natural Woman." That title has the advantage of underlining the fact that these essays are grounded far more in Laclos' emulation of

Rousseau's *Discourses* than they are in some biographical event imagined as prompting on his part a changed and more sympathetic attitude toward women. That biographical approach most often argues that Laclos' newly solicitous concern for woman's education was the response by a mellowing forty-three-year-old to the pregnancy of his twenty-three-year-old mistress, Marie-Solange Duperre, who would give birth to their first child in May 1784 and whom Laclos would marry two years later. This rather Victorian perspective is articulated at length in Georges Poisson, *Choderlos de Laclos ou l'obstination* (Paris: Grasset, 1985). For an analysis of these essays that builds on Poisson's thesis but which reads his concern with women's education as evidence of a "feministic" (as opposed to "feminist") Laclos, see Suellen Diaconoff, "Resistance and Retreat: A Laclosian Primer for Women," *University of Toronto Quarterly* 58, no. 3 (1989): 391–408.

8. On the complexity of the debates concerning make-up during this period and its importance within eighteenth-century esthetics, see Hyde, *Making Up the Rococo*.

9. Charles Baudelaire, "Notes sur *Les Liaisons dangereuses*," in *Œuvres complètes*, ed. Claude Pichois (Paris: Éditions Gallimard, Bibliothèque de la Pléiade, 1975), 2:66–75.

10. Following out Baudelaire's view of this work as a "manual of sociability," one could read Laclos' novel as a kind of satiric "conduct book." On that subject, see my "Educating Women: Laclos and the Conduct of Sexuality," in *The Ideology of Conduct: Essays on Literature and the History of Sexuality*, ed. Nancy Armstrong and Leonard Tennenhouse (New York: Methuen, 1987): 150–53.

11. On the relative importance of female and male characters in Laclos' novel, see Anne Deneys, "The Political Economy of the Body in the *Liaisons dangereuses* of Choderlos de Laclos," in *Eroticism and the Body Politic*, ed. Lynn Hunt (Baltimore: Johns Hopkins University Press, 1991), 41–62; and Jean-Marie Goulemot, "Le Lecteur-voyageur et la mise en scène de l'imaginaire viril dans *Les Liaisons dangereuses*," in *Laclos et le libertinage*, ed. René Pomeau (Paris: Presses Universitaires de France, 1983), 163–75.

12. Friedrich Melchior Grimm, *Correspondance littéraire, philosophique et critique*, ed. Maurice Tourneux, 16 vols. (Paris: Garnier, 1877–82), 13:110 (April 1782).

13. Laclos, *Les Liaisons dangereuses*, in *Œuvres complètes*, 167. All subsequent quotations from the novel will be followed by parentheses enclosing the page number according to this edition. My translations loosely follow those of P. W. K. Stone, in *Les Liaisons Dangereuses* (London: Penguin Books, 1961).

14. Given Merteuil's status as the ultimate avatar of socialized woman, it is not surprising that the perfect control with which she transforms every aspect of her appearance into a mask should make her the antithesis of natural woman. Describing the physiognomy of natural woman, Laclos writes: "She does not yet know how to simper, but she knows even less how to restrain herself. Her soul is legible on her face. It expresses her anger and terror with force, while her desire and voluptuousness are painted there with no less energy" (403).
15. Tzvetan Todorov, *Littérature et signification* (Paris: Éditions Larousse, 1967).

CHAPTER 7. RECASTING THE EPICUREAN NOVEL

1. As a historical figure, the Vicomte de Mirabeau was given a surprisingly important role in the first part of the six-hour television epic *La Révolution française*, done by Robert Enrico and Richard T. Heffron as part of France's state-sponsored celebration of the Revolution's bicentennial. In that first part, titled *Les Années Lumière*, the late Peter Ustinov played the Vicomte superbly.
2. Antoine de Baecque goes so far as to describe Mirabeau as fomenting "guerilla warfare of counter-revolutionary laughter" in the very midst of the National Assembly. See his *Les Éclats du rire: La Culture des rieurs au XVIIIième siècle* (Paris: Calmann-Levy, 2000), 217.
3. The best known of his satiric writings are *La Lanterne magique nationale*, *Le Pot-pourri national*, *Les Quatre Repas*, and the five *Bulletin de couches de M. Target, père et mère de la constitution des ci-devant français*. The catalog of the Bibliothèque Nationale attributes almost a hundred such polemical tracts to Mirabeau.
4. For Mirabeau's biography, see Joseph-Victor Sarrazin, *Mirabeau Tonneau: Ein Condottiere aus der Revolutionszeit* (Leipzig: Gebhardt und Wilisch, 1893); and Eugène Berger, *Le Vicomte de Mirabeau (Mirabeau-Tonneau), 1754–1792* (Paris: Hachette, 1904).
5. The full title for the 1792 edition was *La Morale des sens ou l'homme du siècle, extrait des mémoires de M. le chevalier de Barville; réédités par Mr. M. . . . D.M . . .* Reedited only once in the nineteenth century (Brussels: Gay et Doucé, 1882) and mistakenly attributed to Mirabeau's more famous older brother, it has recently been republished as Vicomte de Mirabeau, *La Morale des sens*, ed. Jane P. Sctrick (Paris: Phébus, 2000). All quotations from this work will be followed by parentheses enclosing the page reference according to that edition.

6. Sctrick, preface to *La Morale des sens*, 12.
7. See May, *Le Dilemme du roman*.
8. Robert Darnton, "Readers Respond to Rousseau: The Fabrication of Romantic Sensitivity," chapter 6 in *Great Cat Massacre*, 228.
9. Rousseau expresses his own mistrust of written language as an inevitably duplicitous sign system in his *Essay on the Origin of Language*, a work never published during his lifetime.
10. For a more extensive treatment of this force of the moment as it relates to the French Enlightenment, see my *Esthetics of the Moment*, 11–25 and passim.
11. I am referring here to the famous passage on the unity of matter and its transformations at the beginning of *Le Rêve de d'Alembert*, where Diderot argues that Falconet's statues of men will, with the passage of time, disintegrate into dust, become one with the soil and plants, and in turn be assimilated by new generations of living men. See *Œuvres*, 1:613.
12. On this subject, see Jacques Roger, *Les Sciences de la vie dans la pensée française du XVIIIe siècle* (Paris: Armand Colin, 1963). Roger's study brings together the period's many variations on this opposition and demonstrates its centrality to Enlightenment thought.

CHAPTER 8. THEATERS OF PLEASURE

1. Henri d'Alméras, *Les Théâtres libertins au XVIIIe siècle* (Paris: H. Daragon, 1905), 1.
2. The most accessible modern reprint of the plays associated with this erotic theater is *Théâtre érotique français au XVIIIe siècle*, ed. Jean-Jacques Pauvert (Paris: Terrain Vague, 1993). This edition of fourteen plays with publication dates ranging from 1726 to 1792 is the most recent avatar of an anonymous collection of eighteenth-century erotic plays first published under the title *Le Théâtre gaillard* in 1776 and regularly reedited throughout the nineteenth century.
3. Léo Claretie, *Histoire des théâtres de société* (Paris: Librairie Molière, 1906), 12–13. For a study of the generic traits which distinguish society theater from official theater in the eighteenth century, see Marie-Emmanuelle Plagnol-Diéval, *Le Théâtre de société: Un Autre Théâtre?* (Paris: Éditions Honoré Champion, 2003). For an entertaining and well-documented account of private theatrical performances during the second half of the eighteenth century, see the final chapter of Maurice Lever, *Théâtre et Lumières* (Paris: Éditions Fayard, 2001).

4. Martine de Rougemont, *La Vie théâtrale en France au XVIIIe siècle* (Paris: Éditions Honoré Champion, 1988; repr., Geneva: Slatkine Reprints, 1996), 306. The term *théâtre de société* is also preferred by David Trott in *Théâtre du XVIIIe siècle* (Paris: Éditions Espaces 34, 2000), 165–80.
5. For Rousseau's description of this event, see *Les Confessions*, in *Œuvres complètes*, 1:376–79.
6. Louis Petit de Bachaumont, *Mémoires secrets pour servir à l'histoire de la République des Lettres en France*, 18 vols. (London: J. Adamson, 1784–89), 5:238 (March 17, 1770).
7. See Rougemont, *La Vie théâtrale*, 308–9.
8. *Mercure de France* (April 1732), 775–76. Quoted in Judith Curtis and David Trott, *Histoire et recueil des Lazzis* (Oxford: Voltaire Foundation, 1996), 27.
9. Grimm, *Correspondance littéraire*, letter 20, 1:158.
10. The residences that drew the largest audiences were the Hôtel de Soyecourt in the faubourg Saint-Honoré, the Hôtel de Clermont-Tonnerre in the Marais, and the Hôtel de Jobak in the rue Saint-Merry.
11. On the proliferation of theaters during this period, see Rougemont, *La Vie théâtrale*, 271–78.
12. This phrase is borrowed from Curtis and Trott, eds., *Histoire et recueil des Lazzis*, 34.
13. Louis-François Métra [also Mettra], *Correspondance littéraire secrète*, 18 vols. (London: J. Adamson, 1787–90), 12:421. For an overview of Métra's career, see Karin Angelike, *Louis-François Mettra: Ein französischer Zeitungsverleger in Köln, 1770–1800* (Cologne: Bohlau Verlag, 2002).
14. For a study of the complex dynamic between theater, theories of acting, self-presentation, and social mobility from the mid-seventeenth century through the Revolution, see Jeffrey Leichman, "Acting Up: Staging the Modern Subject in Eighteenth-Century France" (Ph.D. diss., Yale University, 2008).
15. Quoted by Claretie, *Histoire des théâtres de société*, 13.
16. Rougemont, *La Vie théâtrale*, 303–4.
17. Quoted by Claretie, *Histoire des théâtres de société*, 13–14.
18. Edmond de Goncourt, *La Femme au dix-huitième siècle* [1862], ed. Elizabeth Badinter (Paris: Flammarion, 1982), 133–34.
19. On the relation of the salon to amateur theatrics, see Rougemont, *La Vie théâtrale*, 311.
20. See Curtis and Trott, *Histoire et recueil des Lazzis*, 26.
21. See Rougemont, *La Vie théâtrale*, 308.

22. On Carmontelle and his theater, see Jean-Hervé Donnard, *Le Théâtre de Carmontelle* (Paris: Armand Colin, 1967).
23. Daniel Gerould, ed., *Gallant and Libertine: Eighteenth-Century French Divertissements and Parades* (New York: Performing Arts Journal Publications, 1983), 9.
24. In her study of society theater, Plagnol-Diéval describes the explicit sexuality of erotic theater as "the first clearly perceptible mark of its differences from official theater." See Plagnol-Diéval, *Le Théâtre de société*, 22.
25. Gaston Capon and Robert Yve-Plessis, *Les Théâtres clandestins* (Paris: Librairie Plessis, 1905); Arthur Maria Rabenalt, *Voluptas ludens: Erotisches Geheimtheater, siebzehntes, achtzehntes und neunzehntes Jahrhundert* (Munich: Verlag Die Schaubühne, 1963).
26. Rougemont, *La Vie théâtrale*, 314 and 307.
27. Gustave Lanson, *Nivelle de La Chaussée et la comédie larmoyante* (Paris: Hachette, 1887), 11–12.
28. Jacques Truchet, ed., *Le Théâtre du XVIIIe siècle*, 2 vols. (Paris: Éditions Gallimard, Collection de la Pléiade, 1974), 1:xxxiv.
29. An interesting variation on the relation between staged performance and printed text can be found in the four-volume *Théâtre d'amour* published by Delisle de Sales in 1780. These plays, with titles like *Junon et Ganymède*, *La Vierge de Babylone*, *Héloyse et Abeilard*, and *Ninette et Finette*, were not intended for stage performance, but as an armchair theater featuring fantastical scenarios of sexuality across different periods and cultures. See Capon and Yve-Plessis, *Les Théâtres clandestins*, 157–75.
30. These police reports are described in Alan Williams, *The Police of Paris, 1718–1789* (Baton Rouge: Louisiana State University Press, 1979); as well as in Camille Piton, *Paris sous Louis XV: Rapports des Inspecteurs de Police au Roi* (Paris: Mercure de France, 1914). For actual police reports, see *Journal des Inspecteurs de M. de Sartines*, ed. Lorédan Larchey, 2 vols. (Brussels: E. Parent, 1863).
31. Details as to the casting for this performance are given in Capon and Yve-Plessis, *Les Théâtres clandestins*, 142–44.
32. The phases of the Duc d'Orléan's theatromania are described in ibid., 90–102.
33. It is to Mlle Gaussin, notorious for the broad and rapid variety of her protectors, that Bachaumont attributes the endearing explanation of her accommodating spirit: "Que voulez-vous! Ça leur fait tant de plaisir et il m'en coûte si peu" (What can I say! It gives them so much pleasure and costs me so little). See Bachaumont, *Mémoires secrets*, 1:31.

34. For the details of this event, see the introduction to Pauvert's *Théâtre érotique français*, 8–9. Pauvert's introduction to this 1993 anthology is a reprint of the introduction to the similar but somewhat edulcorated anthology published by B. de Villeneuve (the pseudonym of Raoul Vèze), *Le Théâtre d'amour au XVIIIe siècle* (Paris: Bibliothèque des Curieux, 1910).
35. For a discussion of literary representations of the prostitute in eighteenth-century France, see Kathryn Norberg, "The Libertine Whore: Prostitution in French Pornography from Margot to Juliette," in *The Invention of Pornography*, ed. Lynn Hunt, 225–52; as well as Pamela Cheek, *Sexual Antipodes, Enlightenment Globalization, and the Placing of Sex* (Stanford, CA: Stanford University Press, 2003), 62–77.
36. Pierre Nicole, *Traité de la comédie et autres pièces d'un procès du théâtre*, ed. Laurent Thirouin (Paris: Éditions Honoré Champion, 1998), 37.
37. Pauvert, *Théâtre érotique français*, 19.
38. For the sake of accessibility, I have limited the choice of the plays discussed here to those available in the Pauvert anthology. All quotations are followed by parentheses enclosing the page references according to that edition.
39. Collé composed this play in response to the Duc de la Vallières's request for a play to be performed at his Château de Champs on Good Friday of 1737. Much to Collé's discomfort, the duke published the play clandestinely in 1739. The episodes surrounding this play are described in his *Correspondance inédite de Collé*, ed. Honoré Bonhomme (Paris: Plon, 1864), 372–78.
40. Both Grandval *père* and *fils* wrote and acted in erotic comedies. Nicolas Racot de Grandval (1676–1753), in addition to producing parodies of Corneille, Racine, and Voltaire, was the organist at the abbey of Saint-Germain-des-Près. Charles-François Racot de Grandval (1710–84) was a playwright and well-known actor within the Comédie-Française. He performed regularly with his mistress, Mlle Dumesnil, in the erotic theater pieces he staged at his *petite maison*.
41. This play's status as a masterpiece should perhaps be qualified by Mérard's notorious plagiarism. Paule Adamy's recent edition of *L'Esprit des mœurs* (Bressac: Plein Chant, 2008) includes the earlier *La Matinée libertine*, often attributed to Andréa de Nerciat, from which Mérard took much of the material for his first act. Adamy also includes in her edition a later, three-act version of *L'Esprit des mœurs*, which she sees as a collective work done by Mérard's enemies with the intention of satirizing his plagiarism by once again stealing everything he had stolen and adding to it still further thefts. Adamy nicely describes Mérard as "less a creator than a sponge."

42. On this question of performance, see Laurence Senelick, "The World Made Flesh: Staging Pornography in Eighteenth-Century Paris," *Theatre Research International* 33, no 2 (2008): 191–203. On the basis of both the preference for bodily action and the actors' freedom in relation to the script, Senelick argues for a similarity between Mérard's theatrical esthetic and Diderot's emphasis on the importance of the tableau in his *Entretiens sur le Fils Naturel* of 1757. See Diderot, *Œuvres*. 4:1131–90.
43. Louis-Benoit Picard, *Les Visitandines, comédie en 2 actes* (Paris: Madaran, 1792). This work is available digitally on the Web site of the Bibliothèque Nationale at www.bnf.fr.
44. On the role of pornography as a preferred weapon in attacks on the monarchy, see Chantal Thomas, *La Reine scélérate: Marie-Antoinette dans les pamphlets* (Paris: Éditions du Seuil, 1989); Lynn Hunt, *The Family Romance of the French Revolution* (Berkeley: University of California Press, 1992), 89–123; and the essay by Maurice Lever, "Marie-Antoinette: icône d'une pornographie politique," in *Anthologie érotique: Le XVIIIe siècle*, ed. Maurice Lever (Paris: Éditions Robert Laffont, 2003), 1029–38.
45. For a provocative study of the respective roles of bodily gesture and verbal utterance in a later form of erotic theater, a genre he sees as expressing "the orgy impulse as a form of utopian desire," see Karl Toepfer, *Theater, Aristocracy, and Pornography: The Orgy Calculus* (New York: PAJ Publications, 1991), 59–80.
46. Michel Delon underlines the importance of what he calls a specifically "erotic energy," in *L'Idée d'énergie au tournant des Lumières, 1770–1820* (Paris: Presses Universitaires de France, 1988), 134. See also on this subject Stéphanie Massé, "Représentation du corps et naturalisme radical dans le théâtre érotique clandestin," in *Les Théâtres de société au XVIIIe siècle*, ed. Marie-Emmanuelle Plagnol-Diéval and Dominique Quéro (Brussels: Éditions de l'Université de Bruxelles, 2005), 225–35.

CONCLUSION

1. On La Mettrie's medical studies and the role they would play in his larger philosophy, see Kathleen Wellman, *La Mettrie: Medicine, Philosophy, and Enlightenment* (Durham, NC: Duke University Press, 1992).
2. The delight Frederick II took in La Mettrie's presence at his court as a consolidation of his image as the benevolent protector of Europe's persecuted philosophers is clear in the *Éloge du Sieur La Mettrie*, which he

published under his own name shortly after his protégé's death and which remains the most complete sources of details as to La Mettrie's life. See Frederick II, King of Prussia, *Éloges de trois philosophes* (London: n.p., 1753), 30–53.

3. Julien Offray de La Mettrie, *Anti-Sénèque, ou le souverain bien*; *L'École de la volupté*; *Système d'Épicure*, ed. Ann Thomson (Paris: Éditions Desjonquères, 1996), 165. Subsequent quotations from this work will be followed by parentheses enclosing the page number according to this edition.

4. Louis Antoine de Saint-Just, "Rapport au nom du Comité de salut public sur le mode du décret contre les ennemis de la Révolution présentée à la Convention Nationale le 13 Ventôse an II (3 mars 1794)," in *Œuvres Complètes*, ed. Anne Kupiec and Miguel Abensour (Paris: Éditions Gallimard, 2004), 673. Subsequent quotations from this address will be followed by parentheses enclosing the page reference according to this edition.

5. On the larger history of happiness, see Darrin M. McMahon, *Happiness: A History* (New York: Atlantic Monthly Press, 2006). McMahon examines the notion of happiness in a much broader sense, looking at how different periods and societies have conceived of well-being. The intention behind his spirited discussion is to trace the genealogies of the many different versions of "happiness" that have punctuated the history of the West, from classical Greece to contemporary America.

6. The new role of happiness and that term's roots in chance find themselves erased in most English translations of the Declaration of 1789 when *le bonheur de tous* becomes the more stolid "the general welfare."

7. Lynn Hunt, *Inventing Human Rights* (New York: W. W. Norton, 2007), 19.

8. The longer history of the shift I am associating with the *cahiers de doléances* is the subject of John Shovlin's *The Political Economy of Virtue: Luxury, Patriotism, and the Origins of the French Revolution* (Ithaca, NY: Cornell University Press, 2006). Looking not at pleasure but at what he calls the "spectacular consumption" associated with luxury goods, Shovlin argues that a crucial change took place in the critique of luxury after midcentury. That critique, which until the 1750s expressed the aristocracy's denunciation of illegitimate consumption by the vulgar, became, in the decades leading to the Revolution, the vehicle with which the rising bourgeoisie attacked aristocratic displays of luxury as abusive markers of social distinction. Shovlin's analysis is particularly helpful for its attention to the decidedly sensationist semiology that underpinned this new challenge leveled against the aristocracy.

9. Rousseau, *Les Confessions*, in *Œuvres complètes*, 1:404; and Sade, *Œuvres*, ed. Delon, 3:152.
10. As Lynn Hunt has put it, "One of the most fateful consequences of the revolutionary attempt to break with the past was the invention of ideology." See her *Politics, Culture, and Class*, 12.
11. Augustin Cochin (1876–1916) was killed in World War I. His major works were published posthumously under the titles *Les Sociétés de pensée et la démocratie moderne* (Paris: Plon-Nourrit, 1921) and *La Révolution de la libre-pensée* (Paris: Plon, 1924). The most extensive study of Cochin available in English is the chapter devoted to him in François Furet, *Interpreting the French Revolution*, trans. Elborg Forster (Cambridge: Cambridge University Press, 1981), 164–204. See also Daniel Gordon, *Citizens without Sovereignty* (Princeton, NJ: Princeton University Press, 1994), 30–34. In his translation of Furet, Forster renders Cochin's *société de pensée* as "philosophical society"—an unfortunate choice which obfuscates the meaning of a term closer to "belief-based society" or "ideology-based society."
12. Émile Durkheim, *The Elementary Forms of the Religious Life*, trans. and intro. Karen E. Fields (New York: Free Press, 1995), 215. The historian Mona Ozouf concludes her 1976 study of the Revolution's festivals with a chapter that qualifies their ultimate function as a "transfer of sacrality" from Christian God to revolutionary Nation. See her *Festivals and the French Revolution*, trans. Alan Sheridan (Cambridge, MA: Harvard University Press, 1988), 262–82. See also McMahon, *Happiness*, 251–67.

Illustration Credits

Fig. 1. Réunion des Musées Nationaux / Art Resource, NY.
Fig. 2. Courtesy of the Académie des Beaux Arts.
Fig. 3. By kind permission of Mr. and Mrs. Stewart Resnick, Los Angeles.
Fig. 4. Scala / Art Resource, NY.
Fig. 5. Courtesy of the Beinecke Rare Book and Manuscript Library, Yale University.
Fig. 6. Courtesy of the Beinecke Rare Book and Manuscript Library, Yale University.
Fig. 7. Bridgeman-Giraudon / Art Resource, NY.
Fig. 8. Courtesy of the J. Paul Getty Museum, Los Angeles.
Fig. 9. Courtesy of the Frick Collection, New York.
Fig. 10. Courtesy of the Ashmolean Museum, Oxford, United Kingdom.
Fig. 11. Courtesy of the National Gallery of Art, Washington, DC.
Fig. 12. Musée des Beaux-Arts, Nancy, France. Photo: Pierre Mignot, Nancy, France.
Fig. 13. Scala / Art Resource, NY.
Fig. 14. Courtesy of the Beinecke Rare Book and Manuscript Library, Yale University.
Fig. 15. Réunion des Musées Nationaux / Art Resource, NY.
Fig. 16. Fine Arts Museums of San Francisco, Achenbach Foundation for the Graphic Arts.
Fig. 17. Fine Arts Museums of San Francisco, Achenbach Foundation for the Graphic Arts.
Fig. 18. Fine Arts Museums of San Francisco, Achenbach Foundation for the Graphic Arts.

Fig. 19. Fine Arts Museums of San Francisco, Achenbach Foundation for the Graphic Arts.
Fig. 20. Courtesy of the J. Paul Getty Museum, Los Angeles.
Fig. 21. Bildarchiv Preussischer Kulturbesitz / Art Resource, NY.

Index

A

Abdera, 173
Académie française, 73, 193
Académie royale de musique, 173, 185
Académie royale de peinture, 74, 98
Addison, Joseph, 73
Adorno, Theodor, 7–8
Ages of Man, the, 111–115, 126
Aix-la-Chapelle, peace treaty of, 175
allegory: of the novel, 12, 22, 28–30; of pleasure, 55, 61–63, 65, 67, 70; in the visual arts, 100, 104, 120; of writing, 24–25
Alphonse l'Impuissant (Collé). *See* Collé, Charles
amateur theater. *See* society theater
American War for Independence, 150
ancien régime: critique of, 149, 199; modern views of, 3, 142, 172; social divisions and institutions of, 82, 151, 167, 184, 199, 212–213
Angola (La Morlière). *See* La Morlière, Jacques Rochette de
Appareilleuse, L' (Grandval *père*). *See* Grandval, Nicolas Racot de
Aretino, Pietro, 195
Argens, Jean-Baptiste de Boyer, marquis d', 53; *Thérèse philosophe*, 53–71, 92, 103, 128–129, 163, 168, 213, 225n3, 225n4, 225n7, 226nn8–11
aristocracy: and class divisions, 6, 165–166; fashions and practices of, 34, 48, 53, 171–174, 177, 180, 188, 199; reactions against, 4, 6, 129, 210–211, 241n8

Aristotle, 72, 93, 107
Art de foutre ou Paris foutant, L' (The Art of Fucking or Paris Fucking), 183
ataraxia, 91
atomism, 5, 8, 203, 205, 215
Aubert, Michel, 96
Augustine, Saint, 107

B

Bachaumont, Louis Petit de, 174, 182, 238n33
Bacon, Francis, 8
Baecque, Antoine de, 235n2
Barthes, Roland, 1
Baudelaire, Charles, 142–143, 147, 234n10
Baudouin, Pierre-Antoine, 42
Beaumarchais, Pierre Augustin Caron de, 172, 174, 179, 192, 196; *The Barber of Seville*, 174; *The Marriage of Figaro*, 179, 192, 196
beauty, female, 17, 43, 133–134, 137, 139–140, 156, 166; genesis of, 138; preferred, 137–138; representation of, 73
Bicêtre, 183, 190, 197–198
Blondel d'Azaincourt, Barthélemy Augustin, 104; *Woman with Bird Cage*, 104–106, 121–123, 125–126
Boccaccio, Giovanni, 83
body: biological needs of, 58–59; and consciousness, 44, 61–63, 70, 88–89, 91; and Epicurean materialism, 5, 8; in erotic theater, 180, 188–189, 193–195, 198–201, 203–204, 206, 240n42; and language, 53,

246   INDEX

body (continued)
    55, 57, 180, 201; and morality, 59–61, 214;
    and pleasure, 2–3, 25, 42–44, 46–47, 51,
    53–54, 56–60, 65, 67–70, 134, 160, 166,
    203, 214; and reading, 25, 42, 44; visual
    representation of, 81, 88–89, 93, 95, 98,
    102, 123. *See also* Church; form
Boergraave, Herman, 208
Borde, Benjamin de la, 185
Bordel ou le Jeanfoutre puni, Le (Caylus).
    See Caylus, Anne-Claude Philippe de
    Tubières, comte de
Boucher, François: *The Abduction of Europe*,
    95–96; *Aurora and Cephalus* 95–97, 230n27;
    The Bird Catchers, 123–125, 164; *The Birth
    and Triumph of Venus*, 88, 90; *The Cage*,
    88–89, 123; center and periphery in art of,
    81, 88–89, 91, 93, 102; critique of, 81–83,
    98–100, 228n11, 229n25; and Du Bos,
    71–76; Epicurean Stoicism of, 90–91, 93,
    102, 157; *Head of a Young Girl*, 94; and the
    human form, 81–83, 88–89, 93–94, 97–99,
    102–103, 230n27, 230n29; *Landscape with
    Hermit*, 83–85, 87–88, 90, 95; *The Pretty
    Cook*, 76–77, 86; *The Rising of the Sun*
    and *The Setting of the Sun*, 98, 230n28;
    and Rousseau, 99, 104, 121–126, 230n3,
    232n20; sensationist art of, 74–75, 81,
    89, 93–102, 164; and synecdoche, 123,
    125–126; *The Toilette of Venus*, 100–101;
    Toilette pastorale, 102; *Two or Three Things,
    Will You Do One of Them?*, 78–79; *Venus
    Asleep*, 96; *Young Girl Seen from Behind*,
    94–95
bourgeoisie, 6, 34, 74–75, 172–174, 188,
    212–213, 241n8
brothel, 183, 187–190, 196, 199
Brothel or The Dickhead Punished, The
    (Caylus). *See* Caylus, Anne-Claude
    Philippe de Tubières, comte de
Brunel, Georges, 82

C

cahiers de doléances, 212, 241n8
Campra, André, 183
Capon, Gaston, 180, 238n29, 238n31
Carmontelle, Louis Carrogis de, 179, 238n22
Cassirer, Ernst, 7–8, 219n5

catharsis, 93, 212
Catholicism, 2, 65, 151, 208
Caylus, Anne-Claude Philippe de Tubières,
    comte de, 189, 194, 201, 204; *Le Bordel ou
    le Jeanfoutre puni* (The Brothel or The
    Dickhead Punished), 180, 189–190, 194,
    201, 204
cercle, 162, 172, 178. *See also* salon
chance, 29–30, 211, 241n6
Christianity: and condemnation of pleasure,
    1–2, 55–56, 61, 103, 106, 126, 128, 169;
    Epicurean rejection of, 4–5, 8, 52, 59,
    107, 218
Church: and condemnation of the body,
    54–57, 62–63, 103, 106–107, 169;
    reactions against, 59–61, 87–88, 150–151,
    163–164, 199, 209–210, 213–214; role of
    in eighteenth-century France, 3, 60, 82,
    151, 163; and theater, 171, 184–185
Claretie, Léo, 173–174
Clermont, Louis de Bourbon Condé,
    comte de, 182
clinamen, 38, 203
Cochin, Augustin, 218, 242n11
Cochin, Charles-Nicolas, 98–99
Coindet, François, 104
Collaert, Hans, 111–115; *The Age of Gold*,
    111–112; *The Age of Silver*, 112–113; *The
    Age of Bronze*, 112–114; *The Age of Iron*,
    113–115
Collé, Charles, 179, 182–183, 186, 239n39;
    Alphonse l'Impuissant (Alphonse the
    Impotent), 186–187; *Isabelle précepteur*
    (Isabelle the Tutor), 183; *Léandre étalon*
    (Leander the Stallion), 183; *La Partie de
    chasse de Henri IV* (The Hunting Party of
    Henri IV), 179
color. *See* line and color
Comédie-Française, 32, 171–172, 175,
    183–184, 239n40
Comédie-Italienne, 172–173
comédie larmoyante, 180–181
community: and civic happiness, 103, 106,
    118, 126; and the general will, 217–218;
    and shared pleasure, 2–4; and Stoicism,
    106, 109
Condillac, Étienne Bonnot, abbé de, 91, 155
Confessions (Rousseau). *See* Rousseau,
    Jean-Jacques

consciousness: and happiness, 212; and language 53, 132; and materialism, 5, 9, 52, 132, 158; of natural man, 110; and pleasure, 65, 68, 70, 141, 212; and reason, 16, 55; and the senses, 53, 55–56, 61–63, 89, 91, 98, 138–139
consolation, 12, 27–28, 121, 134, 146, 198
Comtesse d'Olonne, La (Grandval *père*). See Grandval, Nicolas Racot de
Corneille, Pierre, 172, 239n40; *Le Cid*, 186
countryside, 88, 164–166
couple: and coupling, 34–40, 42, 44–46, 48–49, 133, 172; and shared pleasure, 34–35, 39, 43–44, 49, 66–67, 69, 111–112, 123–124, 160, 195–196. *See also* reading
Courbet, Gustave, 203–204
Crébillon, Claude Prosper Jolyot de, 34, 58, 92, 184, 193, 222n3; *Les Égarements du cœur et de l'esprit*, 58, 92
crime, in context of Revolution, 216–217
Crow, Thomas, 102, 227n6
Cusset, Catherine, 225n3, 226n10

D

d'Alméras, Henri, 171
Damrosch, Leo, 111
d'Arnaud, Baculard, 183
Darnton, Robert, 51, 153, 225nn2–3, 226n10, 236n8
Declaration of the Rights of Man and the Citizen, 150, 211, 213
DeJean, Joan, 221n5
Delisle de Sales, Jean-Baptiste Isouard, 238n29
Delon, Michel, 56, 240n46
Democritus, 8
Démoris, René, 47–48, 230n4
Descartes, René, 3, 5, 8, 52, 90, 154–155, 160, 208
determinism, 60, 64, 208
Diderot, Denis: on Boucher, 81–82, 98–99, 228n11; and the *drame bourgeois*, 172; *Éloge de Richardson*, 50; Epicurean materialism of, 158, 236n11; on Epicureanism and Stoicism, 4–5, 219n4; on La Morlière, 222n3; and Mérard, 240n42; *La Religieuse*, 197; *Le Rêve de d'Alembert*, 236n11; and Rousseau, 123, 230n1, 231n9; on sentimental

identification, 50–51, 53; *Supplément au voyage de Bougainville*, 233n6
Diogenes Laërtius, 4
Discourse on the Origin of Inequality (Rousseau). See Rousseau, Jean-Jacques
Discourse on the Sciences and Arts (Rousseau). See Rousseau, Jean-Jacques
disguise, 31, 93, 165; and crossdressing, 160, 180, 182, 197–198
drame bourgeois, 172
Du Bos, Jean-Baptiste, 72–78, 80–81, 83, 93, 227n1, 227n3, 232n15; *Histoire des quatre Gordiens*, 72; *Réflexions critiques sur la poésie et sur la peinture*, 72–75, 93, 232n15
dualism, 3, 5, 8, 52, 55, 107, 208
Duflos, Claude-Augustin-Pierre, 102
Durkheim, Émile, and *Elementary Forms of the Religious Life*, 218

E

Edict of Nantes, 2
Eisen, Charles, 85–86; *The Hermit*, 85–86
Encyclopédie, 4, 91, 98
Enlightenment, French: critique of, 106, 111, 116; myth of, 6–8, 219n5; philosophies of, 4, 8, 52–53, 218; values and culture of, 2, 103, 109, 173, 175, 220n7, 236n10
Enlightenment self, 52
Epictetus, 8
Epicurean Stoicism, 3–6, 8, 38, 58–60, 94, 102, 109, 129, 145–148, 157; as alternative to *libertinage*, 90–91, 93
Epicureanism: concept and evolution of, 3–5, 8, 218; and eighteenth-century France, 3–5, 8, 51, 149, 167, 185–186, 218; and erotic theater, 185–186, 203–206; and the libertine novel, 48–49, 128; as life-style, 31–32, 209; as male, 146, 148; and materialism, 4–5, 18, 138–139, 151, 158, 160–161, 166, 203–205, 207, 209, 215; and reciprocal pleasure, 36–37, 40, 66, 162–163, 169, 203; Sade's reinterpretation of, 215–216; and Stoicism, 3–5, 8, 27, 38, 60, 71, 169–170, 218; tenets of, 15–16, 63, 65, 67, 70, 103, 106–107, 109–110, 132, 160, 166, 203, 214
Epicurus, 4

epistemology, 7, 9, 103, 158
erotic theater, 171–172, 180–207, 238n24;
and the body, 180, 188–189, 193–195,
198–201, 203–204, 206, 240n42, 240n45;
as Epicurean, 185–186, 203–206; as
genre, 186–187, 191, 200–201; language
and esthetics of, 201–205; and male
impotence, 186–187, 194–195, 199–201;
performance spaces of, 182–185; and
prostitution, 183–185, 188–190, 197–198,
202; publishing of, 181, 193, 236n2,
238n29; in context of the Revolution, 197,
199; and women, 180, 182–183, 199
*Esprit des mœurs au XVIIIe siècle, ou la
petite maison, L'* (Mérard de Saint
Just). *See* Mérard de Saint Just,
Simon-Pierre
Essay on the Origin of Languages (Rousseau).
See Rousseau, Jean-Jacques
Estates General, 150, 212
esthetics: of the novel, 47, 67, 152, 154, 157,
168; of pleasure, 9, 71–73, 75, 89–90, 100,
103, 212; theories of, 73–75, 102, 120,
227n3, 232n15, 232n18, 234n8
ethics: of happiness, 212; of pleasure, 9, 103,
110, 208–209, 211
eudemony, 103, 105–110, 117–118, 121, 126
exemplarity, novelistic, 11, 14, 29, 31, 40–41,
155–157, 160

F

failure, 11, 14, 20, 29–30
Falconet, Étienne-Maurice, 72, 236n11
Favart, Charles Simon, 32, 222n2
Flaubert, Gustave, 51
Fleury, Jacques, 177
For-l'Évêque, 190
form (in painting): female, 81–83, 99;
male, 99
Foucault, Michel, 220n7
Fougeret de Monbron, and *Margot la
ravaudeuse* (Margot the Mender), 62,
129, 184
Fragonard, Jean-Honoré, 75, 85–87, 185,
228n9; *The Hermit*, 85–87
Frankfurt School, 7–8
Frederick the Great [Frederick II of
Prussia], 208, 240n2

Freud, Sigmund, 1–2, 100, 204
Furet, François, 242n11

G

gallery, 11, 71, 167–168
gambling, 32, 37, 178, 182
Gassendi, Pierre, 4, 8, 91, 219n4
Gay, Peter, 219n5
gender: assumptions and stereotypes of, 17,
48–49, 162, 165–166; divisions and
distinctions of, 83, 131, 135–136,
141–142, 146–147, 160, 162–164,
199–200; mobility of, 166, 195; and
society, 132, 142–145, 147, 161.
See also disguise
general will, 118; in the Revolution,
126–127, 217–218
Genlis, Stéphanie Félicité du Crest de
Saint-Aubin, comtesse de, 179
Gerould, Daniel, 179
Goncourt, Edmond de, 177
Goncourt, Jules and Edmond de, 100
Goulemot, Jean-Marie, 41–42, 49, 223n12,
234n11
Grandval, Charles-François Racot
de [Grandval *fils*], 184–185, 201,
239n40; *L'Eunuque, ou la Fidèle
infidélité* (The Eunuch, or The Faithful
Infidelity), 184–185; *La Médicine de
Cythère* (Cythera's Medicine), 185;
Sirop au cul (Syrup-up-the-Ass), 185;
Le Tempérament (Temperament),
201–202
Grandval, Nicolas Racot de [Grandval *père*],
187, 200, 239n40; *L'Appareilleuse* (The
Lady Brothel Keeper), 187–190, 203;
La Comtesse d'Olonne (The Countess of
Olonne), 200–201
Greuze, Jean-Baptiste, 98–100
Grimm, Friedrich Melchior, 143, 175
Guerrier philosophe, Le (Jourdan).
See Jourdan, Jean-Baptiste
Gueullette, Thomas-Simon, 174

H

happiness: civic, 211–212, 216, 218; and
community, 106; and desire, 49–50;

history of, 241n5; and individuality, 66; as a new idea for Europe, 2–3, 209–211, 216, 241n6; as opposed to pleasure, 105–107, 128, 207, 209, 212–213; and sentiment, 100
harmony. *See* melody
Hegel, George Wilhelm, 10
Helvétius, Claude-Adrien, 53, 155, 158, 231n9
Hesiod, 114; and *Works and the Days*, 111, 232n12
Hobbes, Thomas, 91
Homer, 11, 72
Horkheimer, Max, 7–8
Huet, Marie-Hélène, 48
Hunt, Lynn, 212, 220n8, 226n10, 240n44, 241n7, 242n10

I

idealism, 7–8, 128, 156
illusion: and desire, 91–92; and language, 53; and reality, 16, 26, 37–39, 45, 47, 56, 70, 140–142; and rhetoric, 116–117; and sentimental identification, 50–51
impotence, 46, 49, 151–152, 186–187, 194–195, 199–201
individual: within community, 54, 108–110; within couple, 35, 66; and the general will, 217; and liberty, 108; and pleasure, 1–4, 8, 109
instinct, 57–58, 133, 163
irony, 149, 154, 164, 176

J

Jansenists, 185, 225n4
Jesuits, 176, 225n4
Jourdan, Jean-Baptiste, 11–13, 31, 52, 71, 220n3, 223n13; *L'École des prudes*, 12; *Le Guerrier philosophe*, 11–31, 33, 52, 71, 168, 221nn4–5; *Lettres du correcteur des bouffons*, 12
Julie, or the New Heloise (Rousseau). *See* Rousseau, Jean-Jacques

K

Kant, Immanuel, 7, 103

L

La Boétie, Étienne de, and *A Discourse of Voluntary Servitude*, 107, 231n6
La Fontaine, Jean de, 83–88; *Contes et nouvelles en vers*, 83
La Mettrie, Julien Offray de, 1, 53, 91, 151, 155, 158, 207–209, 211, 215, 240nn1–2; *L'Art de jouir*, 1; *Histoire naturelle de l'âme*, 208; *L'Homme machine*, 208; *Système d'Épicure*, 208–209
La Morlière, Jacques Rochette de, 31–33, 53, 169, 221n1, 222n3, 223n7; *Angola*, 31–51, 53, 71, 92, 169, 222n3, 223nn8–9
La Pouplinière, Alexandre-Jean-Joseph Le Riche de, 184
La Rochefoucauld, François, duc de, 15
Laclos, Pierre-Ambroise-François Choderlos de, 51, 92–93, 99–100, 128–148, 151, 153–154, 223n11, 224n21, 233nn5–7, 234nn10–11; *Les Liaisons dangereuses*, 51, 92–93, 99–100, 128–130, 142–149, 151, 153–154, 162, 182, 223n11, 224n21, 233n5, 234nn10–11, 235n14; *On the Education of Women*, 131–143, 233nn5–7
Lady Brothel Keeper, The (Grandval *père*). *See* Grandval, Nicolas Racot de
Lafayette, Marie Madeleine Pioche de La Vergne, comtesse de, and *La Princesse de Clèves*, 11, 31, 71, 221n4
Lancret, Nicolas, 75, 78; *A Young Lady on a Sofa*, 78–80, 228n10
language: and consciousness, 132; and duplicity, 153–154, 236n9; in erotic theater, 201–205; and identity, 52–53; and illusion, 53; and pleasure, 57; and senses, 52–53, 57, 134
Lanson, Gustave, 181
Laujon, Pierre, and *La Gageure des trois commères* (The Three Gossips' Bet), 182
Law, John, 1, 6
Le Brun, Charles, 74, 89, 232n17
Leblanc, Jean-Bernard, 95–96
Lecat, Claude-Nicolas, 120
Ledoux, Claude-Nicolas, 185
Legrand, Marc-Antoine, 190, 202, 204; *Le Luxurieux* (The Rake), 180, 190, 201–206
Lépicié, François-Bernard, 96–97
lettre de cachet, 150, 184, 196

Lévi-Strauss, Claude, 110–111, 231n9, 231n10
Liaisons dangereuses, Les (Laclos). See Laclos, Pierre-Ambroise-François Choderlos de
libertinage, 3, 6, 47–49, 90–93, 107, 161, 169, 219n2
liberty: and equality, 105; and happiness, 104–105, 107–108; illusion of, 120; and libertinage, 91–92; natural, 110; and pleasure, 103–105, 108, 120; Rousseau's religion of, 111, 117–118, 120–121, 126
life-writing, 53, 63–64, 69–70; and exemplarity, 64; and pleasure, 64–65; and reader, 69–70. See also memoir
Ligne, Charles-Joseph, prince de, 177
line and color, 73–74, 89, 119, 126
Locke, John, 8, 73, 91, 155
Louis XIV, 2, 5–6, 174
Louis XV, 37, 72, 81–82, 173
Louis XVI, 150
love, 13–14, 16, 18–21, 155–156; as female, 146–147; possessive, 137; as illusion, 45, 134, 147; and imagination, 141; and nature, 159, 165
Lucretius, 3, 5, 8, 91, 203
Luxurieux, Le (Legrand). See Legrand, Marc-Antoine

M

Macfall, Haldane, 82
make-up, 35, 140–141, 174–175, 177, 234n8
Malesherbes, Guillaume-Chrétien de Lamoignon de, 109
Marie-Antoinette, 174, 199
Marivaux, Pierre Carlet de Chamblain de, 23, 33–34, 93, 172, 178, 193; Le Jeu de l'amour et du hazard (The Game of Love and Chance), 178; La Vie de Marianne (The Life of Marianne), 33
marriage: as dénouement, 48–49, 168–169; laws of, 184
Marseillaise, La, 216
materialism: Epicurean, 18, 138, 151, 158, 160–161, 166, 203, 205, 207, 209, 215; of Epicureanism and Stoicism, 4–5; and the legitimacy of pleasure, 8, 103; and

libertinage, 107; as monism, 8, 52; and the primacy of the senses, 53, 154–155; of Sade, 214
Mauzi, Robert, 48, 222n3
May, Georges, 152
melody, 118, 122; and harmony, 119
memoir, 13–15, 31, 52–53, 58. See also life-writing
memory (faculty), 53–54, 56; and eudemony, 118; and pleasure, 19, 104, 122, 125–126, 138–140
Mérard de Saint Just, Simon-Pierre, vi, 181, 191–193, 196, 199, 201, 239n41, 240n42; L'Esprit des mœurs au XVIIIe siècle, ou la petite maison (The Spirit of Mores in the 18th Century, or The Little House), 181, 191–197, 199, 203, 239n41
Mercure de France, 109, 175
Métra, Louis-François, 175–176
Michaud, Louis-Gabriel, 13
Milam, Jennifer, 78, 229n9
Miller, Nancy K., 48–49
mimesis, 50–51, 68, 70, 119, 199
Mirabeau, André Boniface Riqueti, vicomte de, 149–170, 207, 217, 235nn1–3, 235n5; La Morale des sens, 149, 151–170, 217, 235n5
Mirabeau, Honoré Gabriel Riqueti, comte de, 149–151, 235n5
Mirabeau, Victor Riqueti, marquis de, 149–150, 158
mirror, 25–26, 35–36, 42–44, 48–49, 78–80, 100–101; the novel as, 14, 35, 40–41, 43–44, 47, 51
mise en abyme, 11, 16, 28, 35, 41–42
misogyny, 190–191, 199
Molière, Jean Baptiste Poquelin, and Tartuffe, 56, 88, 173, 185
moment. See pleasure: of the moment
monarchy, 6, 8, 48, 116, 149, 151, 215, 231n6, 240n44
Montesquieu, Charles-Louis de Secondat, baron de la Brède et de, and De l'esprit des lois, 191
Morale des sens, La (Mirabeau). See Mirabeau, André Boniface Riqueti, vicomte de
morality: and Boucher, 81–82, 88, 98–99; conflict between private and public,

59–61; and education, 130; and the general will, 217; and happiness, 211–212; and Laclos, 130, 142–143; and moralism, 14–15, 152, 169–170, 176, 185, 216; and the novel, 10, 14, 31, 48–50, 64; and pleasure, 128; political, 117; in the context of the Revolution, 215–216; and Rousseau, 50, 108–109, 114–115, 117, 129, 142; and Sade, 214–216; secular, 8–9

N

National Assembly, 150–151, 235n2
naturalism, 8, 81, 88
nature: and art, 100–101; and God, 59, 61; man of, 110–111, 118, 131, 166, 231n10, 232n12; and society, 134–135; and virtue, 108, 165; woman of, 131–133, 135, 142, 235n14
nature morte, 88
Necker, Jacques, 212–213
Newton, Isaac, 8
Nicole, Pierre, 185
Nietzsche, Friedrich, 7
nobility, 13, 48, 74–75, 213; of the robe, 32; of the sword, 192
nostalgia, 125–126, 151, 165
novel: of education, 155, 158, 160–161; of eighteenth-century France, 10–11, 33–34; as genre, 22, 51, 152, 154, 160–161, 169; libertine form and conventions of, 47–48, 53, 58, 92, 158, 162; as model, 41, 49–50; and pleasure, 12, 28, 32, 36, 40–44, 67–68, 149, 154, 157–158; and reader, 45, 50–51, 67–70, 153–158, 160–161, 169–170, 217; of seventeenth-century France, 31, 157; of types, 166–168. *See also* allegory; exemplarity; mirror

O

On the Education of Woman (Laclos). *See* Laclos, Pierre-Ambroise-François Choderlos de
opera, 12–13, 39, 65, 71, 119, 122, 175, 184, 197
Opéra, 71, 92, 173, 184
Opéra-Comique, 71, 173, 195
Ovid, 8, 91, 111, 126, 158

P

parades, 174–175, 179
parody: of dualism and idealism, 51, 156; in erotic theater, 186–188, 197–199, 239n40; of rhetoric, 58, 150, 156, 158, 216; of the *roman*, 46, 48, 55
Pascal, Blaise, 15, 158
peasants, 165, 212–213
performative discourse, 211, 217
petite maison, 39, 145, 182–184, 190, 192, 195–196, 199, 239n40
Philippe d'Orléans, 6, 182–184
Philippe-Égalité, 81, 182
Philosophy of the Bedroom (Sade). *See* Sade, Donatien Alphonse François de
Picard, Louis-Benoit, 197; *Les Visitandines* (The Sisters of the Visitation), 197–198
Pierre, Jean-Baptiste, and frontispiece to *Discourse on the Sciences and Arts* (Rousseau), 104–105, 120–121, 125, 230n1
Piles, Roger de, 74, 89, 232n17
Piron, Alexis, 174, 199–200; *Métromania*, 174; *Vasta, reine de Bordélie* (Vasta, Queen of Bordelloland), 199–200
plaire et instruire, 10, 12, 29, 31
Plato, 107
Platonism, 5, 8, 29, 156
pleasure: and anticipation, 20–21, 26–27, 43, 88, 137–139; and beauty, 138–140, 156; and the body, 2–3, 25, 42–44, 46–47, 51, 53–54, 56–60, 65, 67–70, 134, 138, 160, 166, 214; and consciousness, 55, 61, 63, 65, 68, 70; and desire, 137, 139; esthetics of, 71–73, 75, 89–90, 100, 212; ethics of, 9, 103, 110, 208–209, 211; female, 128–129, 133, 137, 143; female manipulation of, 141–148; and imagination, 137–138; and inaccessibility, 28; intensification of, 118; and language, 57; and love, 14, 16, 38, 134, 158; of the moment, 118, 121, 125, 139, 156, 209, 227n4; and music, 119, 122; as opposed to happiness, 105–107, 128, 207, 209, 212–213, 216, 218; and reason, 18, 55, 61; repetition of, 53, 69; representation of, 9–10, 60, 67–71, 157; as solitary, 106, 108, 212; spaces of, 39–40, 182, 185; and the visual arts, 68, 71–74, 81, 93, 98–100,

pleasure (continued)
    102, 119, 122, 125–126; and voyeurism,
    25–27; and writing, 63–65
pleasure principle, 2
Plutarch, 104
poetry: of eighteenth-century France, 172;
    and painting, 72–73, 75, 78, 80, 93,
    95–96; reading of, 15, 20–21, 174
Pompadour, Jeanne-Antoinette Lenormand
    d'Etiolles, marquise de, 37, 72, 81, 98,
    173–174
pornography, 41–42, 56, 68, 82, 102, 128,
    180, 199, 240n44
portrait, 21, 24, 36, 44–45, 47 50, 71, 92, 197,
    221n4, 223n13. *See also* pleasure: and the
    visual arts; senses: and the visual arts
Poussin, Nicolas, 74, 89, 119
preciosity, 146, 157
pregnancy, 85, 188, 233n7; as dénouement,
    169; fear of, 60–61, 66–69
Prévost, Antoine-François, abbé de, 92;
    Manon Lescaut, 92, 129
property: confiscation of, 210–211, 216;
    private, 110, 112, 115–116; women as,
    136, 161
prostitution, 62, 65–66, 81, 122, 128, 215;
    and erotic theater, 183–185, 188–190,
    197–198, 202, 215, 233n1, 239n35
Protestantism, 2, 208, 231n6
Proust, Marcel, 63
proverbes, 179
puberty, female, 54, 132–3, 163, 203;
    male, 37
pudeur, 163, 165, 196
Putains cloîtrées, les (The Cloistered
    Whores), 180, 197–199, 201, 203

Q

querelle des bouffons, 13, 119
quietism, 55

R

Rabelais, François, 47
Rabenalt, Arthur Maria, 180
Racine, Jean, 172, 239n40
Rake, The (Legrand). *See* Legrand,
    Marc-Antoine

reading: as a couple, 35, 40–42, 49; of
    exemplary fiction, 11, 14; of images,
    75–76, 78, 80, 123–124; and pleasure, 2,
    4, 10, 20–22, 25–27, 40; programs of, 15,
    67–68, 157, 162, 233n6; purpose of,
    49–50; ways of, 12, 153–155
reality principle, 2
*Réflexions critiques sur la poésie et sur la
    peinture* (Du Bos). *See* Du Bos, Jean-
    Baptiste
Renoir, Pierre-Auguste, 81
representation: of beauty, 73; of pleasure,
    9–10, 60, 67–71, 157; versus reality,
    11–12, 41, 53, 99
Reveries of the Solitary Walker, The
    (Rousseau). *See* Rousseau, Jean-Jacques
Revolution, French, 5, 207–218; and class
    conflict, 241n8; and crime, 216–217; and
    Epicureanism, 149, 167, 172; and erotic
    theater, 197, 199; and the general will,
    126–127, 217–218; and ideology, 217–218,
    242n10; and Mirabeau, 150, 161, 167,
    235nn1–2; and new idea of civic happiness
    as opposed to pleasure, 3, 209–213, 216,
    218; and sentiment, 6; as telos, 8, 220n8;
    and theater, 172, 175; and the valorization
    of Stoicism, 4, 218
Ricconboni, Marie-Jeanne Laboras de
    Mézières, 129
Richardson, Samuel, 50
Robespierre, Maximilien François Marie
    Isidore de, 218
rococo: as style, 6, 74; codes of, 76, 78, 80–81
Rougemont, Martine de, 173, 180, 237n7,
    237n11, 237n16, 237n19, 237n21
Rousseau, Jean-Jacques: and the Ages of
    Man, 111–114, 232n12; and Boucher, 99,
    104, 121–126, 230n3, 232n20; *Confessions*,
    52, 122, 174, 214, 237n5; critique of
    Enlightenment philosophy, 109–111,
    116–117; and Diderot, 123, 230n1, 231n9;
    Discourse on the Origin of Inequality,
    108–111, 114–118, 126–127, 130–131,
    141–142, 164, 233n7; *Discourse on the
    Sciences and Arts*, 104, 108–110, 119–120,
    126, 131, 230n1, 233n7; and the eighteenth-
    century novel, 33, 128, 149, 151, 169; *Emile*,
    118; *Essay on the Origin of Languages*, 74,
    112, 118–119, 122, 236n9; esthetic theories

of, 74, 119–120, 232nn16–18; *Julie, or the New Heloise*, 49–51, 99, 118, 123, 128–130, 141, 149, 151, 153–154, 157, 169, 207, 217, 232n20; and Laclos, 128–133, 135, 138, 141, 142, 153–154, 233n7; and language, 53, 236n9; and Mirabeau, 151, 153–154, 157, 164–166, 169; and pleasure, 1–2, 42, 103–104, 106, 109, 112, 117–118, 120–121, 125–126, 128, 166; political theories of, 91, 103, 105–106, 108–110, 114–115, 117, 120, 126–127, 130–132, 135, 138, 207, 217, 231nn9–10; posthumous role of in revolutionary ideology, 127, 217–218; and reading, 42, 49–51, 130, 153; and religion, 110–111, 117; *The Reveries of the Solitary Walker*, 1, 108, 118, 121–122, 126; *The Social Contract*, 118, 127, 217; and theater, 171, 174; and totalitarianism, 126–127; and valorization of sentimentality, 99–100, 149, 157; *The Village Soothsayer*, 122, 174

Rubens, Peter Paul, 81, 89, 119

Russo, Elena, 227n5

S

sacralization, of the state, 217–218, 242n12

Sade, Donatien Alphonse François de, 207, 213–218, 225n7, 226n9; "Frenchmen, yet one more effort if you wish to be Republicans," 214–216; *Philosophy of the Bedroom*, 214–216

Saint-Just, Louis Antoine de, 207, 209–211, 213, 215–218

salon, 27–28, 173–174, 178–179, 221n5, 237n19

satire, 34, 53, 56, 150–151, 192–193, 199, 207, 223n7, 239n41

Scarron, Paul, 33

Schnitzler, Arthur, 190

Sctrick, Jane P., 151

Second Empire, 6

secularism, 8–9, 59, 103–104, 110–111

seduction, 2, 28, 34–35, 43–44, 163, 177

sensation, 1–3, 88, 98, 103–104, 134, 158–159, 209, 232n18

sensationism, 9, 91, 98–99, 132, 138–139, 154–155, 241n8

senses: and consciousness, 53, 55–56, 61–63, 89, 91, 98, 138–139; and empiricism, 2–3, 8; excitement of, 57, 68–69, 132–133; and imagination, 51, 55–56, 140; and knowledge, 2, 8–9, 53, 61, 73, 103, 145; and language, 52–53, 57, 134; and pleasure, 2, 9–10, 73, 92, 100, 103, 144–145, 152, 156, 209–210; and reason, 55; repression of, 2, 29, 51, 56–57, 99, 103; and sentiment, 51, 134; and subjectivity, 53, 73; and the visual arts, 73, 88–90, 94–96, 99–100, 102; and writing, 52–53, 63, 93

sentimentalism: Mirabeau's rejection of, 153, 169–170, 207, 217; rise of, 99, 128, 217; of Rousseau, 149, 153, 157, 207, 217. See also *comédie larmoyante*

servitude: La Boétie on, 107, 108; as opposed to *libertinage*, 91, 107; Rousseau on, 103, 108, 113–114, 116–117, 120; of women, according to Laclos, 131–132, 135–138, 141–142, 147

sexuality, 37, 57–58, 60, 66–67, 134–136, 152, 163–164, 214, 225n7, 226n8; and erotic theater, 172, 179–180, 186, 199, 203, 206, 238n24

Sisters of the Visitation, The (Picard). See Picard, Louis-Benoit

sociability, 15, 53, 108, 110, 132, 143, 173

Social Contract, The (Rousseau). See Rousseau, Jean-Jacques

société de pensée, 218, 242n11

society theater, 173–180, 236n3, 238n24

Soubise, Prince de, 185

Soyer, Louis-Charles, 82

Spinoza, Baruch, 60

Spirit of Mores in the 18th Century, or The Little House, The (Mérard de Saint Just). See Mérard de Saint Just, Simon-Pierre

stereotypes: characters as, 166, 189; cultural, 165, 172; of gender, 48–49, 162, 165–166; of the libertine novel, 48, 92–93; national, 176

Stoicism: and community, 106, 109; concept and evolution of, 3–5, 8, 170, 218; and Epicureanism, 3–5, 8, 27, 38, 60, 169–170; and esthetic distance, 3–4, 71, 218; as female, 145–148; and happiness, 22, 218; and materialism, 4–5, 152; and self-control, 16–18, 38, 58–60, 152–153

Strauss, Leo, 108, 118
subjectivity, 9, 53, 61, 63–65; and the novel, 153–155, 157, 160, 166
symbolism, in the visual arts, 76–78, 113
synecdoche, 123, 125–126, 137, 139–140
synesthesia, 89
syphilis, 190–191, 198

T

taste (*goût*), 73–74, 81–83, 137, 175, 181, 229*n*25
Tempérament, Le (Grandval *fils*). *See* Grandval, Charles-François Racot de
Terror, the, 1, 8, 126–127, 216
theater: and audience, 185, 193, 199; and education, 176–177; of eighteenth-century France, 39, 93, 171–186, 199, 207, 237*n*11, 237*n*14. *See also* erotic theater; society theater
théâtre de la foire, 71, 171, 173–174
théâtre de société. *See* society theater
Théâtre italien, 12, 32
theatricality, 171, 175–177
Third Republic, 6
Thérèse philosophe (Argens). *See* Argens, Jean-Baptiste de Boyer, marquis d'
Thomas Aquinas, Saint, 107
Thomas, Chantal, 132, 226*n*9, 240*n*44
Todorov, Tzvetan, 147
totalitarianism, 6–8, 126–127
Trott, David, 178, 237*n*4, 237*n*12
Truchet, Jacques, 181

U

Urfé, Honoré d', 33; *L'Astrée*, 45, 157

V

Van Loo, Carle, 75
Vasta, reine de Bordélie (Piron). *See* Piron, Alexis
Ventôse decrees, 210
Versailles, 37, 48, 150, 173–174
Versailles, Treaty of, 210
Versini, Laurent, 146, 223*n*7, 233*n*4, 233*n*6
Vèze, Raoul de [B. de Villeneuve], 185–186, 239*n*34
Village Soothsayer, The (Rousseau). *See* Rousseau, Jean-Jacques
Virgil, vi, 11, 152
virtue: bourgeois, 172; civic, 1–2, 6, 99, 169, 210–211; moral, 15, 48; and pleasure, in Epicurean Stoicism, 8, 12, 106–107, 109, 129, 170; and Rousseau, 50, 99, 108–109, 129–130, 149, 217
Visitandines, Les (Picard). *See* Picard, Louis-Benoit
Voltaire, 32, 135, 171, 179, 231*n*9, 239*n*40
voyeurism, 25–27, 54–57, 61, 69, 221*n*4, 225*n*3

W

War of the Polish Succession, 13, 20
War of the Spanish Succession, 72
wars of religion, 2, 114, 116, 164, 231*n*6
Watteau, Antoine, 111, 124–125; *Departure for Cythera*, 124–125
Wildenstein, Daniel, 82, 100
women: beauty of, 133–134, 137, 139–140, 156, 166; condition of, 136–138, 141–143, 147, 161–162, 184, 197–198; education of, 130–131, 161, 163, 176, 233*n*5, 233*n*7; and erotic theater, 180, 182–183, 199; natural, 131–133, 135, 142, 235*n*14; and pleasure, 128–129, 133, 137, 143; Stoicism of, 145–148; and theater, 176–178, 184
writing: act of, 63–65, 147–148; and painting, 80. *See also* life-writing

Y

Yve-Plessis, Robert, 180, 238*n*29, 238*n*31

Z

Zeno of Citium, 4, 8